How the Internet Works

Fourth Edition

How the Internet Works

Fourth Edition

Preston Gralla

Illustrated by Sarah Ishida, Mina Reimer, and Stephen Adams

A division of Macmillan Computer Publishing, USA
201 W. 103rd Street
Indianapolis, IN 46290

Copyright© 1998 by Que® Corporation
First printing: September 1998

Executive Editor	Karen Reinisch
Acquisitions Editor	Renee Wilmeth
Development Editor	Noelle Gasco
Technical Editor	Doug Klippert
Managing Editor	Thomas F. Hayes
Project Editor	Karen A. Walsh
Copy Editors	Barbara Hacha and Julie McNamee
Illustrators	Sarah Ishida, Mina Reimer, and Stephen Adams
Book Designers	Carrie English and Bruce Lundquist
Production	Betsy Deeter, Lisa England, John Etchison, and Trina Wurst
Indexers	Sandra Henselmeier and Cheryl Jackson

Library of Congress Catalog No.: 98-85292

ISBN: 0-7897-1726-3

00 99 98   6 5 4 3 2 1

Interpretation of the printing code: The rightmost double-digit number is the year of the book's printing; the rightmost single-digit number, the number of the book's printing. For example, a printing code of 98-1 shows that the first printing of the book occurred in 1998.

THIS book, like the Internet, is a collaborative work. My name may be on the cover, but I am far from the only person involved in its creation.

Development Editor Noelle Gasco managed to pull together all the elements of a complex project, all the while keeping a cool head, improving the illustrations, and offering editorial insight and help. Renee Wilmeth, once again, helped shape this book and was instrumental in getting it off the ground.

Without Mina Reimer, Sarah Ishida, and Stephen Adams, the illustrators, there would be no book because this book is such a visual experience. And many thanks to the entire team at Que who produced the book including Karen Walsh, project editor; and Barbara Hacha, copy editor.

Thanks also have to go to the many, many people I interviewed for this book. People from Quarterdeck Corporation, Chaco Communications, Progressive Networks, White Pine Software, Microsoft, Netscape, Headspace, SurfWatch Software, WebTV, Accrue, VDONet Corporation, America Online, Yahoo!, Hilgraeve, and Nuborn Technologies are only a few of the folks who gave their time to help me understand the nitty-gritty of how various Internet technologies work. Tim Smith and Jonathan Spewak from ZDNet offered me vital help as well.

I gleaned much information from the many FAQs and similar documents widely available on the Internet. I'd like to thank the anonymous authors of those documents, whoever they are.

Many thanks go to Doug Klippert, the technical editor for the book, who did a superb job of ensuring that I always got the information right.

Finally, big thanks have to go to my wife, Lydia. She put up with those occasional glassy-eyed looks that were replies to simple questions like, "Did you leave your keys in the refrigerator again?" She also endured my extreme absent-mindedness while I was figuring out ways to explain how firewalls, ISDN, or Web robots work when I should have been concentrating on more immediate matters.

IN the course of cruising the World Wide Web and clicking on a link, have you ever wondered, "How does that work?" Or perhaps this question popped into your mind while you were transferring a file to your computer via FTP, or reading a newsgroup message, or when you first heard about technologies such as Spam, cookies, and firewalls. Maybe you've wondered how a message sent from your computer travels through the vastness of cyberspace and ends up in the right email box halfway across the world. Have you ever wanted to know how search tools find the exact piece of information you want out of the millions of pieces of information on the whole Internet? How can you listen to music and view animations while surfing the Web?

This book is designed for everyone interested in the Internet. Its guiding principle is this: No matter how much of a cyberpro you are—or how much of a novice—there's a lot you don't understand about the Internet. Here's just one small example. I have a friend who has made his living with companies involved with the Internet for many years. He's a complete cyberpro who lives and breathes the Internet. One day, he almost whispered to me, "I don't like to admit this, but I don't know what a proxy server is. How *does* it work, anyway?"

He's not alone. The Internet changes so quickly, and the technology advances so rapidly, that it can seem almost impossible to keep up with all of it. If you're like just about everyone else involved in the Internet, your questions are similar to those of my friend. You'll find your answers here.

In Part 1, I explain the underlying basics of the Internet: who runs it, how TCP/IP works, how to understand Internet addresses and domains, and similar topics.

Part 2 covers the Internet's underlying architecture. Here's where you'll find out about things such as routers and how the client/server architecture underpins virtually every aspect of the Internet.

Part 3 depicts the various ways that you can connect your computer to the Internet. Here's where to turn if you're interested in any of the following topics: how a cable modem, Digital Subscriber Line (DSL), or ISDN works; how online services connect to the Internet; how Network Computers (NCs) work; and a host of similar subjects.

Part 4 covers every aspect of Internet communications. It shows how email and newsgroups work, how IRC chat works, what email "Spam" is and what you can do to prevent it, how instant messaging works, and how you can use the Internet to make telephone calls anywhere in the world.

Part 5 shows how the common Internet tools and services work. Here's where you'll find out how gophers and Telnet work, how search engines and search tools work, and what happens when you use FTP to download a file to your computer.

Part 6 covers what has become by far the most popular part of the Internet—the World Wide Web. You'll learn virtually every aspect of how the Web works. It delves into how browsers work, how Web server software works, and how Hypertext Markup Language (HTML) works. This section also covers the ways in which the Web is becoming integrated directly into your computer, how Web pages are published and organized on a site, and every other aspect of the Web that is likely to be of interest to you.

Part 7 takes a close look at advanced Internet tools. Here's the place to learn about cutting-edge Internet technology. You'll find out about how push technology works, how the Java and ActiveX programming languages work, how JavaScript works, how agents can silently do your bidding for you, and how the Common Gateway Interface (CGI) works, which is a little-known but vital part of the Internet.

Part 8 shows you how some of the most exciting parts of the Internet works—the various multimedia technologies. Whether you want to know how virtual reality or animations work, how streaming video works, how videoconferencing works, or how similar technologies work, you'll find it all here.

Part 9 covers intranets and how the Internet works with the outside world. We'll see how companies use Internet technologies to build their own private networks called *intranets*. We'll take a close look at the underlying technologies that let you shop on the Web, which account for billions of dollars a year in sales.

Finally, Part 10 covers security concerns. It explains the controversial *cookie* technology that lets Web servers put bits of information on your hard disk and use that information to track you. It shows how firewalls work, how viruses can attack your computer, and how cryptosystems allow confidential information to be sent across the Internet. It delves into how hackers can attack Internet service providers (ISPs) using so-called "smurf attacks." And it covers the issue of pornography on the Internet and shows how parental-control software can prevent children from seeing objectionable material.

So, come along and see how the vast Internet works. Even if you're a cyberpro (and especially if you're not), you'll find out a lot you never knew.

P A R T

WHAT IS THE INTERNET?

FOR the first time ever, the world is truly at your fingertips. From your computer you can find information about anything you can name or even imagine. You can communicate with people on the other side of the world. You can set up a teleconference, tap into the resources of powerful computers anywhere on the globe, search through the world's best libraries, and visit the world's most amazing museums. You can watch videos, listen to music, and read special multimedia magazines. You can shop for almost anything you can name. You can do all this by tapping into the largest computer network in the world—the Internet.

The Internet isn't a single network; it is a vast, globe-spanning network of networks. No single person, group, or organization runs the Internet. Instead, it's the purest form of electronic democracy. The networks communicate with each other based on certain protocols, such as the Transmission Control Protocol (TCP) and the Internet Protocol (IP). More and more networks and computers are being hooked up to the Internet every day. Tens of thousands of these networks exist, ranging from university networks to corporate local area networks to large online services such as America Online and CompuServe. Every time you tap into the Internet, your own computer becomes an extension of that network.

We'll spend the first section of this book defining the Internet. We'll also examine the architectures, protocols, and general concepts that make it all possible.

In Chapter 1, "The Wired World of the Internet," we will examine how the Internet runs. We'll look at who pays for the high-speed data backbones that carry much of the Internet's traffic, and at the organizations that make sure that standards are set for networks to follow so that the Internet can run smoothly. We'll also look at the various kinds of networks that are connected to the Internet.

Chapter 2, "How Information Travels Across the Internet," explains how information travels across the Internet and describes how hardware such as routers, repeaters, and bridges sends information among networks. It also shows how smaller networks are grouped into larger regional networks—and how those large regional networks communicate among themselves.

In Chapter 3, "How TCP/IP Works," we'll look at the Internet's basic protocols for communications and learn a little about basic Internet jargon, such as TCP/IP (short for Transmission Control Protocol and Internet Protocol). The chapter will explain how those protocols work and how special software such as Winsock enables personal computers to get onto a network originally designed for larger computers.

Chapter 4, "Understanding Internet Addresses and Domains," takes the mystery out of the Internet's often confusing addressing scheme. You'll learn about Internet domains and addresses and will even be able to make sense of them.

Chapter 5, "Anatomy of a Web Connection," covers the basics of what has become the most popular portion of the Internet—the World Wide Web. We'll look at the anatomy of a Web connection and see how hardware, such as Web servers, and software, such as Web browser client software, talk to one another and let you surf through the entire known world.

Chapter 6, "Internet File Types," will give you an understanding of the most common types of files you'll come across as you browse the Net. Compressed files, video files, graphics files—you'll learn about almost every kind of file you might encounter.

Whether you're a newbie or cyberpro, this section will teach you the basics of the Internet.

CHAPTER

1

The Wired World of the Internet

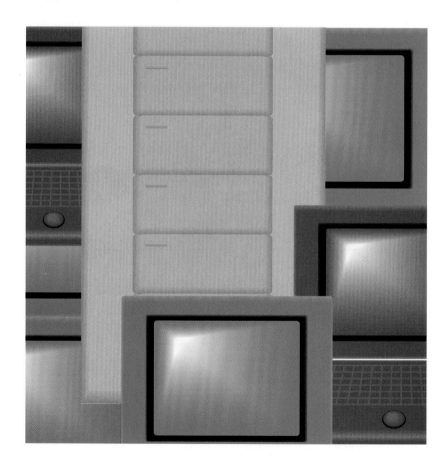

ONE of the most frequently asked questions about the Internet is: Who runs it? The truth is that no centralized management of the Internet exists. Instead, it is a collection of thousands of individual networks and organizations, each of which is run and paid for on its own. Each network cooperates with other networks to direct Internet traffic so that information can pass among them. Together, these networks and organizations make up the wired world of the Internet. For networks and computers to cooperate in this way, however, a general agreement must take place about things such as Internet procedures and standards for protocols. These procedures and standards are laid out in RFCs (requests for comment) agreed upon by Internet users and organizations.

A variety of groups guide the Internet's growth by helping to establish standards and by educating people on the proper way to use the Internet. Perhaps the most important is the Internet Society, a private, nonprofit group. The Internet Society supports the work of the Internet Activities Board (IAB), which handles much of the Internet's behind-the-scenes and architectural issues. The IAB's Internet Engineering Task Force is responsible for overseeing how the Internet's TCP/IP protocols evolve. (See Chapter 3, "How TCP/IP Works," for details on protocols.)

The World Wide Web Consortium (W3C) develops standards for the evolution of the fastest-growing part of the Internet, the World Wide Web. The W3C is an industry consortium run by the Laboratory for Computer Science at the Massachusetts Institute of Technology (MIT).

Private companies, such as www.zdnet.com, oversee the registering of Internet domains. These companies are overseen by boards made up of people from business, the government, and individual Internet users.

Although these organizations are important as a kind of glue for holding together the Internet, at the heart of the Internet are individual local networks. These networks can be found in private companies, universities, government agencies, and online services. They are funded separately from each other and in a variety of manners, such as fees from users, corporate support, taxes, and grants. Many Internet service providers (ISPs), which provide Internet access for individuals, have networks as well. Individuals who want to access the Internet pay ISPs a monthly connection rate, so in that sense, everyone who uses the Internet helps pay for it.

The networks are connected in a variety of ways. For efficiency's sake, local networks join in consortiums known as regional networks. A variety of leased lines connect regional and local networks. The leased lines that connect networks can be as simple as a single telephone line or as complex as a fiber-optic cable with microwave links and satellite transmissions.

Private companies who make money by selling access to their lines build backbones, which are very high-capacity lines that carry enormous amounts of Internet traffic. Government agencies, such as NASA, and large private corporations pay for some of these backbones. The National Science Foundation also pays for some backbones.

How the Internet Runs

1 Because the Internet is a loose organization of networks, no single group runs it and pays for it. Instead, many private organizations, universities, and government agencies pay for and run parts of it. They all work together in a democratic, loosely organized alliance. Private organizations range from small, homegrown networks to commercial online services, such as America Online and CompuServe, and private Internet service providers (ISPs) that sell access to the Internet.

2 Through agencies such as the National Science Foundation, the federal government pays for some high-speed backbones that carry Internet traffic across the country and the world. The extremely high-speed vBNS (very high-speed Backbone Network Services), for example, provides a high-speed infrastructure for the research and education community by linking together supercomputer centers. The government is also building an even faster backbone, which will transmit data at 9.6 billion bits per second (bps). Often, a large corporation or organization such as NASA will provide backbones to link sites across the country or the world.

Regional Network

vBNS Backbone

3 Regional networks provide and maintain Internet access within a geographic area. Regional nets may consist of smaller networks and organizations within the area that have banded together to provide better service.

Supercomputer Center

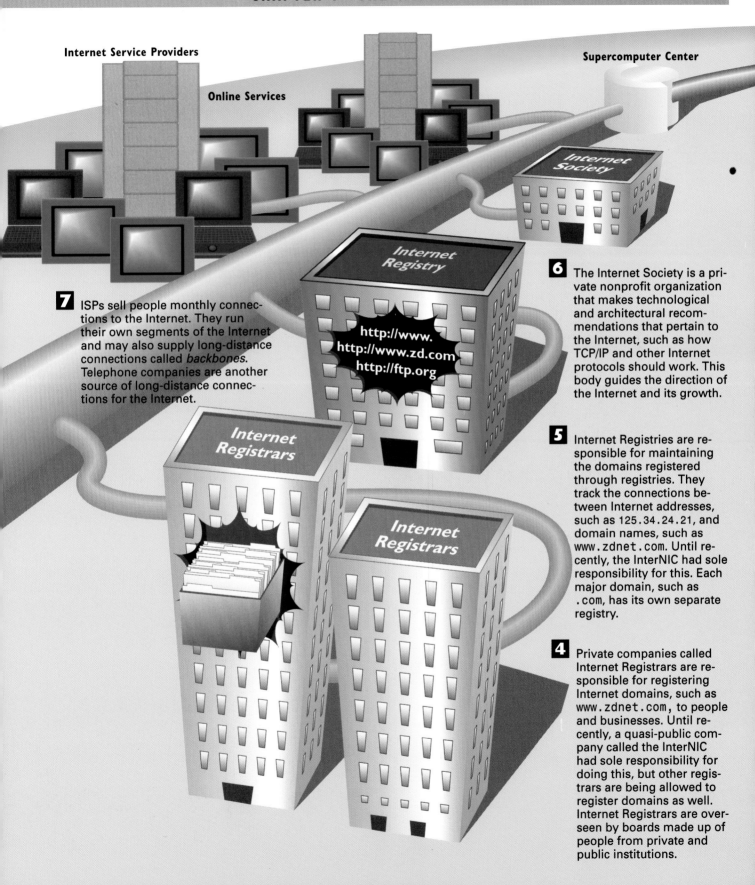

Internet Service Providers

Online Services

Supercomputer Center

Internet Society

Internet Registry

http://www.
http://www.zd.com
http://ftp.org

Internet Registrars

Internet Registrars

7 ISPs sell people monthly connections to the Internet. They run their own segments of the Internet and may also supply long-distance connections called *backbones*. Telephone companies are another source of long-distance connections for the Internet.

6 The Internet Society is a private nonprofit organization that makes technological and architectural recommendations that pertain to the Internet, such as how TCP/IP and other Internet protocols should work. This body guides the direction of the Internet and its growth.

5 Internet Registries are responsible for maintaining the domains registered through registries. They track the connections between Internet addresses, such as 125.34.24.21, and domain names, such as www.zdnet.com. Until recently, the InterNIC had sole responsibility for this. Each major domain, such as .com, has its own separate registry.

4 Private companies called Internet Registrars are responsible for registering Internet domains, such as www.zdnet.com, to people and businesses. Until recently, a quasi-public company called the InterNIC had sole responsibility for doing this, but other registrars are being allowed to register domains as well. Internet Registrars are overseen by boards made up of people from private and public institutions.

CHAPTER

2

How Information Travels Across the Internet

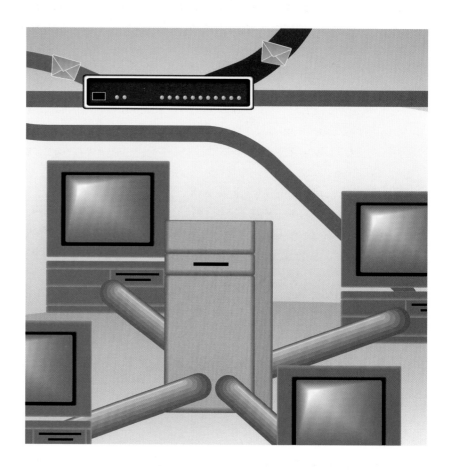

YOU may take for granted that when you send a piece of information across the Internet, it will always reach its intended destination. However, the process of sending that information is remarkably complex.

When you send information across the Internet, the Transmission Control Protocol (TCP) first breaks it up into packets. Your computer sends those packets to your local network, Internet service provider (ISP), or online service. From there, the packets travel through many levels of networks, computers, and communications lines before they reach their final destination, which may be across town or around the world. A variety of hardware processes those packets and routes them to their proper destinations. This hardware is designed to transmit data between networks and makes up much of the glue that holds the Internet together. Five of the most important pieces of hardware are hubs, bridges, gateways, repeaters, and routers.

Hubs are important because they link groups of computers to one another and let computers communicate with each other. *Bridges* link local area networks (LANs) with one another. They enable data destined for another LAN to be sent there, while keeping local data inside its own network. *Gateways* are similar to bridges, but they also translate data from one kind of network to another.

When data travels across the Internet, it often crosses great distances, which can be a problem because the signal sending the data can weaken over the distance. To solve the problem, *repeaters* amplify the data at intervals so the signal doesn't weaken.

Routers play a key role in managing Internet traffic. Their job is to make sure the packets always arrive at the proper destination. If data is being transferred among computers that are on the same LAN, routers often aren't needed because the network itself can handle its internal traffic. Routers come into play when the data is sent between two different networks. Routers examine packets to determine their destination. They take into account the volume of activity on the Internet, and they send the packets to another router—one that is closer to the packet's final destination.

Midlevel networks hook LANs together using high-speed telephone lines, ethernet, and microwave links. A regional network is a midlevel network in a geographic area. A wide area network (WAN) is another kind of midlevel network. A WAN consists of an organization with many networked sites linked together.

When a packet travels from a computer on a LAN in a midlevel network to a computer somewhere else on the midlevel network, a router (or a series of routers) sends the packets to their proper destination. However, if the destination lies outside the midlevel network, the packets are sent to a NAP (Network Access Point), where they are sent across the country or the world on a backbone. High-speed backbones such as the vBNS (very high-speed Backbone Network Services) can transmit enormous amounts of data—155 megabits (millions of bits) per second (Mbps). Even faster backbones are being built that will transmit data at an astonishing 9.6 billion bits per second.

Linking Networks to the Internet

1 The Internet comprises networks that are attached to one another via pathways that facilitate the exchange of information, data, and files. Being connected to the Internet means having access to these pathways. Your computer can send packets of data over these pathways to any other computer connected to the Internet.

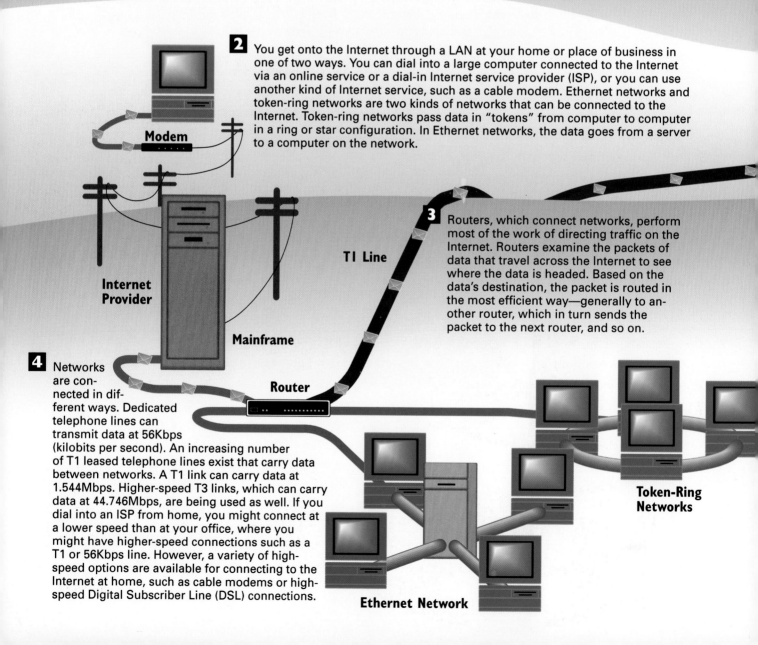

2 You get onto the Internet through a LAN at your home or place of business in one of two ways. You can dial into a large computer connected to the Internet via an online service or a dial-in Internet service provider (ISP), or you can use another kind of Internet service, such as a cable modem. Ethernet networks and token-ring networks are two kinds of networks that can be connected to the Internet. Token-ring networks pass data in "tokens" from computer to computer in a ring or star configuration. In Ethernet networks, the data goes from a server to a computer on the network.

Modem

Internet Provider

Mainframe

T1 Line

3 Routers, which connect networks, perform most of the work of directing traffic on the Internet. Routers examine the packets of data that travel across the Internet to see where the data is headed. Based on the data's destination, the packet is routed in the most efficient way—generally to another router, which in turn sends the packet to the next router, and so on.

4 Networks are connected in different ways. Dedicated telephone lines can transmit data at 56Kbps (kilobits per second). An increasing number of T1 leased telephone lines exist that carry data between networks. A T1 link can carry data at 1.544Mbps. Higher-speed T3 links, which can carry data at 44.746Mbps, are being used as well. If you dial into an ISP from home, you might connect at a lower speed than at your office, where you might have higher-speed connections such as a T1 or 56Kbps line. However, a variety of high-speed options are available for connecting to the Internet at home, such as cable modems or high-speed Digital Subscriber Line (DSL) connections.

Router

Ethernet Network

Token-Ring Networks

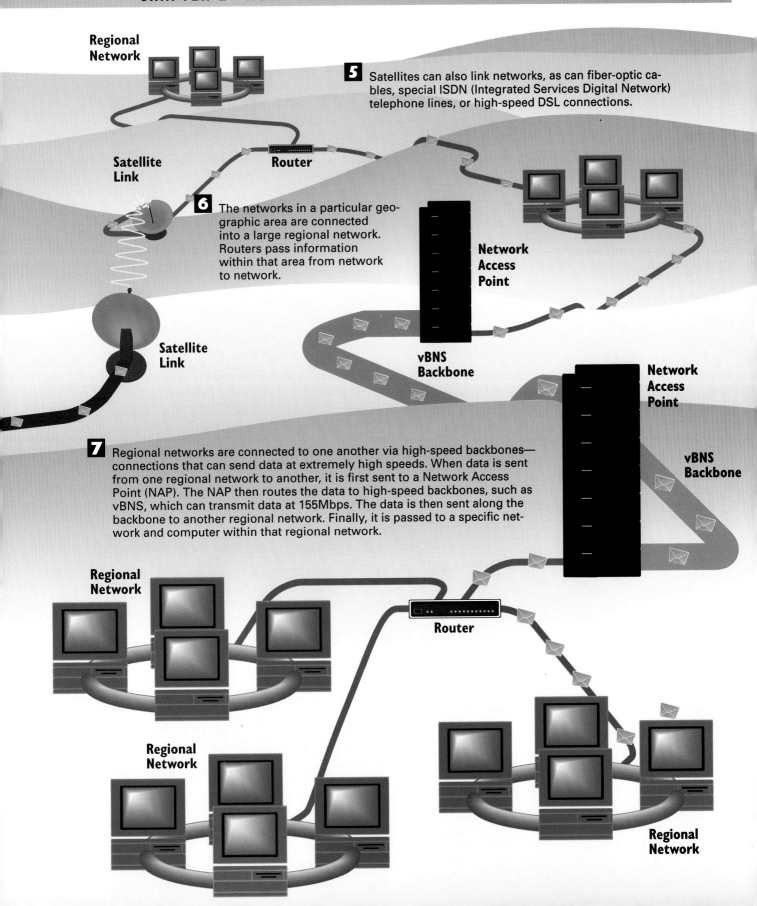

Regional Network

5 Satellites can also link networks, as can fiber-optic cables, special ISDN (Integrated Services Digital Network) telephone lines, or high-speed DSL connections.

Satellite Link

Router

6 The networks in a particular geographic area are connected into a large regional network. Routers pass information within that area from network to network.

Network Access Point

Satellite Link

vBNS Backbone

Network Access Point

vBNS Backbone

7 Regional networks are connected to one another via high-speed backbones—connections that can send data at extremely high speeds. When data is sent from one regional network to another, it is first sent to a Network Access Point (NAP). The NAP then routes the data to high-speed backbones, such as vBNS, which can transmit data at 155Mbps. The data is then sent along the backbone to another regional network. Finally, it is passed to a specific network and computer within that regional network.

Regional Network

Router

Regional Network

Regional Network

CHAPTER

3

How TCP/IP Works

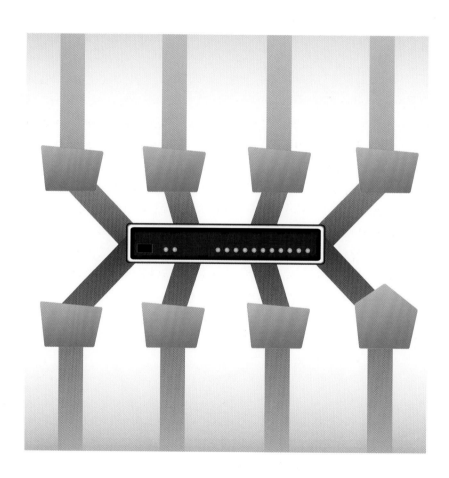

A seemingly simple set of ideas makes it possible for computers and networks all over the world to share information and messages on the Internet: Break up every piece of information and message into pieces called *packets*, deliver those packets to the proper destinations, and then reassemble the packets into their original form after they've been delivered so the receiving computer can view and use them. That's the job of the two most important communications protocols on the Internet—the Transmission Control Protocol (TCP) and the Internet Protocol (IP). They are frequently referred to as TCP/IP. TCP breaks down and reassembles the packets, whereas IP is responsible for making sure the packets are sent to the right destination.

TCP/IP is used because the Internet is what is known as a packet-switched network. In a *packet-switched network*, there is no single, unbroken connection between sender and receiver. Instead, when information is sent, it is broken into small packets, sent over many different routes at the same time, and then reassembled at the receiving end. By contrast, the telephone system is a circuit-switched network. In a *circuit-switched network*, once a connection is made (as with a telephone call, for example), that part of the network is dedicated only to that single connection.

In order for personal computers to take full advantage of the Internet, they need to use special software that understands and interprets the Internet's TCP/IP protocols. This software is referred to as a *socket* or a *TCP/IP stack*. For PCs, the required software is called Winsock. There are many different versions of Winsock available for PCs. For Macintoshes, the software is called MacTCP. In both cases, this software serves as an intermediary between the Internet and the personal computer. Personal computers can take advantage of the simplest, most rudimentary parts of the Internet without using Winsock or MacTCP. For full access to the Internet, TCP/IP stacks are necessary.

A computer can be connected to a LAN (local area network) with a network card. In order to communicate with the network, the network card requires a hardware driver—software that mediates between the network and the network card. If a computer is not physically connected to a LAN with a network card, it can instead connect to the Internet by dialing in and using a modem. The computer will still need a TCP/IP stack in order to use the TCP/IP protocols. However, it won't require a network card or a hardware driver. Instead, the computer needs to use one of two software protocols: either SLIP (Serial Line Internet Protocol) or PPP (Point-to-Point Protocol).

SLIP and PPP are designed for computers connected to the Internet over a serial connection via a modem. In general, the newer PPP provides a more error-free connection than does the older SLIP. Computers can also dial into the Internet without using TCP/IP stacks, SLIP, or PPP. However, they won't be able to tap into the full power of the Internet, most specifically, the World Wide Web. To make full use of the Web, you need a computer that is part of the Internet, which requires a TCP/IP stack. The SLIP or PPP must then be used when dialing into an ISP for Web access.

How TCP/IP Works

1 The Internet is a packet-switched network, which means that when you send information across the Internet from your computer to another computer, the data is broken into small packets. A series of switches called routers send each packet across the Net individually. Once all the packets arrive at the receiving computer, they are recombined into their original, unified form. Two protocols do the work of breaking the data into packets, routing the packets across the Internet, and then recombining them on the other end: The Internet Protocol (IP), which routes the data, and the Transmission Control Protocol (TCP), which breaks the data into packets and recombines them on the computer that receives the information.

2 For a number of reasons, including hardware limitations, data sent across the Internet must be broken up into packets of less than about 1,500 characters each. Each packet is given a header that contains a variety of information, such as the order in which the packets should be assembled with other related packets. As TCP creates each packet, it also calculates and adds to the header a *checksum*, which is a number that TCP uses on the receiving end to determine whether any errors have been introduced into the packet during transmission. The checksum is based on the precise amount of data in the packet.

3 Each packet is put into separate IP "envelopes" which contain addressing information that tells the Internet where to send the data. All the envelopes for a given piece of data have the same addressing information so they can all be sent to the same location to be reassembled. IP "envelopes" contain headers that include information such as the sender address, the destination address, the amount of time the packet should be kept before discarding it, and so on.

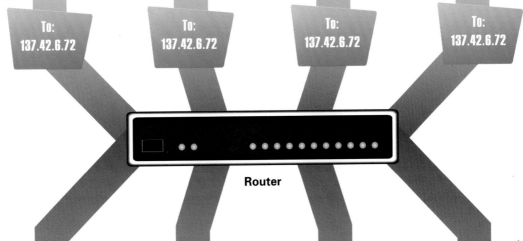

To:
137.42.6.72

To:
137.42.6.72

To:
137.42.6.72

To:
137.42.6.72

Router

4 As the packets are sent across the Internet, routers along the way examine the IP envelopes and look at their addresses. These routers determine the most efficient path for sending each packet to the next router closest to its final destination. After traveling through a series of routers, the packets arrive. Because the traffic load on the Internet changes constantly, the packets may be sent along different routes and the packets may arrive out of order.

18,713

CORRUPTION

ORIGINAL PACKET RETRANSMITTED

17,136

To:
137.42.6.72

To:
137.42.6.72

To:
137.42.6.72

To:
137.42.6.72

5 As the packets arrive at their destination, TCP calculates a checksum for each packet. It then compares this checksum with the checksum that has been sent in the packet. If the checksums don't match, TCP knows that the data in the packet has been corrupted during transmission. It then discards the packet and asks that the original packet be retransmitted.

6 When all the non-corrupt packets are received by the computer to which the information is being sent, TCP assembles them into their original, unified form.

TCP

1011101010101
0011001010
1001000111
1011000101
1100101001

CHAPTER 4

Understanding Internet Addresses and Domains

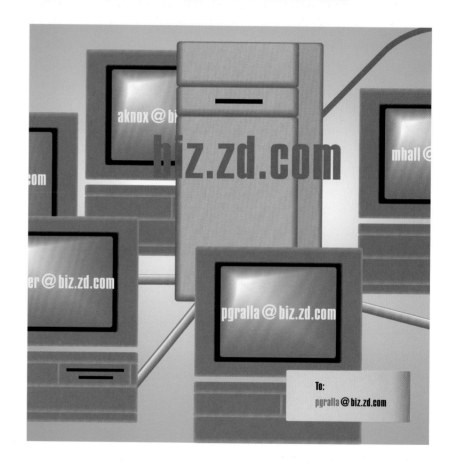

TO do just about anything on the Internet, and especially to send email, you'll need to understand Internet addresses. The Internet Protocol (IP) uses Internet address information to deliver mail and other data from computer to computer. Every IP address on the Internet is actually a series of four numbers separated by periods (called dots), such as 163.52.128.72. It would be difficult, if not impossible, for you to remember numeric addresses when you wanted to get in touch with someone. Also, numeric IP addresses sometimes change. This means not only would it be impossible for people to keep track of the original numeric addresses, but it would also be impossible to know every time those numeric addresses were altered.

Sun Microsystems developed the Domain Name System (DNS) in the early 1980s as an easier way to keep track of addresses. It has been the addressing system on the Internet ever since. The DNS establishes a hierarchy of *domains*, which are groups of computers on the Internet. The DNS gives each computer on the net an Internet address, or domain name, using easily recognizable letters and words instead of numbers. The domains at the top level of the hierarchy maintain lists and addresses of the domains just beneath them. Those subordinate domains have similar responsibilities for the domains just beneath them, and so on. In this way, every computer on the net gets an Internet address. The DNS also helps Internet computers send email to the proper destination by converting the textual Internet address into its IP numeric equivalent.

An Internet address is made up of two major parts separated by an @ (at) sign. One example is pgralla@ziffdavis.com

The first part of the address—to the left of the @ sign—is the user name, which usually refers to the person who holds the Internet account and is often that person's login name. The second part of the address, to the right of the @ sign, is the host name or domain name, which identifies the specific computer where the person has an Internet email account. If the email account is located at the person's work, this host or domain name may reflect the name of the company, such as pgralla@ziffdavis.com. Otherwise, it will probably reflect where the person has an Internet account—either with an Internet service provider (ISP) or online service, such as jjcale@tic.net or jonejoan@aol.com.

The rightmost portion of the domain section of the address identifies the largest domain and kind of organization where the person has his or her address. Common domains in the United States are .com for commercial; .edu for education; .gov for government; .mil for military; .net for network (most commonly used by ISPs, but also for companies and groups concerned with the organization of the Internet); and .org for organization. A variety of plans have been proposed for seven or more domains to be added, such as .web for Web. Outside the United States, only two letters are used to identify the domains, such as .au for Australia; .ca for Canada; .uk for United Kingdom; and .fr for France.

How Internet Addresses and Domains Work

1 The Internet Protocol (IP) delivers mail based on the specific email address. This address is expressed as four numbers, separated by periods (called dots), such as 163.52.128.72. However, because it would be difficult to remember such complex addresses, you can instead use Internet addresses made up of words and letters. Computers called *domain name servers* translate the alphabetical address into a numerical address, so email can be sent to the proper location.

2 An Internet address is made up of two major parts separated by an @ (at) sign. The address can tell you a good deal of information about the person who "owns" the address. The first part of the address (to the left of the @ sign) is the username, which usually refers to the person who holds the Internet account and is often that person's login name or in some way identifies him or her. The second part of the address (to the right of the @ sign) contains the hostname (which can refer to a specific server on a network), followed by the Internet address, which together identify the specific computer where the person has an Internet email account.

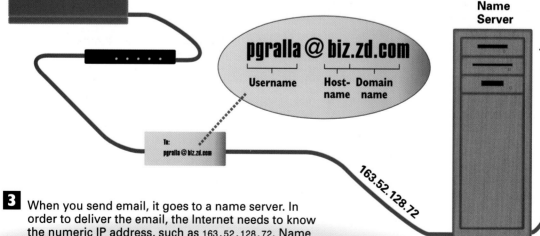

Name Server

pgralla @ biz.zd.com

Username   Host- Domain
name   name

To:
pgralla @ biz.zd.com

163.52.128.72

3 When you send email, it goes to a name server. In order to deliver the email, the Internet needs to know the numeric IP address, such as 163.52.128.72. Name servers look up the alphabetical address and substitute the numeric IP address for it so the email can be delivered properly.

4 The Domain Name System (DNS) divides the Internet into understandable groups, or domains. Note the portion of the domain section at the far right of the address. It identifies the largest domain names and kind of organization where the person's address resides. The domain names and host-names identify the host computer where the Internet should deliver the email. The receiving host computer looks at the username and delivers the mail to the proper email box.

5 To the left of the largest domain is specific information about the organization, which tells routers to which network the email should be sent. It can be a single Internet address, such as zd (for Ziff-Davis), or it can be a group of domains and subdo-mains, such as mfsc.nasa.

6 To the left of the Internet address is the hostname, which tells routers to which specific computer within the domain the email should be delivered.

7 The domain and hostnames tell the Internet to which computer the email should be delivered. The receiving host computer looks at the username and delivers the mail to the proper email box.

pgralla @ biz.zd.com

pgralla @ biz.zd.com

zd.com

To:
pgralla @ biz.zd.com

To:
pgralla @ biz.zd.com

To:
pgralla @ biz.zd.com

pgralla @ biz.zd.com

aknox @ bi

biz.zd.com

mhall @ bi

vperry @ biz.zd.com

ajones @ biz.zd.com

sweber @ biz.zd.com

pgralla @ biz.zd.com

To:
pgralla @ biz.zd.com

ORGANIZATION

CHAPTER

5

Anatomy of a Web Connection

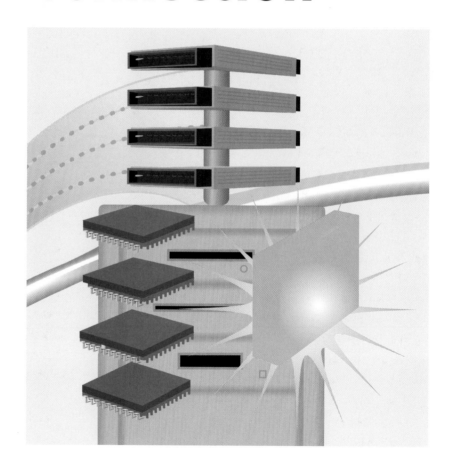

A typical Web connection consists of four basic parts: the desktop, client computer, or similar device; the Internet access provider; the host or server computer at the other end of the connection; and the communications networks that link together the first three components. The desktop is the command and control station from which you direct your navigation of the Web. If you're getting onto the Internet via a personal computer and a modem, at the starting point of the connection, you need a few basic hardware components—the personal computer, a fast modem and a telephone line, Web "browser" software, and an integrated communications program. The browser sends instructions to the communications program to contact a specific computer on the Web and retrieve a specific Web document or page. The communications program dials the modem, which enables the browser to send the request using TCP/IP. To reach the Internet, most desktop computers call an intermediary computer at a company that serves as an Internet access provider, also known as the Internet service provider, or ISP. The ISP acts as a conduit for individuals to dial in before getting patched through to the Internet backbone.

If you're connecting from work, your connection might look somewhat different. A personal computer on a network can share a modem with other computers on the network, for example, or the business may be directly connected to the Internet via a LAN (local area network) or other connection. In the latter case, an ISP wouldn't be needed to get onto the Web. You can get onto the Internet at home in a variety of ways, as well, without using a traditional modem—you can use a cable modem or not even use a computer at all; instead, you can go onto the Internet via your television set with a service such as WebTV. And even personal digital assistants (PDAs)—little handheld digital devices—can get you onto the Web these days.

After you're connected to the Internet and you want to get to a Web site, you'll need to know that Web site's specific domain, such as zdnet.com. After you type in that domain, preceded by www., you'll be sent to the site. You won't see it, but when you type in those letters, some nearly instantaneous electronic wizardry takes place. The computers that run the Internet can't understand letters and names such as zdnet.com, and so the plain English name is changed to an Internet IP address (such as 205.181.112.65) before you're sent to the site. Names are "resolved" to IP addresses using the Domain Name System, which is covered in Chapter 4, "Understanding Internet Addresses and Domains." By the way, anyone can own a domain on the Internet. All an individual needs to do is pay a small fee to an Internet registrar, and if the desired name isn't already taken, he or she can own it. To set up a site with that domain name, the new owner will need to get a company such as an Internet service provider (ISP) to host the site.

Host computers spread throughout the Internet house Web pages. Hosts differ from desktop computers in that they can handle multiple telecommunications connections at one time. Usually, they also have gigabytes of hard-disk storage, considerable random access memory (RAM), and a high-speed processor. In fact, some host systems may actually be several computers linked together, with each handling incoming Web page requests.

How Web Connections Work

1 A fast connection is essential for Web cruising. You may use a 28.8Kbps (kilobits per second) or faster modem that converts digital information from the computer into the analog signals transmitted by ordinary phone lines (sometimes called POTS, or plain old telephone service). ISDN lines that transfer digital data at speeds up to 128Kbps are available in some residential areas. Faster still are ADSL (asynchronous digital subscriber line) lines that transmit and receive digital data at 1.5Mbps or faster. And cable modems also can receive data at 1.5Mbps.

2 If you're using the telephone system to get onto the Internet, your telecommunications connection follows either the normal phone system (POTS) or an ISDN or ADSL line until it reaches the telephone company's central office. The central office routes calls either through its own network of copper, fiber-optic, or satellite links, or to a long distance carrier's point of presence, or POP. (The POP is the point at which a local call is handed off to a long distance company.) The call is then routed to the central office nearest your Internet service provider, also called an ISP.

Local Telephone Company

Page 3
Page 2
Page 1

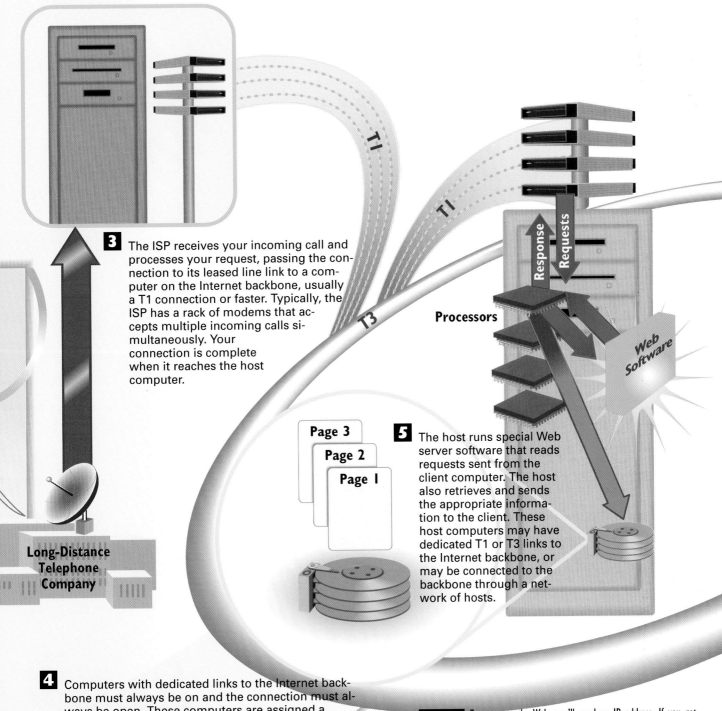

3 The ISP receives your incoming call and processes your request, passing the connection to its leased line link to a computer on the Internet backbone, usually a T1 connection or faster. Typically, the ISP has a rack of modems that accepts multiple incoming calls simultaneously. Your connection is complete when it reaches the host computer.

Long-Distance Telephone Company

Processors

Web Software

Response

Requests

T1

T1

T3

Page 3
Page 2
Page I

5 The host runs special Web server software that reads requests sent from the client computer. The host also retrieves and sends the appropriate information to the client. These host computers may have dedicated T1 or T3 links to the Internet backbone, or may be connected to the backbone through a network of hosts.

4 Computers with dedicated links to the Internet backbone must always be on and the connection must always be open. These computers are assigned a permanent IP (Internet Protocol) address, which is a multidigit number. This address enables other machines to find it. When you connect to the Internet via an ISP, your connection to the Internet backbone is opened, and your computer is assigned a temporary IP address—although some ISPs give you a permanent IP address, which is always yours whenever you connect to the Internet.

NOTE To get onto the Web, you'll need an IP address. If you get onto the Web at work via a LAN, the odds are you have a single IP address that is used every time you go onto the Internet. However, when you dial in from home, your IP address need not be the same every time you dial in. Often, the ISP you use will assign you a temporary IP address every time you dial in. By doing this, ISPs keep down the number of IP addresses they need to maintain.

CHAPTER
6

Internet File Types

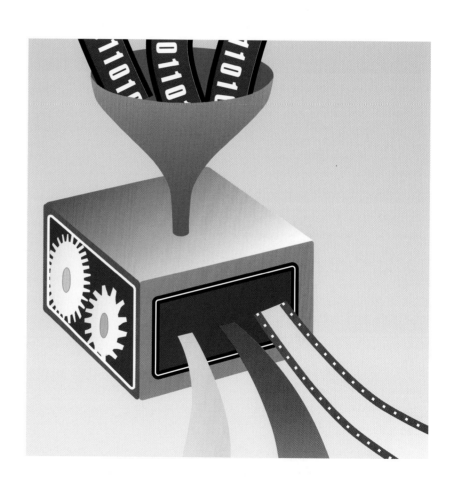

THERE are millions of files on the Internet that show you pictures, let you hear music and sounds, allow you to watch videos, and let you read articles and run software on your computer. Some of these files can be used on any computer, regardless of whether it is a Macintosh or an IBM-compatible PC. Graphics files, sound files, and video files, for example, can be played on many different kinds of computers, as long as those computers have the special software (often called *players* or *plug-ins*) required to view, run, or listen to them. Some files require special hardware in order to work. Other files, such as software programs that you download, can only run on a PC or a Mac, or they may require extra memory.

In general, on the Internet you'll find three kinds of files: ASCII (American Standard Code for Information Interchange); EBCDIC (Extended Binary Coded Decimal Interchange Code); and binary. ASCII and EBCDIC are ways of organizing data into something we can understand. ASCII codes are computer codes that represent the characters on your screen, such as the uppercase letter A or a dollar sign ($). ASCII text files contain nothing but simple character data. They lack the sophisticated formatting commands that word processing or desktop publishing programs can apply to a document. EBCDIC is like ASCII but you won't normally find EBCDIC files because they're primarily used by mainframe computers. Binary files contain special coded data and can only be run or read by specific computers and software.

In contrast to plain ASCII text files, there are files that contain sophisticated formatting and graphical information in them. Files that adhere to the PostScript page description language are of this type. These files are in fact ASCII files, but they contain information about how to format and print the file. There are other kinds of files that contain formatting and graphical information, such as those in the Adobe Acrobat PDF format, but many of them are binary files instead of ASCII files. In order to view or print either of these types of files, you'll need special software readers. In the case of PostScript files, you'll generally need a special PostScript printer that can print files in that language. Files of this type can be viewed in two ways: either when you're online and connected to the Internet, or when you're offline and not connected. To view the files when online, you'll use special plug-in modules or helper applications for your Web browser. To view the files when offline, you'll need software readers.

Sound, visual image, animation, and video files are also common on the Internet. These files are all binary files, which are made up of bits that are represented by 0s and 1s. Files of this type are often large, requiring special software readers, players, and sometimes hardware in order to play and read them. Some of these files can only be played or viewed on a specific type of computer, whereas others can be played or viewed on many types of computers if you have the right software. Some of the files, such as streaming audio files and streaming video files, can be viewed while you're online, connected to the Internet. Other types of files need to be viewed with special readers or players when you're off line.

File Types on the Internet

1 There are many different types of files on the Internet. Each file has information contained in its header. The header is simply the first line of a file or a specific number of bytes at the beginning of a file. Software that can read or view the files looks into the header of a file to distinguish what kind of file it is, and then processes the file accordingly.

2 You'll find graphics files in many formats, including GIF, JPEG, PNG, PCX, and TIF. GIF and JPEG are two of the most common graphics formats. They allow the exchange of image files between different kinds of computers and can be downloaded to your computer quickly. A GIF reader or JPEG reader can read binary GIF and JPEG files and display them on your computer. Graphics programs will typically read both types of files. A GIF file contains the binary data that will display an image when viewed with the proper reader. Your computer's video card takes information from the reader and displays it on your computer's monitor. Both GIF and JPEG are the commonly used graphics formats in Web pages. Your Web browser has the ability to read and display these files on Web pages without needing any added software.

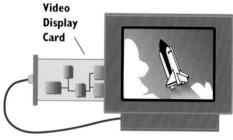

Video Display Card

Software Engine

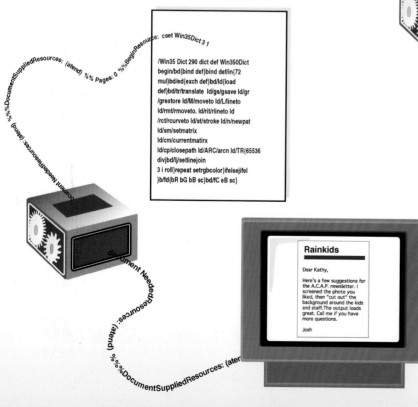

```
cset Win35Dict 3 1

/Win35 Dict 290 dict def Win350Dict
begin/bd{bind def}bind def/in{72
mul}bd/ed{exch def}bd/ld{load
def}bd/tr/translate  ld/gs/gsave ld/gr
/grestore ld/M/moveto ld/L/lineto
ld/rmt/rmoveto. ld/rit/rlineto ld
/rct/rcurveto ld/st/stroke ld/n/newpat
ld/sm/setmatrix
ld/cm/currentmatirx
ld/cp/closepath ld/ARC/arcn ld/TR{65536
div}bd/lj/setlinejoin
3 i roll}repeat setrgbcolor}ifelsejifel
}b/ld{bR bG bB sc}bd/fC eB sc}
```

Rainkids

Dear Kathy,

Here's a few suggestions for the A.C.A.P. newsletter. I screened the photo you liked, then "cut out" the background around the kids and staff. The output loads great. Call me if you have more questions.

Josh

3 Several different file types, such as PostScript (which ends in a .PS extension) and Adobe Acrobat (.PDF) files, contain complex information about documents. This includes placement of pictures, size and type of fonts, and the complex shapes and formatting information that is needed in order to view the page. You'll need specific readers for PostScript and Acrobat files. These readers allow you to see the fully formatted pages on your screen over the Internet and print them if you wish.

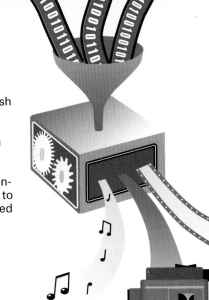

4 You'll find many different kinds of binary multimedia files on the Internet that let you listen to or play sounds, music, and videos. Windows sound files (which end in a .WAV extension) and Macintosh sound files are common types of files that you can download to your computer and play with a sound player. Other sound files, such as those created by Real Audio software, allow you to listen to the sounds while the file is downloading. This process is called *streaming audio*. Windows .AVI files are common animation files. Macintosh QuickTime and MPEG files (which end in an .MPG extension) are common video formats. Other animation files allow you to watch the video while the file is downloading. This process is called *streaming video*. You'll need special software to use all of these types of files.

Uncompression Engine

5 There are many executable programs you'll find on the Internet that you can download to your computer and use just like any other kind of software. Because these software files can be large and take a long time to download, it is often compressed to make it download faster. Once it's on your computer, you uncompress it with special decompression software and run it like any other program. Frequently, PC software has been compressed with PKZIP and has a .ZIP extension, whereas Macintosh software can be compressed with a variety of compression software. In general, PC files can only be used with PCs, while Macintosh files can only be used with Macintoshes.

6 You'll find many ASCII text files on the Internet that you can read with a text editor or word processor. These can be articles, FAQs (frequently asked questions and their answers), or any other kind of informational files.

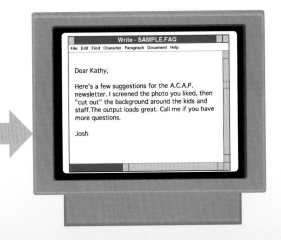

Dear Kathy,

Here's a few suggestions for the A.C.A.P. newsletter. I screened the photo you liked, then "cut out" the background around the kids and staff. The output loads great. Call me if you have more questions.

Josh

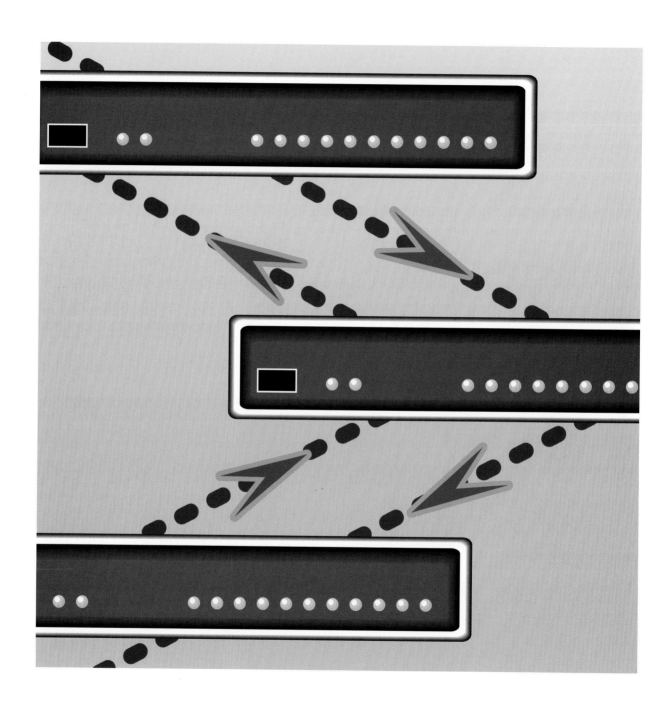

P A R T

THE INTERNET'S UNDERLYING ARCHITECTURE

AS you browse the World Wide Web or do anything else on the Internet, you take for granted that all information will be handled in a timely way. When you send data, you expect it to get to its proper location quickly. It all appears so seamless, as simple as the U.S. mail being delivered to the proper address. In fact, though, every time you do the simplest thing, such as contacting a Web site, you rely upon a remarkably complex architecture made up of complicated hardware and software spread across the planet—architecture that has been developed over the years and continues to be refined. This architecture is made up of your own computer and the software it runs; hardware, such as powerful servers that take your requests and then relay information to you; routers that examine every packet being sent across the Internet and ensure that it is sent to its proper destination; name servers that translate between alphanumeric Internet addresses, such as `pgralla@ziffdavis.com`, and IP addresses, such as `123.22.22.112`; and sets of rules that govern how computers on the Internet communicate with each other. When you look at it this way, it appears a remarkable feat that a simple piece of email you send to a friend manages to circumnavigate the globe and is received in a single piece.

Consider what has to happen for that piece of email to be sent to your friend. After you compose it on your computer and send it, it has to be broken down into many small pieces, and every one of those pieces has to be sent to the proper place and reassembled in the proper order. The email address, `myfriend@hishome.com`, for example, must be translated into its IP address, such as `123.22.22.112`, so that the Internet's hardware and software can figure out how to get it to its proper destination. That translation has to occur in every single packet in the message. After the IP address is known, the packets have to travel through many routers across the Internet, each of which sends the packets on their way, closer to their final destination. Your email software and your friend's email software have to communicate with mail servers to send and receive the mail. When you look at it this way, it's not quite so simple a task.

The chapters in this section cover the underlying architecture of the Internet—the hardware, the software, and the general organization that you rarely see or think of, but without which the Internet would not exist.

Chapter 7, "How the Domain Name System Works," covers the *Domain Name System (DNS)* and *domain name servers.* The DNS and its associated servers perform the most basic of tasks for the Internet—translating between the common alphanumeric Internet addresses with which we're all familiar, such as `prepg@tiac.com`, and the IP addresses that Internet computers use, such as `112.45.45.113`. Computers and people "think" differently; we think in letters as well as numbers, but computers can handle only numbers. So the DNS translates between human-speak and computer-speak. It ensures that when you send email or try to contact a Web site, the site you think you're contacting matches the one on the Internet.

Chapter 8, "How the Routers Work," details how the most basic piece of hardware on the Internet—a router—works. *Routers* are combinations of hardware and software that perform the job of making sure that all data is sent to the proper destination. Think of routers as the traffic cops of the Internet. They use the IP addresses that the name servers have translated to route the data. Routers look at the address and then send the data to the next-closest router to the destination and so on, until the data is finally delivered. They use *routing tables* to determine how to route the traffic, and they can also adjust the routes as the traffic on the Internet changes, ensuring that the data is routed in the most efficient way possible.

Finally, Chapter 9, "The Internet's Client/Server Architecture," looks at the Internet's client/server architecture. *Servers*—also called *hosts*—are powerful computers that perform functions such as delivering information or Web pages, hosting databases, or handling email. A *client* is your own computer and the software that sits on it, such as a Web browser or a piece of email software. Clients request information from servers, which do the heavy-duty processing and then send the information back to the client, which displays the information.

So the next time you send a piece of email or view a Web page, realize that a lot is going on behind the scenes.

7

How the Domain Name System Works

THE heart of how the Internet works is the Domain Name System (DNS), the way in which computers can contact each other and do things such as exchange email or display Web pages. When someone on the Internet wants to contact a location—for example, to visit a Web site—he or she will type in an address, such as www.metahouse.com. The Internet Protocol (IP) uses Internet address information and the DNS to deliver mail and other information from computer to computer.

The DNS translates the plain English address, www.metahouse.com, for example, into numbers that Internet computers can understand, such as 123.23.43.121. In order to do this efficiently, the Internet has been organized into a number of major domains. Major domains refer to the letters at the end of a plain English address, such as .com. A number of common domains are used in the United States: .com (commercial); .edu (education); .gov (government); .mil (military); .net (Internet service providers and networks—companies and groups concerned with the organization of the Internet); and .org (organization). Because the number of Internet sites has been growing exponentially, the domain name system is being expanded and may also include at least seven additional domains, such as .web for Web. Only two letters are used outside the United States to identify the domains; for example, .au for Australia; .ca for Canada; .uk for United Kingdom; and .fr for France.

Domains are organized in a hierarchical manner, so that beneath major domains are many minor domains. As an example of how the DNS and domains work, look at NASA's SPACElink Internet address: spacelink.msfc.nasa.gov. The top domain is .gov, which stands for government. The domain just below that is .nasa, which is the NASA domain. Then below that, .msfc (Marshall Space Flight Center) is one of NASA's many computer networks. Spacelink identifies the NASA computer that runs the SPACElink program. SPACElink's numeric IP address has changed through the years, but its Internet address has stayed the same.

The DNS system keeps track of changes such as the one just mentioned so that even when an IP address changes, if the Internet address is used, email will always be delivered to the proper place. Computers called *name servers* are responsible for keeping track of such changes and translating them between IP addresses and domain addresses. Name servers also work with the DNS to ensure that mail is delivered to the right person. They make sure that when you type in a Web Uniform Resource Locator (URL) you're sent to the proper location. Lastly, they're responsible for properly routing all messages and traffic on the Internet.

The Internet can't understand alphanumeric Internet addresses such as pgralla@ziff-davis.com, so name servers translate that address into its proper numeric IP address, such as 163.52.128.72. Name servers contain tables that match alphanumeric Internet addresses to numeric IP addresses.

How Domain Name System (DNS) Servers Work

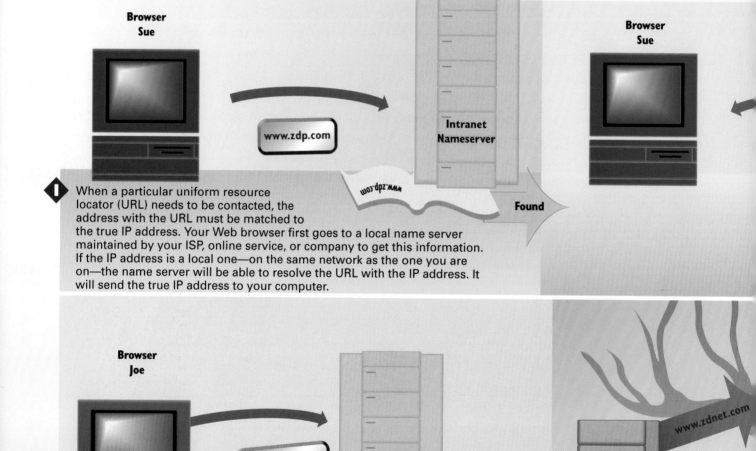

Browser Sue

www.zdp.com

Intranet Nameserver

www.zdp.com

Found

Browser Sue

1 When a particular uniform resource locator (URL) needs to be contacted, the address with the URL must be matched to the true IP address. Your Web browser first goes to a local name server maintained by your ISP, online service, or company to get this information. If the IP address is a local one—on the same network as the one you are on—the name server will be able to resolve the URL with the IP address. It will send the true IP address to your computer.

Browser Joe

www.zdnet.com

Intranet Nameserver

NOT Found...Asks

www.zdnet.com

interNic Internet Nameserver

3 If the information you have requested isn't on a local network, the local name server may not have the address you're looking for. In that instance, the local name server must get the information from a name server on the Internet. The local name server contacts the root domain server. The root domain server tells the local server which primary name server and secondary name server have the information about the requested URL.

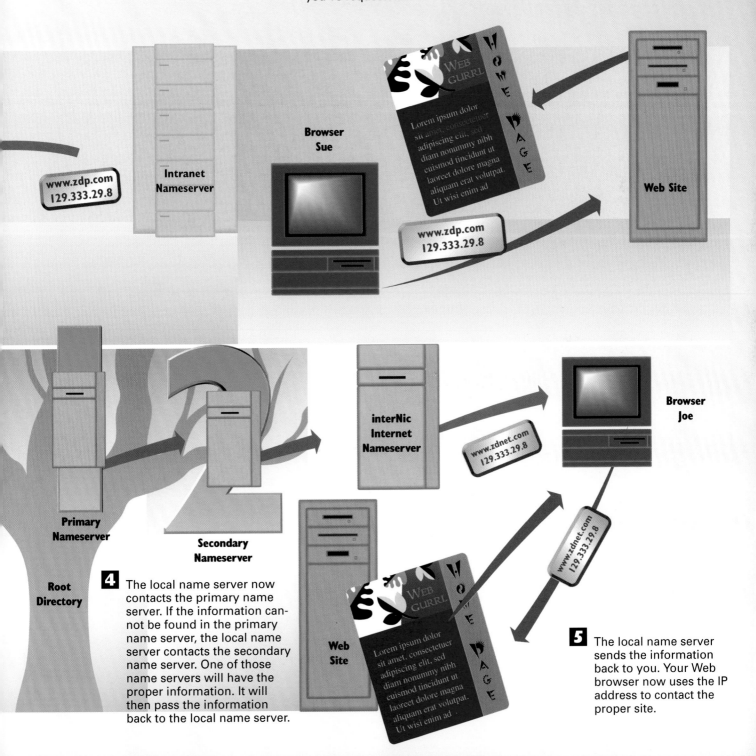

2 Your Web browser now has the true IP address of the place you're trying to locate. It uses that IP address and contacts the site. The site sends you the information you've requested.

www.zdp.com
129.333.29.8

Intranet
Nameserver

Browser
Sue

WEB GURRL HOME PAGE

Lorem ipsum dolor sit amet, consectetuer adipiscing elit, sed diam nonummy nibh euismod tincidunt ut laoreet dolore magna aliquam erat volutpat. Ut wisi enim ad

www.zdp.com
129.333.29.8

Web Site

interNic
Internet
Nameserver

www.zdnet.com
129.333.29.8

Browser
Joe

www.zdnet.com
129.333.29.8

Primary
Nameserver

Secondary
Nameserver

Root
Directory

Web
Site

WEB GURRL HOME PAGE

Lorem ipsum dolor sit amet, consectetuer adipiscing elit, sed diam nonummy nibh euismod tincidunt ut laoreet dolore magna aliquam erat volutpat. Ut wisi enim ad

4 The local name server now contacts the primary name server. If the information cannot be found in the primary name server, the local name server contacts the secondary name server. One of those name servers will have the proper information. It will then pass the information back to the local name server.

5 The local name server sends the information back to you. Your Web browser now uses the IP address to contact the proper site.

8

How the Routers Work

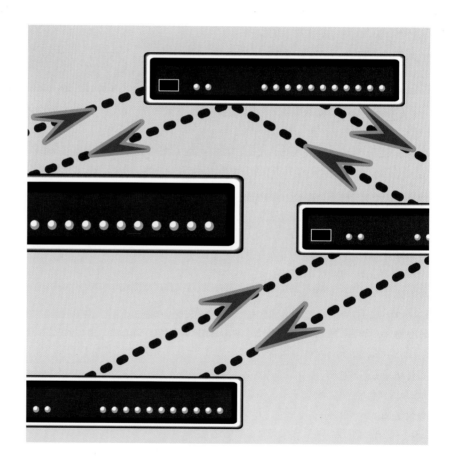

ROUTERS are the traffic cops of the Internet. They make sure all data gets sent to where it's supposed to go via the most efficient route. When you sit down at your computer on the Internet and send or receive data, generally that information must first go through at least one router and often more than one router before it reaches its final destination.

Routers open the IP packets of data to read the destination address, calculate the best route, and then send the packet toward its final destination. If the destination is on the same network as the sending computer, such as within a corporation, the router will send the packet directly to the destination computer. If the packet is destined for a destination outside the local network, the router will instead send the packet to another router closer to the destination. That router in turn will send the packet to a yet-closer router, and so on, until the packet reaches its final destination.

When routers determine the next router to receive packets, factors such as traffic congestion and the number of *hops* (routers or gateways on any given path) come into play. The IP packet carries a segment that holds the maximum hop counts it can travel and a router will not use a path that would exceed that predefined number of hops.

Routers have two or more physical ports: receiving (input) ports and sending (output) ports. In actuality, every port is bidirectional and can receive or send data. When an input port receives a packet, a software routine called a *routing process* is run. This process looks inside the header information in the IP packet and finds the address where the data is being sent. It then compares this address against an internal database called a *routing table*. The routing table has detailed information about the ports to which packets with various IP addresses should be sent. Based on what it finds in the routing table, the router sends the packet to a specific output port. This output port then sends the data to the next router or to the destination itself.

At times, packets are sent to a router's input port faster than the port can process them. When this happens, the packets are sent to a special holding area called an *input queue*, which is an area of RAM on the router. That specific input queue is associated with a specific input port. A router can have more than one input queue. Each input port processes packets from the queue in the order in which they were received so the first packets sent in are the first to get processed and sent out.

If the number of packets received exceeds the capacity of the queue (called the *length* of the queue), packets may be lost. When this happens, the TCP protocol on the sending and receiving computers will have the packets re-sent.

How Routers Work

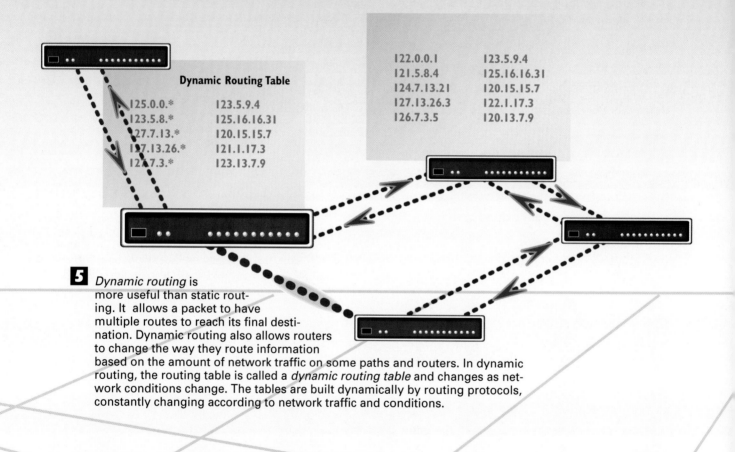

1 A router has *input ports* for receiving IP packets and *output ports* for sending those packets toward their destination. When a packet comes to an input port, the router examines the packet header and checks the destination in it against a *routing table*—a database that tells the router how to send packets to various destinations.

Dynamic Routing Table

125.0.0.*	123.5.9.4
123.5.8.*	125.16.16.31
127.7.13.*	120.15.15.7
127.13.26.*	121.1.17.3
126.7.3.*	123.13.7.9

122.0.0.1	123.5.9.4
121.5.8.4	125.16.16.31
124.7.13.21	120.15.15.7
127.13.26.3	122.1.17.3
126.7.3.5	120.13.7.9

5 *Dynamic routing* is more useful than static routing. It allows a packet to have multiple routes to reach its final destination. Dynamic routing also allows routers to change the way they route information based on the amount of network traffic on some paths and routers. In dynamic routing, the routing table is called a *dynamic routing table* and changes as network conditions change. The tables are built dynamically by routing protocols, constantly changing according to network traffic and conditions.

6 There are two broad types of routing protocols: interior and exterior. *Interior routing protocols* are typically used only on routers in a company's *intranet*, or internal network. These interior routing protocols route traffic bound only for inside the intranet. A common interior routing protocol is the Routing Information Protocol (RIP). *Exterior protocols* are typically used for routers located on the Internet. A common exterior routing protocol is the Exterior Gateway Protocol (EGP).

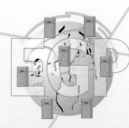

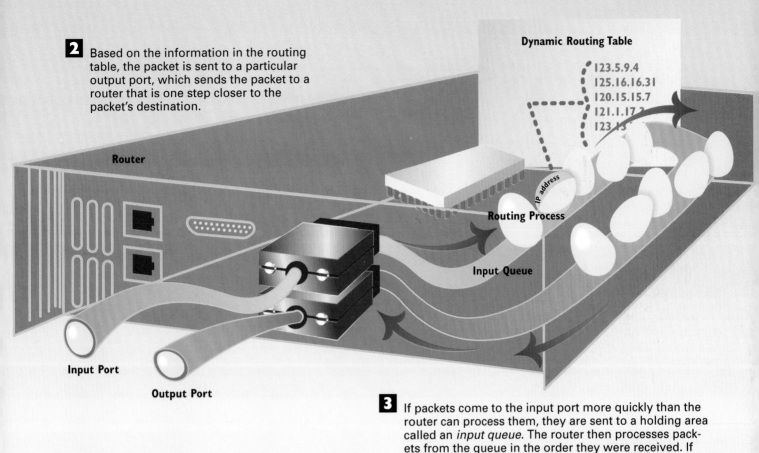

2 Based on the information in the routing table, the packet is sent to a particular output port, which sends the packet to a router that is one step closer to the packet's destination.

Dynamic Routing Table

123.5.9.4
125.16.16.31
120.15.15.7
121.1.17.3
123.13

Router

Routing Process

IP address

Input Queue

Input Port

Output Port

3 If packets come to the input port more quickly than the router can process them, they are sent to a holding area called an *input queue*. The router then processes packets from the queue in the order they were received. If the number of packets received exceeds the length of the queue, packets may be lost. When this happens, the TCP protocol on the sending and receiving computers will have the packets re-sent.

4 A simple kind of routing table is called a *static routing table*. In static routing, the routing table has specific ways of routing data to other networks. Only those pathways can be used. New routes can be added to the routing table. Static routing can't adjust routes as network traffic changes so it isn't an optimal alternative for many routers.

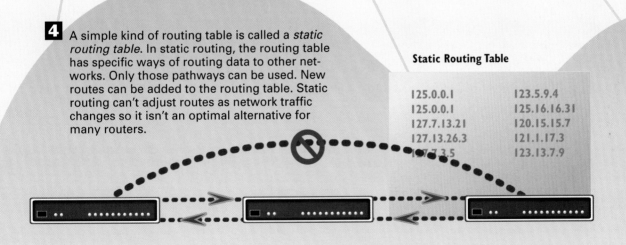

Static Routing Table

125.0.0.1	123.5.9.4
125.0.0.1	125.16.16.31
127.7.13.21	120.15.15.7
127.13.26.3	121.1.17.3
127.7.3.5	123.13.7.9

CHAPTER

9

The Internet's Client/Server Architecture

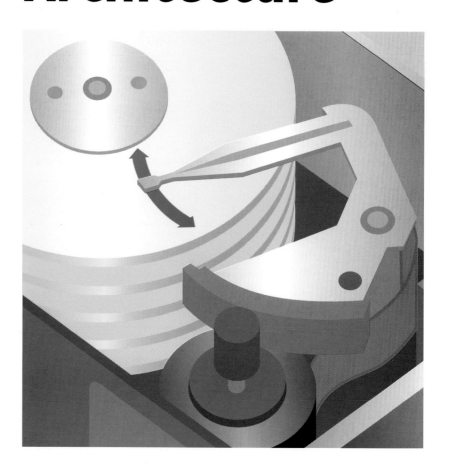

THE Internet works on the client/server model of information delivery. In this model, a client computer connects to a server computer on which information resides; the client depends on the server to deliver information. In effect, the client requests the services of the larger computer. These services may involve searching for information and sending it back to the client, such as when a database on the Web is queried. Other examples of these services are delivering Web pages, and handling incoming and outgoing email. Whenever you use the Internet, you're connected to a server computer and requesting the use of that server's resources.

Typically, the client is a local personal computer and the server (also known as the *host*) is usually a more powerful computer that houses the data. These computers can be of many different kinds: powerful Windows-based PCs, Macintoshes, and a wide variety of hardware that runs the UNIX operating system, such as computers made by the Digital Equipment Corporation.

The connection to the server is made via a LAN (local area network), a phone line, or a TCP/IP-based WAN (wide area network) on the Internet. A primary reason to set up a client/server network is to allow many clients to access the same applications and files that are stored on a server.

In the case of the Internet's World Wide Web, the client is actually the browser on your PC and the server is a host computer located somewhere on the Internet. Typically, the browser sends the server a request for a specific Web page. The server processes that request and sends an answer back to the browser (again, most often in the form of a Web page).

The connection between the client and server is maintained only during the actual exchange of information. Thus, after a Web page is transferred from the host (or server) computer, the HTTP connection between that computer and the client is broken. (HTTP stands for Hypertext Transfer Protocol; it's the protocol used by the World Wide Web.) Even though the HTTP connection is closed, the ISP maintains the TCP/IP connection to the Internet.

The client/server model enables the desktop PC to run the browser software to search the Web, yet still access host servers around the Internet to execute search and retrieval functions. In essence, this architecture enables the Web to be conceived of as a limitless file storage medium and database, distributed among thousands of host computers, all accessible by any individual PC.

The following illustration shows how the Web runs on a client/server architecture. Keep in mind that all other resources on the Internet run on the client/server model as well. For example, in email transactions the client would be the email software on your computer while the server would be the email server into which you connect.

How Client/Server Architecture Works

1 The PC-based browser software controls the client end of the Web application. Using TCP/IP, the browser issues HTTP requests to the host server. The browser can request a specific Web page or it can ask the host server to perform a database query. In either instance, the request is broken into HTTP packets that are sent across the Internet's TCP/IP communications infrastructure to the host computer.

HTTP

TCP/IP HTTP

TCP/IP HTTP

Site

2 The host computer runs the server software that enables the host to separate the actual request from the packets and perform the asked-for services. This will either involve retrieving and sending back to the client PC the specified Web page, or executing a database search and sending back to the client the result in the form of a Web page.

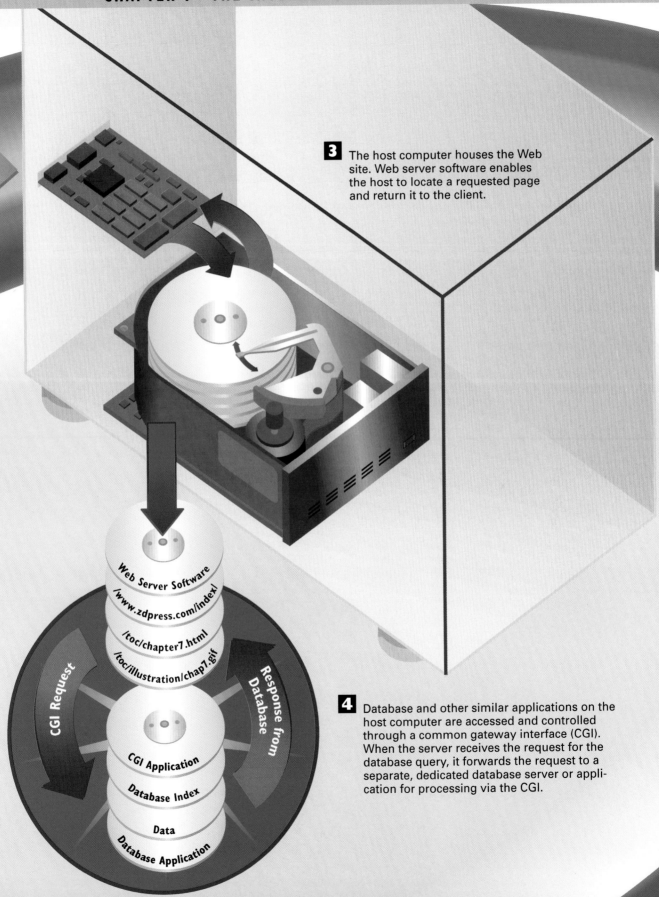

3 The host computer houses the Web site. Web server software enables the host to locate a requested page and return it to the client.

Web Server Software

/www.zdpress.com/index/

/toc/chapter7.html

/toc/illustration/chap7.gif

CGI Request

Response from Database

CGI Application

Database Index

Data

Database Application

4 Database and other similar applications on the host computer are accessed and controlled through a common gateway interface (CGI). When the server receives the request for the database query, it forwards the request to a separate, dedicated database server or application for processing via the CGI.

P A R T

CONNECTING
TO THE
INTERNET

NOW you know the basics of what the Internet comprises, and you know about its underlying architecture. So how do you actually connect to it?

You can connect to the Internet in many ways—and many more pop up practically every day. They range from simple telephone dial-in connections to special ISDN high-speed dial-ins, to television connections, Digital Subscriber Lines, and more. You can have a direct connection at your place of work or your university. You can browse the World Wide Web through a telephone line connection at home. Your computer can be merely a "dumb terminal" that can gain access to only a few Internet resources, such as a library database, or your computer can be a full Internet computer with access to everything the Internet has to offer. In this part of the book, we'll look at the myriad ways that people and computers gain access to the Internet.

One general rule is true about Internet connections: the faster the better. People want the fastest connection possible because many pictures, sounds, and videos are available on the Internet. Today, the two most common ways you can connect to the Internet are through a corporate or university LAN (local area network) or over telephone lines. Direct connections over LANs are generally faster than telephone line connections—although a new telephone technology called Digital Subscriber Lines (DSL) is changing that. Tomorrow, television and cable connections may be just as common.

In this section we'll look at all the ways that computers can connect to the Internet. Chapter 10, "Connecting Your Computer," gives an overview of the types of Internet connections that are possible. Not only will we examine different kinds of network connections and phone-line connections, but we'll also look at newer, high-speed connections that are becoming available; cable modems and DSL are two such examples.

Online services, such as CompuServe, America Online, and the Microsoft Network, at one time competed directly with the Internet for users. Now, instead of competing, those online services have joined the Internet club and provide Internet access to users. An online service can be one of the simplest ways to get an Internet connection. When you connect to an online service, you also get a full connection to the Internet. Chapter 11, "Connecting to the Internet from Online Services," examines how online services make that Internet connection.

Someday, we all expect to have extremely high-speed connections to the Internet, possibly via fiber-optic cabling in our homes. In fact, some communities are already installing such fiber optics. However, for the whole country to be wired will cost billions of dollars, and that capability appears to be at least several years away, if not longer. A quicker solution to reasonably priced, high-speed connections is ISDN (Integrated Services Digital Network). ISDN enables us to connect at high speeds to the Internet via normal, existing telephone lines. Not every area in the country has ISDN yet. In some areas it can be an expensive option, but in others it is reasonably priced. It requires a special modem, as well. However, it is an increasingly popular way to get to the Internet at very high speeds—much faster than even the highest-speed modems. Chapter 12, "How ISDN Works," explains that new technology.

Chapter 13, "The Internet/Television Connection," looks at what may become one of the primary ways that many of us connect to the Internet—through some kind of television connection. The chapter looks at the most common types of television connections, using cable television as a way to get onto the Internet, and how to use an ordinary television to browse the Internet. A cable connection allows you to use your normal cable TV wires to hook up your PC to the Internet—and does it at exceedingly high speeds, far beyond even what ISDN has to offer. Meanwhile, services such as WebTV go a different route—they enable you to browse the Web using a normal TV, although they often make the Internet connection using telephone wires instead of cable wires.

Chapter 14, "How Network Computers (NCs) Work," details one of the more intriguing ways to hook yourself into the Internet, via Network Computers, or NCs (sometimes also called information appliances). This calls for very low-cost computers—at perhaps $500 or so—that have no local storage or software; instead, all software and storage are held on the Internet.

Chapter 15, "How the Digital Subscriber Line (DSL) Works," looks at one of the newer high-speed ways to connect to the Internet—DSLs. These connections enable you to use existing telephone lines to hook up to the Internet at extremely high speeds. To use it, you'll need a special DSL modem, and your phone company needs the special modems as well.

As you'll see in this part of the book, it will become increasingly easy to connect to the Internet—and at increasingly higher speeds. Not only will you be able to do things faster on the Internet, but you will also be able to access entirely new services that will contain video, animation, and other high-bandwidth content.

CHAPTER

10

Connecting Your Computer

THERE are many different ways your computer can connect to the Internet, ranging from dial-in connections to LANs (local area networks) to connections over cable TV wires. If you are connected to a LAN or campus network at your business or school, you may already be connected to the Internet. If the LAN or campus network that you're on is connected to the Internet via a router or bridge, that means your computer is also connected to the Internet. Often, this offers higher-speed access than when you dial into the Internet. If you're not connected to the Internet via a network, there are a variety of options for accessing the Internet and many more appear every day.

One option is to find a network or ISP (Internet service provider) that lets you dial into it with your home computer. You can do this with terminal emulation software that makes your computer function like a "dumb terminal." In this case, the Internet software doesn't actually run on your computer. Instead, you run it on the computer you've connected to and your screen merely shows what's happening on the computer you've dialed into. If you connect in this way, the Internet services you can access are severely limited. For example, you generally won't be able to see graphics while you browse the most popular part of the Internet, the World Wide Web.

If you want to tap the full power of the Internet over telephone lines, you'll need full Internet connections, such as those that are available with SLIP (Serial Line Internet Protocol) and PPP (Point-to-Point Protocol). When you dial into the Internet with these protocols, your computer becomes a part of the Internet and you can use all the processing power you've got. PPP is newer and more stable than SLIP and can retransmit packets if they get garbled, which is a fairly common situation you'll encounter when sending information over telephone lines.

ISDN (Integrated Services Digital Network) lines provide high-speed connections to the Internet. Typically, these speeds range from 64Kbps to 128Kbps. You'll need a special ISDN modem and an ISP that offers ISDN access. Asymmetric Digital Subscriber Line (ADSL), a newer technology, allows for very high-speed connections over existing telephone wires, but your ISP will have to support the technology.

Another option is a special cable modem that allows you to use your coaxial television cable to access the Internet. Your local cable company may be able to provide you with this service. Speeds can be up to 100 times faster than regular modem speeds.

There are many different kinds of connections you can use to hook up to the Internet. Start at your local college or library. Contact an ISP and find out about their fees. There are many national and local service providers, so shop around. Lastly, the major online services now include Internet access, so you can easily use them to connect to the Net.

Connecting Your Computer to the Internet

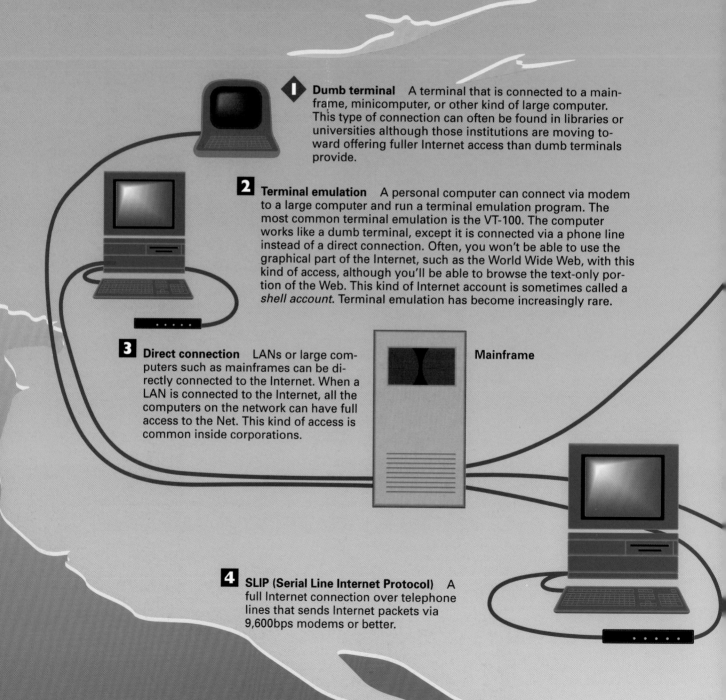

1 **Dumb terminal**   A terminal that is connected to a mainframe, minicomputer, or other kind of large computer. This type of connection can often be found in libraries or universities although those institutions are moving toward offering fuller Internet access than dumb terminals provide.

2 **Terminal emulation**   A personal computer can connect via modem to a large computer and run a terminal emulation program. The most common terminal emulation is the VT-100. The computer works like a dumb terminal, except it is connected via a phone line instead of a direct connection. Often, you won't be able to use the graphical part of the Internet, such as the World Wide Web, with this kind of access, although you'll be able to browse the text-only portion of the Web. This kind of Internet account is sometimes called a *shell account*. Terminal emulation has become increasingly rare.

3 **Direct connection**   LANs or large computers such as mainframes can be directly connected to the Internet. When a LAN is connected to the Internet, all the computers on the network can have full access to the Net. This kind of access is common inside corporations.

Mainframe

4 **SLIP (Serial Line Internet Protocol)**   A full Internet connection over telephone lines that sends Internet packets via 9,600bps modems or better.

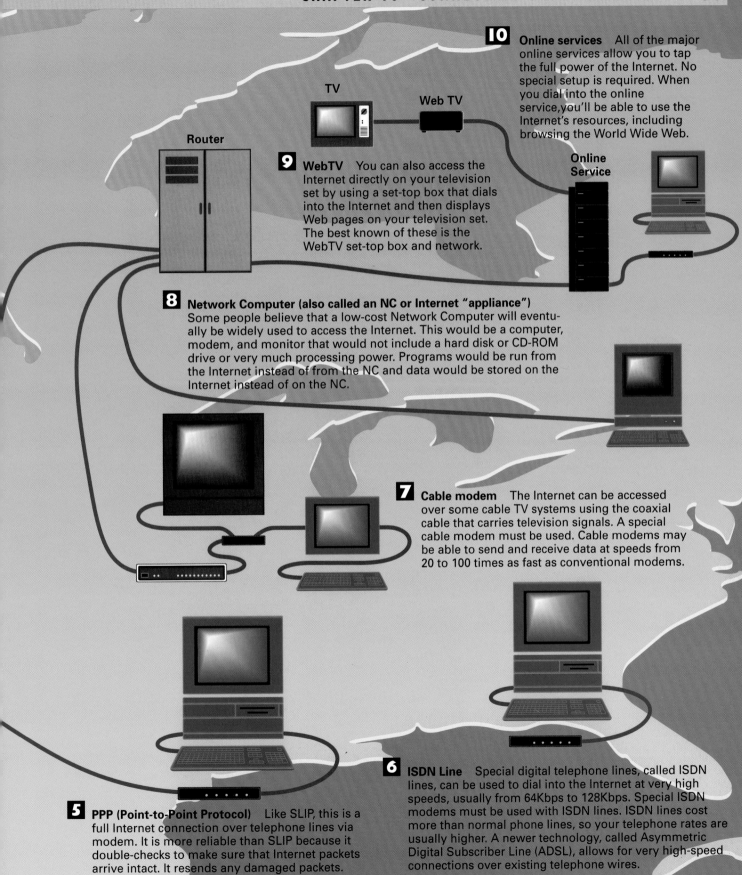

10 **Online services** All of the major online services allow you to tap the full power of the Internet. No special setup is required. When you dial into the online service, you'll be able to use the Internet's resources, including browsing the World Wide Web.

TV

Web TV

Router

Online Service

9 **WebTV** You can also access the Internet directly on your television set by using a set-top box that dials into the Internet and then displays Web pages on your television set. The best known of these is the WebTV set-top box and network.

8 **Network Computer (also called an NC or Internet "appliance")** Some people believe that a low-cost Network Computer will eventually be widely used to access the Internet. This would be a computer, modem, and monitor that would not include a hard disk or CD-ROM drive or very much processing power. Programs would be run from the Internet instead of from the NC and data would be stored on the Internet instead of on the NC.

7 **Cable modem** The Internet can be accessed over some cable TV systems using the coaxial cable that carries television signals. A special cable modem must be used. Cable modems may be able to send and receive data at speeds from 20 to 100 times as fast as conventional modems.

6 **ISDN Line** Special digital telephone lines, called ISDN lines, can be used to dial into the Internet at very high speeds, usually from 64Kbps to 128Kbps. Special ISDN modems must be used with ISDN lines. ISDN lines cost more than normal phone lines, so your telephone rates are usually higher. A newer technology, called Asymmetric Digital Subscriber Line (ADSL), allows for very high-speed connections over existing telephone wires.

5 **PPP (Point-to-Point Protocol)** Like SLIP, this is a full Internet connection over telephone lines via modem. It is more reliable than SLIP because it double-checks to make sure that Internet packets arrive intact. It resends any damaged packets.

CHAPTER

11

Connecting to the Internet from Online Services

THERE are many ways to get access to the Internet; one is by using an online service such as CompuServe or America Online. These online services have long provided their own unique content, special areas, and services available only to their subscribers. They use proprietary software and interfaces to give subscribers access to their resources. Unlike most of the Internet, the content, areas, and services the online companies provide are not always free. In order to get them, you may have to pay a monthly subscription fee to the online service. These online services are different from Internet service providers (ISPs) that offer only access to the Internet and don't have their own private areas and services.

The services let you access the Internet in a number of ways. To make it easier to use the Internet's resources, the services often use their own proprietary software or "user interface." The user interface requires you to issue a command that is then sent out over a gateway to the Internet. The information you've asked for is retrieved, sent back over the gateway to your online service, and is displayed for you using the online service's proprietary software.

Most online services also allow you to use your own client software to get to the Internet. To do this, you essentially bypass the online service's proprietary interface. You use the online service as you would a dial-in ISP. First, you dial into the online service to establish a TCP/IP connection. Then you launch the client software on your computer. It is the TCP/IP connection that gives you access to the Internet's resources.

Online services also let you browse the Web. Some let you use only their own proprietary Web browsers. Others have their own proprietary Web browsers, but also allow you to browse the Web using any Web browser of your choice. To use your own Web browser, you first dial into the service to establish a TCP/IP connection. Then you launch your own Web browser and you can browse the Web just as you would with any other dial-in ISP.

In addition to letting you browse the Web, online services also let you use other Internet resources such as Telnet (which lets you gain access to a distant computer on the Internet), Gopher (a menuing system that gives you access to a great deal of information and resources), IRC (chat on the Internet), and Usenet newsgroups (public Internet discussion areas). In some instances, you'll gain access to those resources using the online service's proprietary software while in other instances you'll use normal Internet client software.

Increasingly, the online services are moving toward eliminating their proprietary architecture altogether. The trend is to build the service on the same framework as the Internet, such as the TCP/IP protocol and related technologies. The Microsoft Network, for example, is now based entirely on TCP/IP and Prodigy has launched an Internet-specific version of its service. America Online and CompuServe are both incorporating elements of Internet technology inside their services and may one day go entirely to an Internet-based model.

How Online Services Connect to the Internet

I Online services such as CompuServe or America Online provide a very convenient way to use Internet resources. These services have their own software that makes it easy to access Internet resources such as Telnet, Gopher, and FTP. Some also allow you to use your own Telnet, FTP, Gopher, or other software instead of theirs. Using these resources, you may browse the World Wide Web, either with their own proprietary Web browser or by using any other Web browser. Finally, some services let you use special software required to access Internet resources such as IRC (Internet Relay Chat).

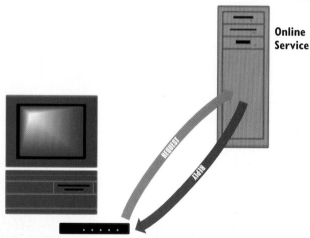

Online Service

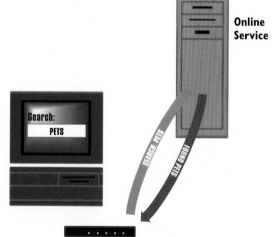

Online Service

2 Each online service has a great deal of resources, content, and special areas that are not available to anyone except people who subscribe to that particular service. These areas use the online service's own proprietary software and interface; they do not work like the Internet. You dial directly into the online service to get at these resources.

3 When you use the resources of an online service, you don't go outside the service to the Internet—instead, you stay behind a firewall. A *firewall* is a security system of accepting or blocking packets as they are transmitted across a network. Individual online services establish firewalls that only let subscribers into the service.

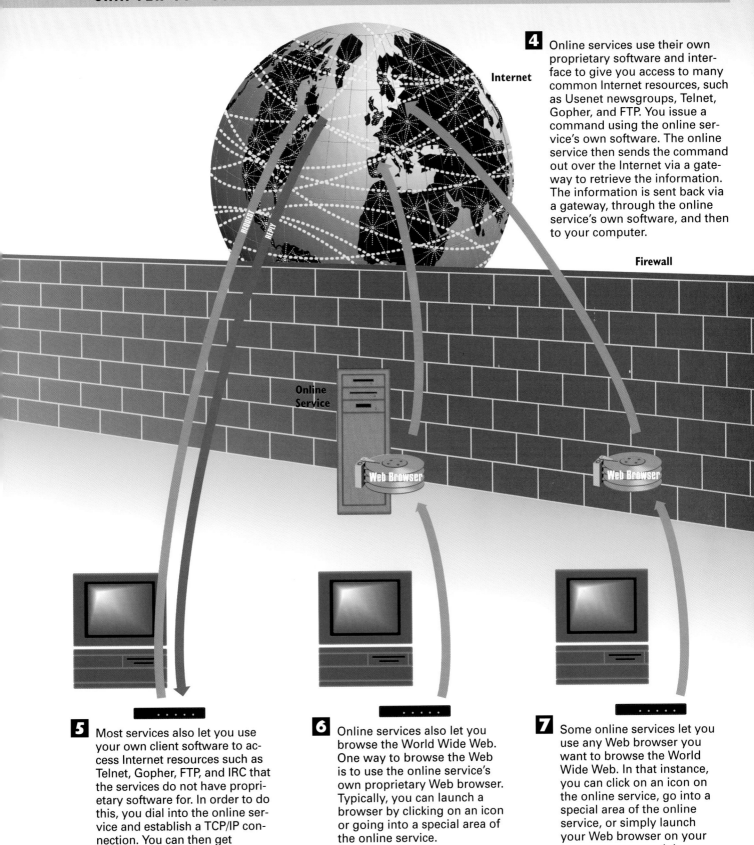

4 Online services use their own proprietary software and interface to give you access to many common Internet resources, such as Usenet newsgroups, Telnet, Gopher, and FTP. You issue a command using the online service's own software. The online service then sends the command out over the Internet via a gateway to retrieve the information. The information is sent back via a gateway, through the online service's own software, and then to your computer.

Internet

Firewall

Online Service

Web Browser

Web Browser

5 Most services also let you use your own client software to access Internet resources such as Telnet, Gopher, FTP, and IRC that the services do not have proprietary software for. In order to do this, you dial into the online service and establish a TCP/IP connection. You can then get directly onto the Internet using your own client software.

6 Online services also let you browse the World Wide Web. One way to browse the Web is to use the online service's own proprietary Web browser. Typically, you can launch a browser by clicking on an icon or going into a special area of the online service.

7 Some online services let you use any Web browser you want to browse the World Wide Web. In that instance, you can click on an icon on the online service, go into a special area of the online service, or simply launch your Web browser on your own computer, and then begin browsing the Web.

CHAPTER
12

How ISDN Works

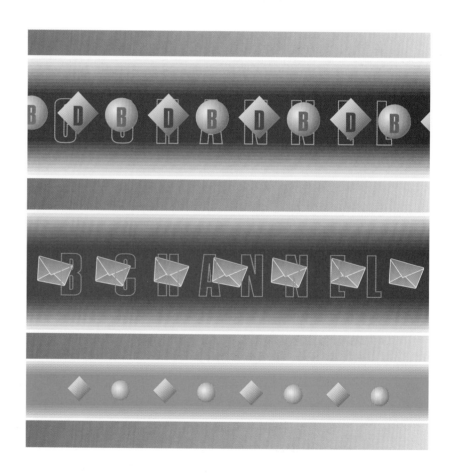

ONE common complaint about the Internet is that ordinary telephone connections are too slow. Even "high-speed" modems that can connect at 28,800Kbps can be too slow to take advantage of the rich graphics now available. The Internet is full of graphics, videos, sounds, and other multimedia files that are very large and take a very long time to be sent across the Internet to your computer.

One affordable way to get a faster Internet connection is to use ISDN (Integrated Services Digital Network). It's a technology that's been around for years, but the advent of the Internet and the need for higher-speed connections has made it more popular.

ISDN allows for high-speed connections to the Internet using existing copper cable telephone wires. It isn't available to everyone in the country yet because it requires telephone companies to install special ISDN digital-switching equipment. However, every day more areas of the country offer ISDN service. If ISDN is available in your area, you'll pay extra for the service compared to a normal telephone line. In order to use ISDN and the Internet, the number you're dialing will have to be equipped for ISDN access. Many private Internet dial-in providers and online services allow for ISDN access.

ISDN also requires that you have an ISDN modem. Although it looks like a modem, an ISDN modem isn't really a modem at all. Instead, it's a terminal adapter, a piece of hardware that lets you send and receive digital signals over ISDN phone lines. Normal modems transform digital signals from your computer into analog signals that can be sent over normal analog telephone lines. Because ISDN is a digital technology, only digital data is sent by the ISDN adapter. Some ISDN devices include the capability to function as a regular modem. This capability is needed because not every place you can dial into with your computer lets you use ISDN; some services presently only allow regular modem access.

There are different kinds of ISDN access, but the most common one is known as Basic Rate Interface (BRI). BRI divides your telephone line into three logical channels. The logical channels are not separate wires, but instead are ways in which data is sent and received over your telephone lines. BRI has two 64Kbps B (bearer) channels and one 16Kbps D (data) channel—commonly referred to as 2B+D. The D channel sends routing information while the two B channels send data. You can talk on one B channel while cruising the Internet on the other channel. Or, if your hardware and ISP or online service allows it, you can combine the two B channels into a single high-speed 128Kbps channel.

How ISDN Works

1 ISDN (Integrated Services Digital Network) is a way of establishing very high-speed connections to the Internet using existing copper telephone wires. No new telephone wires are needed in order for you to use ISDN. To allow you to use ISDN, your local telephone company will need to have installed special ISDN digital switches. In ISDN, all the information sent between your computer and the Internet is digital. Not all areas of the country have ISDN access yet. Call your telephone company to find out if it is available to you.

2 In order to use ISDN service, a computer requires an ISDN modem. In fact, this "modem" isn't really a modem at all and should be called a terminal adapter instead. A normal modem (short for modulator/demodulator) converts the information inside your computer from digital signals into analog signals that can be sent over telephone lines. ISDN is a digital technology so there is no need to convert information from digital to analog. Instead, the ISDN "modem" sends digital information from your computer over ISDN telephone lines and receives digital information from telephone lines.

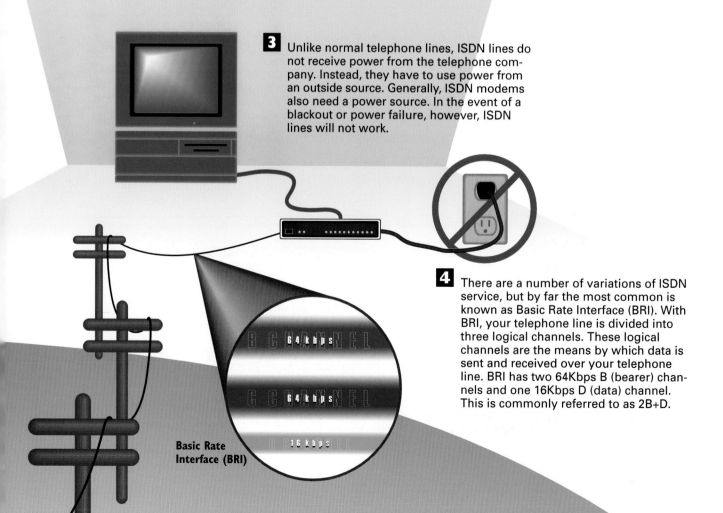

3 Unlike normal telephone lines, ISDN lines do not receive power from the telephone company. Instead, they have to use power from an outside source. Generally, ISDN modems also need a power source. In the event of a blackout or power failure, however, ISDN lines will not work.

Basic Rate Interface (BRI)

B CHANNEL — 64 kbps
B CHANNEL — 64 kbps
D CHANNEL — 16 kbps

4 There are a number of variations of ISDN service, but by far the most common is known as Basic Rate Interface (BRI). With BRI, your telephone line is divided into three logical channels. These logical channels are the means by which data is sent and received over your telephone line. BRI has two 64Kbps B (bearer) channels and one 16Kbps D (data) channel. This is commonly referred to as 2B+D.

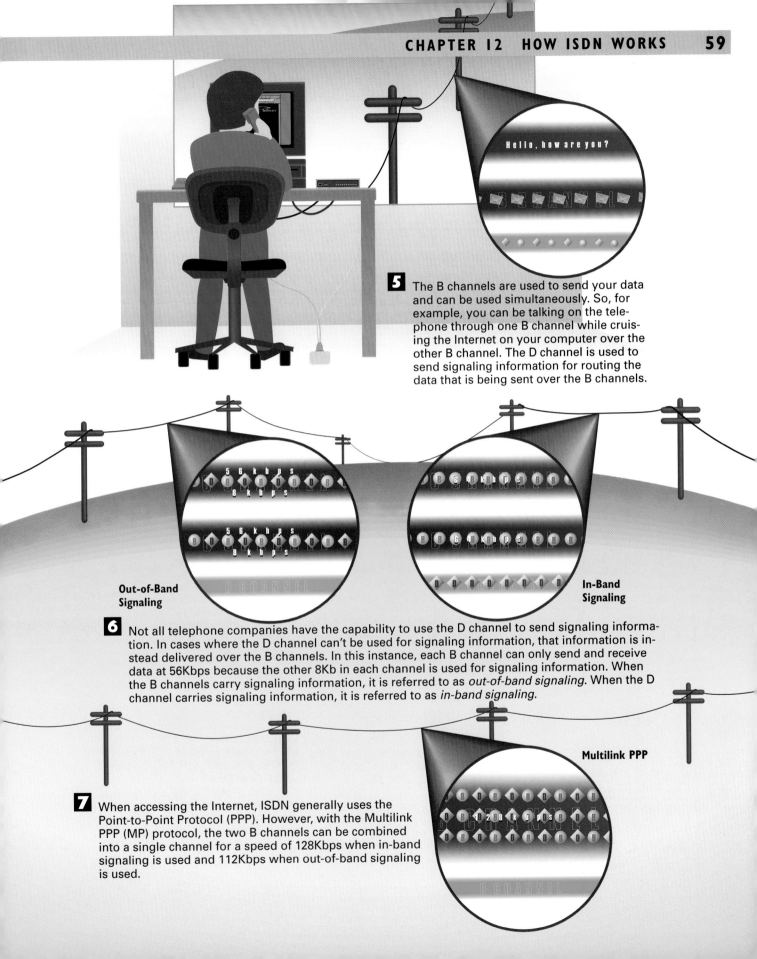

5 The B channels are used to send your data and can be used simultaneously. So, for example, you can be talking on the telephone through one B channel while cruising the Internet on your computer over the other B channel. The D channel is used to send signaling information for routing the data that is being sent over the B channels.

Out-of-Band Signaling

In-Band Signaling

6 Not all telephone companies have the capability to use the D channel to send signaling information. In cases where the D channel can't be used for signaling information, that information is instead delivered over the B channels. In this instance, each B channel can only send and receive data at 56Kbps because the other 8Kb in each channel is used for signaling information. When the B channels carry signaling information, it is referred to as *out-of-band signaling*. When the D channel carries signaling information, it is referred to as *in-band signaling*.

Multilink PPP

7 When accessing the Internet, ISDN generally uses the Point-to-Point Protocol (PPP). However, with the Multilink PPP (MP) protocol, the two B channels can be combined into a single channel for a speed of 128Kbps when in-band signaling is used and 112Kbps when out-of-band signaling is used.

CHAPTER

13

The Internet/Television Connection

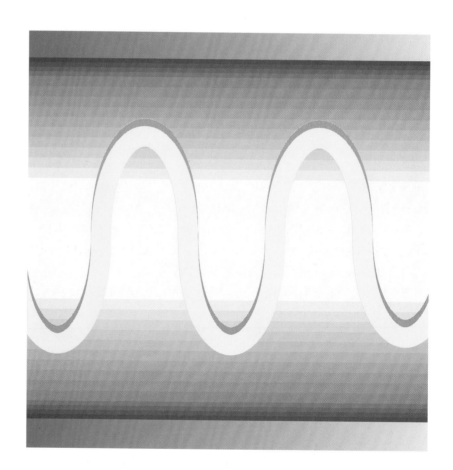

WHEN people first began talking about the "information superhighway" about five years ago, it wasn't the Internet they were talking about. Instead, it was television—and specifically cable television—that they believed would change the way we lived and worked. There were visions of 500 TV channels, "interactive television," shopping from home, and customized news available whenever you wanted it. This information superhighway was going to hook us all together electronically so we could more easily communicate and get information, services, goods, and entertainment. It didn't pan out that way. Instead, the Internet has become an information superhighway that can do almost everything people imagined could be done by using cable TV.

How much longer the Internet will be the sole driving force behind the information superhighway remains to be seen. Every day, TV and the Internet are drawing closer to one another. The Internet is gaining more TV-like qualities, such as the capability to play videos and music, and even the capability to broadcast live video feeds. Television technology is also developing in ways that will make it more interactive, like the Internet.

Eventually, the Net and TV will most likely merge in some way. Here's one example of how this might work. You may be able to watch a sporting event and simultaneously chat with others while you're watching—all on the same screen. Furthermore, when a batter came up to bat during a baseball game, you would be able to use the Net to get detailed statistics about the batter, and even past videos and highlights of his career.

Television and the Internet have already begun to merge in a very real way, primarily through two different technologies: cable modems and TVs that connect to the Net, allowing you to browse the Net through your TV set, such as WebTV.

Cable modems offer extremely high-speed access to the Internet. They allow you to access the Net using the existing coaxial TV cable that comes into your house. Cable modems can receive data at up to 1.5 million bits per second and can send data at up to 300,000bps—far faster than normal modems and ISDN lines. They offer T1-like speeds, but at a fraction of the cost of T1 lines. They can deliver these high speeds because they are sent through high-capacity cable lines. Because Internet data and the normal cable signal coexist on the same lines, you can access the Net and watch TV simultaneously. The illustration in this chapter describes how MediaOne provides cable modem access to its customers.

A different technology allows you to browse the Web using your television set. A *set-top box* connects your TV to the Net via a modem, takes the signal from the modems, and sends it to the TV. A remote control-like device allows you to browse the Web while watching TV at the same time. As of this writing, the connection is still made via normal modem speeds, so access is far slower than with a cable modem. That, however, may change in the future.

How Cable Modems Work

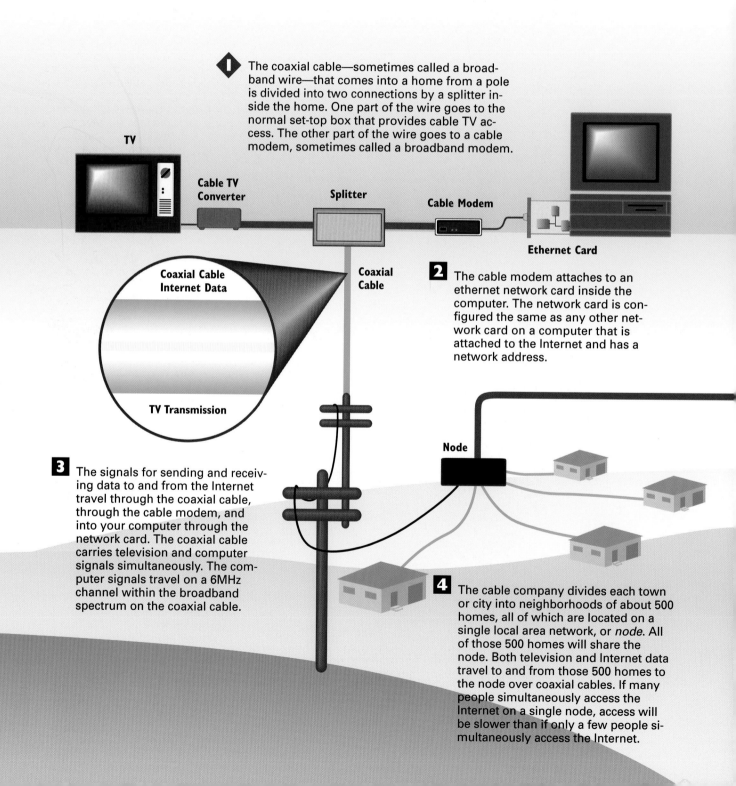

1 The coaxial cable—sometimes called a broad-band wire—that comes into a home from a pole is divided into two connections by a splitter inside the home. One part of the wire goes to the normal set-top box that provides cable TV access. The other part of the wire goes to a cable modem, sometimes called a broadband modem.

TV

Cable TV Converter

Splitter

Cable Modem

Ethernet Card

Coaxial Cable Internet Data

Coaxial Cable

TV Transmission

2 The cable modem attaches to an ethernet network card inside the computer. The network card is configured the same as any other network card on a computer that is attached to the Internet and has a network address.

Node

3 The signals for sending and receiving data to and from the Internet travel through the coaxial cable, through the cable modem, and into your computer through the network card. The coaxial cable carries television and computer signals simultaneously. The computer signals travel on a 6MHz channel within the broadband spectrum on the coaxial cable.

4 The cable company divides each town or city into neighborhoods of about 500 homes, all of which are located on a single local area network, or *node*. All of those 500 homes will share the node. Both television and Internet data travel to and from those 500 homes to the node over coaxial cables. If many people simultaneously access the Internet on a single node, access will be slower than if only a few people simultaneously access the Internet.

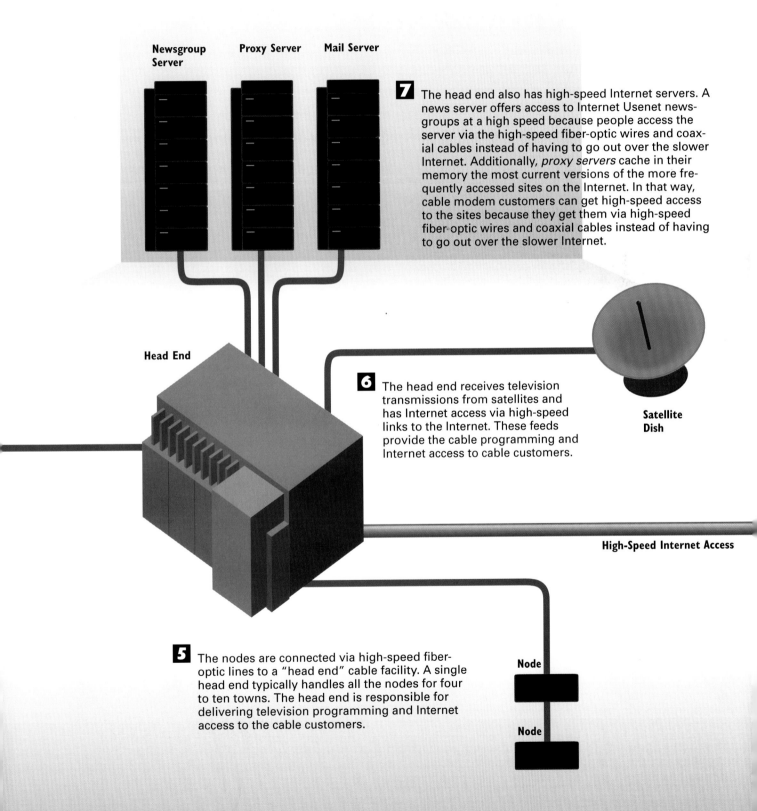

Newsgroup Server

Proxy Server

Mail Server

7 The head end also has high-speed Internet servers. A news server offers access to Internet Usenet newsgroups at a high speed because people access the server via the high-speed fiber-optic wires and coaxial cables instead of having to go out over the slower Internet. Additionally, *proxy servers* cache in their memory the most current versions of the more frequently accessed sites on the Internet. In that way, cable modem customers can get high-speed access to the sites because they get them via high-speed fiber-optic wires and coaxial cables instead of having to go out over the slower Internet.

Head End

6 The head end receives television transmissions from satellites and has Internet access via high-speed links to the Internet. These feeds provide the cable programming and Internet access to cable customers.

Satellite Dish

High-Speed Internet Access

5 The nodes are connected via high-speed fiber-optic lines to a "head end" cable facility. A single head end typically handles all the nodes for four to ten towns. The head end is responsible for delivering television programming and Internet access to the cable customers.

Node

Node

How WebTV Works

1 WebTV allows people to browse the Internet through a TV set and watch television at the same time. A special WebTV set-top box sits next to a television set. The box has normal connectors to the television and/or cable service, and special connectors to a modem and phone line. It also has the memory required to run a Web browser along with other hardware and software.

2 The WebTV set-top box has the capability to accept add-ons in a similar way to how computers can accept add-ons. The first add-on is a printer, but others are expected to follow.

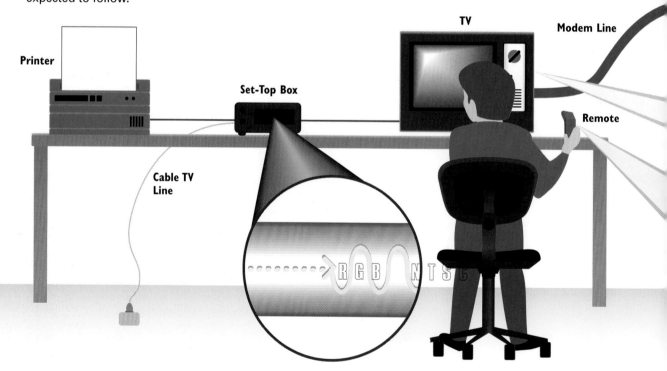

Printer

TV

Modem Line

Set-Top Box

Remote

Cable TV Line

RGB   NTSC

3 Television screens and computer monitors use different technologies to display pictures and information. Computer monitors use Red-Green-Blue (RGB) technology in which the three colors are combined to form all the colors you see on your monitor. Televisions use NTSC (National Television Standards Committee) technology. The WebTV set-top box converts the signal from the RGB of the Web to the NTSC used by televisions so that the signal will be as clear as possible.

5 To speed up access to Internet sites, the WebTV network runs a series of proxy servers. These proxy servers cache commonly accessed Web pages. When someone who uses WebTV goes to one of those pages, the page will be delivered from the proxy server, which will deliver the page at a higher speed than if it were accessed from the Internet.

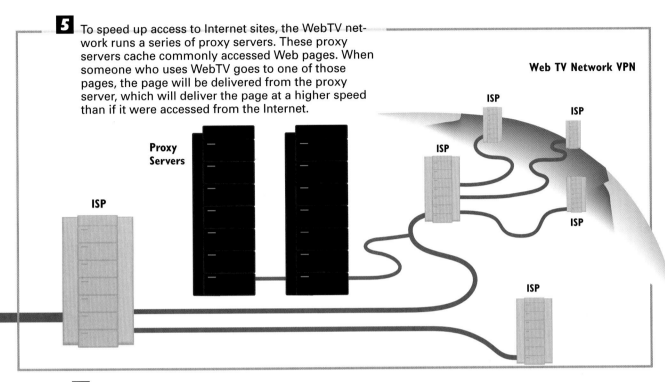

Web TV Network VPN

Proxy Servers

ISP

4 When you want to access the Internet, the WebTV box connects to the WebTV network to get access to the Internet. The WebTV network is not a single network, but instead a Virtual Private Network (VPN). WebTV makes deals with ISPs (Internet service providers) across the country to provide access via local POPs (points of presence); encryption technology knits it all together into what appears to be a single network. This VPN has many Web servers on it to provide capabilities such as email and other services.

6 WebTV uses its own proprietary Web browser, which adheres to HTML standards and can run common plug-ins. The browser is designed for optimal display on a television set. Some sites, such as *TV Guide,* have developed Web sites that make the best use of the browser.

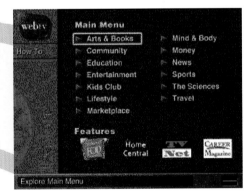

7 The ability to browse the Web is controlled by a simple remote control unit that allows people to scroll, move around the screen, and "click" on objects. The control also allows people to either browse the Web, watch television, or to view the Web and television simultaneously.

C H A P T E R

14

How Network Computers (NCs) Work

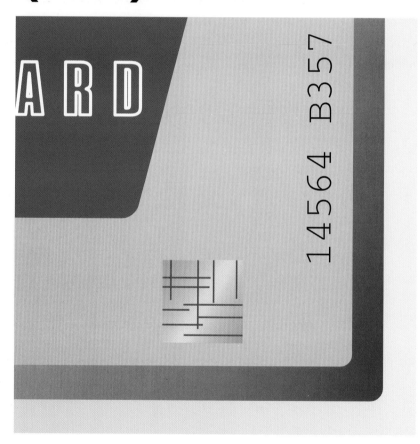

THERE are those who believe that because of the widespread use of the Internet, the days of traditional computers are numbered. To some, it stands to reason that the Network Computer (NC) could take over. The NC will cost less than the traditional systems and will be able to do anything you need it to do because of its intimate tie-in to the Net. Some NCs are available now and their use is expected to grow in the future.

The NC can cost $500 or less because it doesn't require nearly as much hardware as a traditional system. It does not include a hard disk or CD-ROM drive, which cuts the cost of the computer significantly.

NCs don't require local storage or CD-ROM drives because the files and software aren't stored locally on the NC. Instead, the files and software are stored on the Internet, on special, secure NC servers. The software is Java-based, so it's portable across a variety of hardware. Rather than being written for a specific computer, such as the Macintosh or PC, Java programs will run on a variety of platforms.

NCs require that sophisticated servers be built to manage storing and serving up software and data. These servers would be accessible via the Internet. For security reasons, NCs may also be used with special "smart cards," credit-sized plastic cards with chips built into them.

To use an NC, you would put your card into a special reader, type in a personal identification number (PIN), and you would then be logged onto the network. A personalized desktop would appear on your NC that took into account your preferences about the kind of software you wanted to run, and the kind of information you wanted to receive. When you ran software, it would be delivered to you over the Internet by the NC server. When you saved files, you would save them to your own secure, private portion of the Internet.

There is no one standard for an NC. Oracle Corporation makes databases for the Internet and has been an early backer of NCs. Oracle would benefit by the NC's widespread adoption because the company would sell the server software to make NCs work.

NCs have a certain lure for corporations. They could cut the cost of buying and maintaining hardware and software dramatically by thousands of dollars per computer. Furthermore, because all software is delivered straight to the NC from a server, corporations could also ensure that everyone in the company used the same standardized software. It may well save significant time and money when systems needed to be configured and upgraded. Instead of upgrading 150 separate machines, a system administrator could merely install new software on the server and all the machines would automatically run that new software.

NCs could also be used in various consumer devices, as a way to bring Internet information into people's living rooms.

How Network Computers (NCs) Work

Network Computers (NCs) are low-cost computers with little or no local storage, and no CD-ROM drives or similar peripherals. The Internet handles all the software they run and the storage of data.

1 To use an NC, you'll need a smart card—a card with a computer chip embedded in it that identifies you to the network, much like a bank Automated Teller Machine (ATM) card identifies you to your bank's network.

2 You put the NC card into a special card reader and will then be asked for a personal identification number (PIN). A server will check that your PIN matches your smart card.

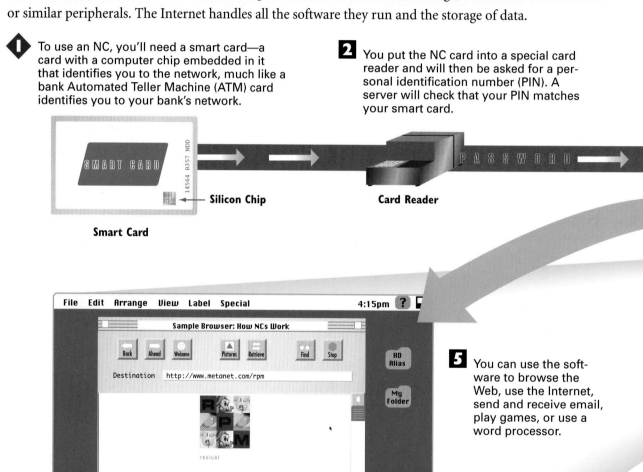

Silicon Chip

Smart Card

Card Reader

5 You can use the software to browse the Web, use the Internet, send and receive email, play games, or use a word processor.

NC

RAM

3 When the server authorizes you to use the NC, the NC will display a personal desktop on it, based on your preferences for things such as news, stock quotes, weather, and entertainment information. The desktop also contains icons for the programs you want to run. This desktop software is sent to you from the server, although alternately, it could also be stored locally on a read-only memory (ROM) chip. The software you want to run isn't stored locally. Instead, it's stored on the NC server.

OK to log on?

Yes, here's software.

4 After you receive the software, it runs locally on the NC in its random access memory (RAM). The software will be either HTML-based, such as a Web browser, or written in the Java programming language.

NC Server

Save my file

6 When you want to save a file, you don't save that file to your NC because it doesn't have a hard disk. Instead, you save it to your own private, secure portion of the Internet that is managed by the NC server. When you want to use the file again, you'll call it up from your own private area.

CHAPTER

15

How the Digital Subscriber Line (DSL) Works

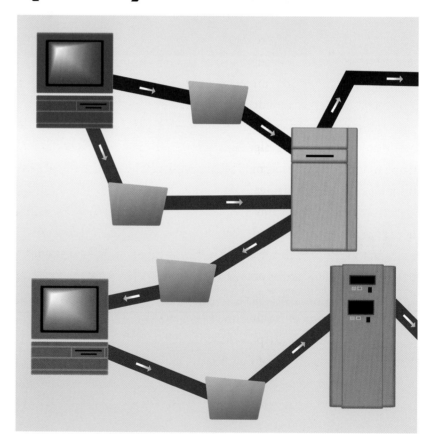

IN recent years, a plethora of options could be found for gaining high-speed access to the Internet. Among the newest, which may eventually prove to be one of the most popular, is the Digital Subscriber Line, or DSL. Several kinds of DSL technologies are available, but they all work on the same principles. They enable you to use your existing telephone lines to access the Internet at very high speeds—potentially as high as 55Mbps—using VDSL (Very high data rate DSL), although that kind of extremely high-speed connection is used primarily by large corporations because of its cost. Home users will probably get speeds of 1.5Mbps, which is still very fast—about 50 times the speed of a 28,800bps modem. Additionally, DSL technologies will enable you to use the Internet at high speeds and simultaneously talk on your telephone, using the same single phone line.

DSL technologies require that DSL modems be used on each end of the phone line. In fact, the term DSL doesn't really refer to a phone line, because an ordinary, existing copper phone line can be used for DSL. Instead, it refers to the DSL modems themselves. More confusing still, DSL "modems" aren't really modems at all. Traditional modems modulate the digital signals from your computer into analog signals so that they can be sent over telephone lines, and then they demodulate them back into digital signals so that your computer can understand them—hence the name modem, from the terms "MOdulate-DEModulate." DSL modems don't convert signals from digital to analog. Instead, they transmit and receive all data as digital signals. Because the signals don't need to be converted and can be sent as digital data instead of analog data, data can be sent at much higher speeds than data sent via traditional modems.

DSL technology has one drawback; it requires that your house (and DSL modem) be located within a certain distance from the telephone company office and its DSL modem. In cities, this should not be a major problem, but it could be a problem in rural areas. The exact distance required will depend on the kind and speed of DSL service you use. Higher speeds require that you be closer to the phone company office.

Although many kinds of DSL service are available, probably the most popular for people at home will be Asymmetric Digital Subscriber Line (ADSL) and DSL Lite. With them, you can receive data at a faster rate than you can send data—for example, you can receive data at 1.5Mbps and send data at 640Kbps.

How Asymmetric Digital Subscriber Line (ADSL) Works

Many kinds of Digital Subscriber Lines (DSLs) exist. One of the most popular for the home will be Asymmetric Digital Subscriber Line, called that because it sends and receives data at different speeds.

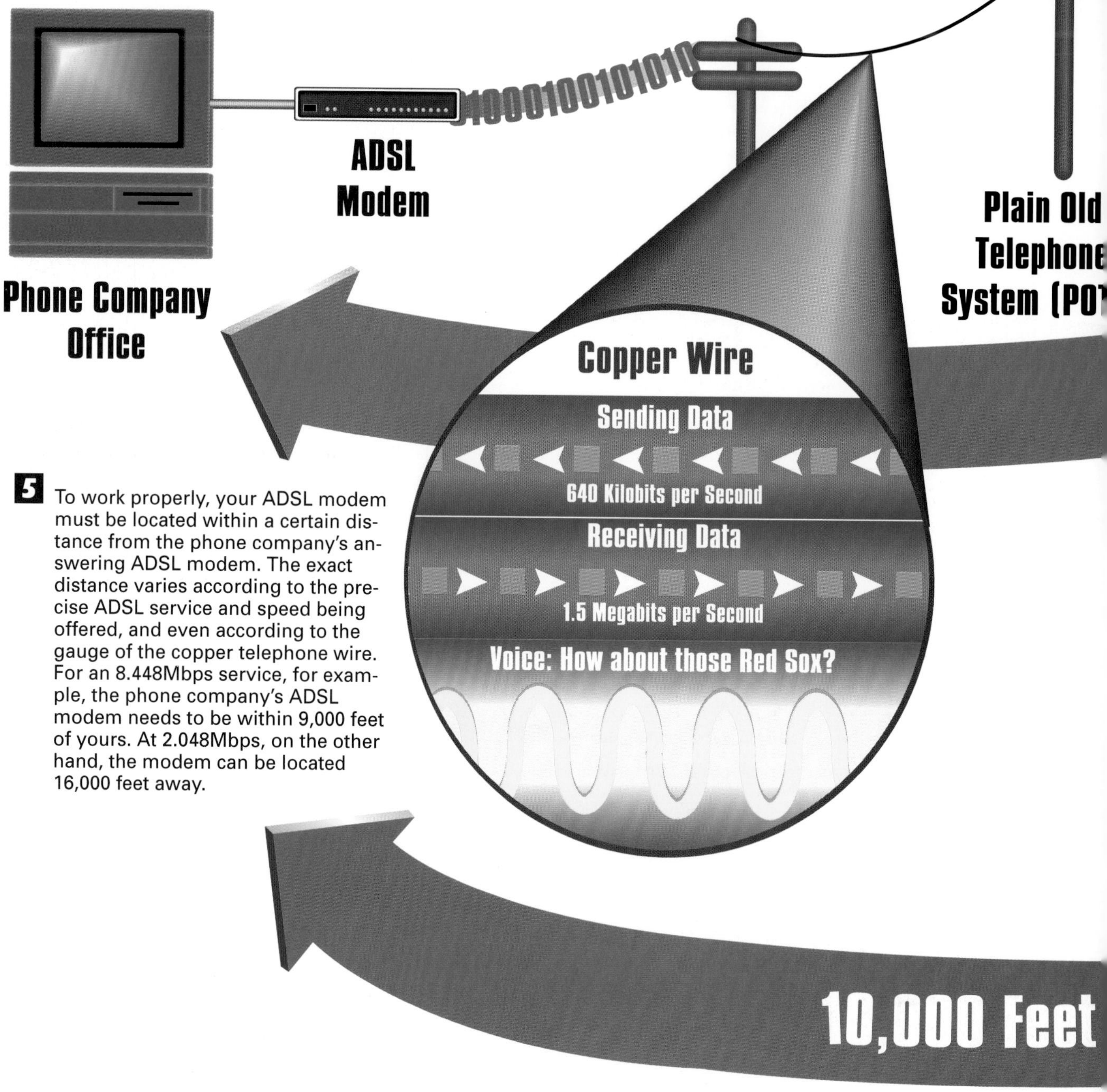

ADSL Modem

10001000101010

Plain Old Telephone System (POT

Phone Company Office

Copper Wire

Sending Data

640 Kilobits per Second

Receiving Data

1.5 Megabits per Second

Voice: How about those Red Sox?

5 To work properly, your ADSL modem must be located within a certain distance from the phone company's answering ADSL modem. The exact distance varies according to the precise ADSL service and speed being offered, and even according to the gauge of the copper telephone wire. For an 8.448Mbps service, for example, the phone company's ADSL modem needs to be within 9,000 feet of yours. At 2.048Mbps, on the other hand, the modem can be located 16,000 feet away.

10,000 Feet

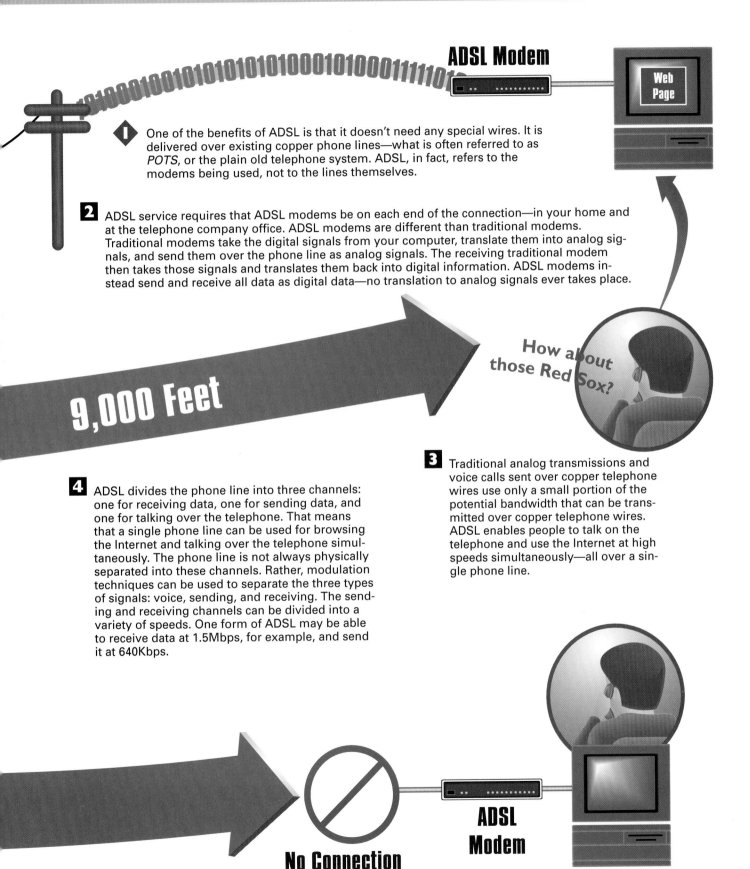

ADSL Modem

Web Page

1 One of the benefits of ADSL is that it doesn't need any special wires. It is delivered over existing copper phone lines—what is often referred to as *POTS*, or the plain old telephone system. ADSL, in fact, refers to the modems being used, not to the lines themselves.

2 ADSL service requires that ADSL modems be on each end of the connection—in your home and at the telephone company office. ADSL modems are different than traditional modems. Traditional modems take the digital signals from your computer, translate them into analog signals, and send them over the phone line as analog signals. The receiving traditional modem then takes those signals and translates them back into digital information. ADSL modems instead send and receive all data as digital data—no translation to analog signals ever takes place.

How about those Red Sox?

9,000 Feet

3 Traditional analog transmissions and voice calls sent over copper telephone wires use only a small portion of the potential bandwidth that can be transmitted over copper telephone wires. ADSL enables people to talk on the telephone and use the Internet at high speeds simultaneously—all over a single phone line.

4 ADSL divides the phone line into three channels: one for receiving data, one for sending data, and one for talking over the telephone. That means that a single phone line can be used for browsing the Internet and talking over the telephone simultaneously. The phone line is not always physically separated into these channels. Rather, modulation techniques can be used to separate the three types of signals: voice, sending, and receiving. The sending and receiving channels can be divided into a variety of speeds. One form of ADSL may be able to receive data at 1.5Mbps, for example, and send it at 640Kbps.

No Connection

ADSL Modem

P A R T

COMMUNICATING ON THE INTERNET

FROM its very earliest days, the Internet has been concerned primarily with one task—making it easier for people to communicate with one another using computers. The Internet was created to enable university researchers to share their thoughts, work, and resources, and for military people to communicate with each other in case of war and even, theoretically, a nuclear attack.

Today, more than two decades after the inception of the first networks that grew into the Internet, it is still primarily a communications medium. Millions of people from all over the world share their thoughts, hopes, work, gossip, and comments on the wires and computers that make up the Internet. Many of the means of communication, such as electronic mail, have changed very little in the past 20 years. Yet other, entirely new ways of communicating have been devised, such as enabling you to use the Internet as your telephone, completely cutting out long-distance charges, even if you're calling to the other side of the world. Technologies enable people to communicate privately, one-on-one; others allow for vast discussion groups that span the globe, and still others allow for both private communication with one person and public communication with large groups.

In this section of the book, we'll look at the main ways that people communicate on the Internet.

In Chapter 16, "How Email Works," we'll take a long look at what continues to be the most popular way for people to communicate on the Internet—electronic mail, or email. Email remains possibly the greatest use of the Internet and is used for business and personal communication. We'll see how email gets routed from your computer through the maze of wires that makes up the Internet, and then ends up in the proper recipient's in-box. We'll look at all the elements of a mail message and learn how you can send binary files, such as pictures and sounds, through email. We'll also explore mailing lists, where you can subscribe to any one of thousands of public discussions via email, or receive what are essentially electronic newsletters delivered to your email in-box. And we'll look at how you can look up anyone's email address using white page directories that use a technology called the Lightweight Access Directory Protocol (LADP).

Chapter 17, "Email Spam and Blocking," covers one of the most controversial modes of communication on the Internet—the use of *Spam*, the equivalent of junk mail via email, that is sent to millions of people each day. Although Spam is a problem on newsgroups as well as email, email is the greatest area of controversy. Spam annoys people and wastes their time while they clean out their mailboxes; it clogs the Internet so that other messages may be delivered late—or not at all; and it can be delivered by piggybacking onto other people's email servers, costing them money. The chapter looks at how Spam is sent, as well as ways that it can be blocked.

Chapter 18, "How Usenet Newsgroups Work," explores *Usenet newsgroups*—public discussion groups in which anyone can participate. Many thousands of these groups focus on every subject conceivable. You'll see how newsgroups work and how you can decipher their often arcane names.

Chapter 19, "How Internet Chat and Instant Messaging Work," covers the different ways people can "chat" on the Internet. The most popular one is *IRC*, or *Internet Relay Chat*. IRC is a way for people to publicly chat with one another on the Internet. They don't actually speak, but type comments on their keyboards instead, and then people all over the world can read and respond to them. The chapter also covers *instant messaging*—ways in which people chat one-on-one with others when they log onto the Internet.

Finally, Chapter 20, "Making Phone Calls on the Internet," details one of the more intriguing new uses of the Internet—using it as your telephone. Today you can dial into your local Internet provider with your computer, and if you have the right hardware and software, you can talk with anyone similarly connected to the Internet anywhere in the world, all without paying long-distance telephone charges. And it covers a new kind of low-cost telephone service that has sprung up: IP Telephony. In *IP Telephony*, you talk over your telephone as you would normally—the phone call appears no different to you. But the Internet, rather than the normal phone system, is used to make the connection to the person you're calling.

16

How Email Works

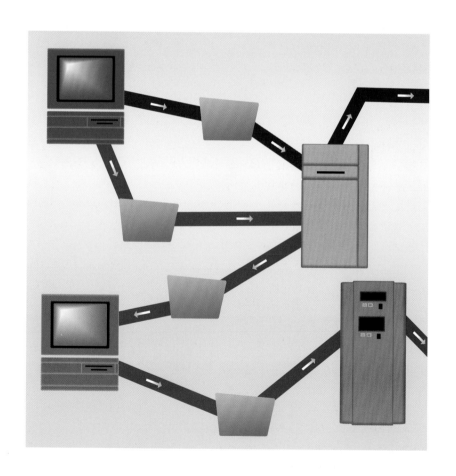

ELECTRONIC mail, or email, may be the most heavily used feature of the Internet. You can use it to send messages to anyone who is connected to the Internet or connected to a computer network that has a connection to the Internet, such as an online service. Millions of people send and receive email every day. Email is a great way to keep up with far-flung relatives, friends, co-workers in different branches of your company, and colleagues in your field.

Email messages are sent in the same way as most Internet data. The TCP protocol breaks your messages into packets, the IP protocol delivers the packets to the proper location, and then the TCP reassembles the message on the receiving end so that it can be read.

You can also attach binary files, such as pictures, videos, sounds, and executable files to your email messages. Because the Internet isn't able to directly handle binary files in email, the file first must be encoded in one of a variety of encoding schemes. Popular schemes are MIME and uuencode. The person who receives the attached binary file (called an attachment) must decode the file with the same scheme that was used to encode the file. Many email software packages do this automatically.

When you send email to someone on the Internet, that message often has to travel through a series of networks before it reaches the recipient—networks that might use different email formats. Gateways perform the job of translating email formats from one network to another so that the messages can make their way through all the networks of the Internet.

A mailing list is one of the most intriguing uses of email. It connects a group of people who are interested in the same topic, such as Japanese cartoons or home schooling. When one person sends email to the mailing list, that message is automatically sent to everyone on the list. You can meet others and talk to them on a regular basis about your shared interests, hobbies, or professions. To get onto a mailing list, you send an email note to the mailing list administrator and include your email address.

Mailing lists can be moderated or unmoderated. A *moderated mailing list* is screened by the list administrator, who may kill duplicate messages or messages that are not related to the list's theme. An *unmoderated mailing list* is wide open; all mail sent to it is automatically sent to everyone on the list.

Often, when you want to subscribe to a mailing list, you send a message to a computer instead of a person. That computer, known as a list server (also called a *listserv*), reads your email and automatically subscribes you to the list. You can unsubscribe to the list in the same way.

In the past, it was very difficult to find the email address of someone if you knew only his or her name. These days, it's not so hard. A variety of "white page" directories have sprung up on the Internet that enable you to look up people's email addresses easily. These sites mainly use a standard called the Lightweight Directory Access Protocol (LDAP), which enables you to find people's email addresses without even having to visit a Web site. Using the protocol, you can search for email addresses on the Internet from directly within your email program.

Anatomy of a Mail Message

1 An email message is made up of binary data, usually in the ASCII text format. ASCII is a standard that enables any computer, regardless of its operating system or hardware, to read the text. ASCII code describes the characters you see on your computer screen.

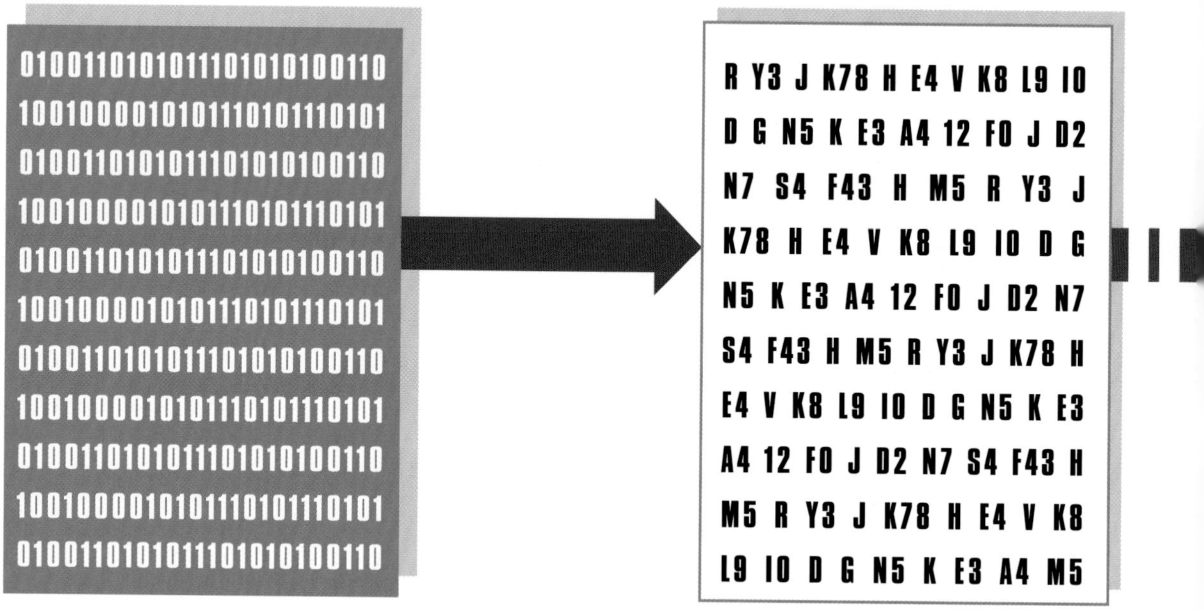

```
010011010101110101010100110
100100001010111010111010 1
010011010101110101010100110
100100001010111010111010 1
010011010101110101010100110
100100001010111010111010 1
010011010101110101010100110
100100001010111010111010 1
010011010101110101010100110
100100001010111010111010 1
010011010101110101010100110
```

R Y3 J K78 H E4 V K8 L9 I0

D G N5 K E3 A4 12 F0 J D2

N7 S4 F43 H M5 R Y3 J

K78 H E4 V K8 L9 I0 D G

N5 K E3 A4 12 F0 J D2 N7

S4 F43 H M5 R Y3 J K78 H

E4 V K8 L9 I0 D G N5 K E3

A4 12 F0 J D2 N7 S4 F43 H

M5 R Y3 J K78 H E4 V K8

L9 I0 D G N5 K E3 A4 M5

2 You can also attach pictures, executable programs, sounds, videos, and other binary files to your email message. To do this, you'll have to encode the file in a way that will enable it to be sent across the Internet. The receiver will also have to be able to decode the file after it is received. A variety of encoding schemes can be used. Some email software will automatically do the encoding for you and will also do the decoding on the receiving end.

3 In the To line, type in the email address of the person to whom you're sending a message. The address must be typed in following very strict rules. If you get a single letter or the syntax wrong, your message won't get to the intended recipient.

4 Your email address will appear on the From line. Using this address, the recipient of your message will be able to respond to you.

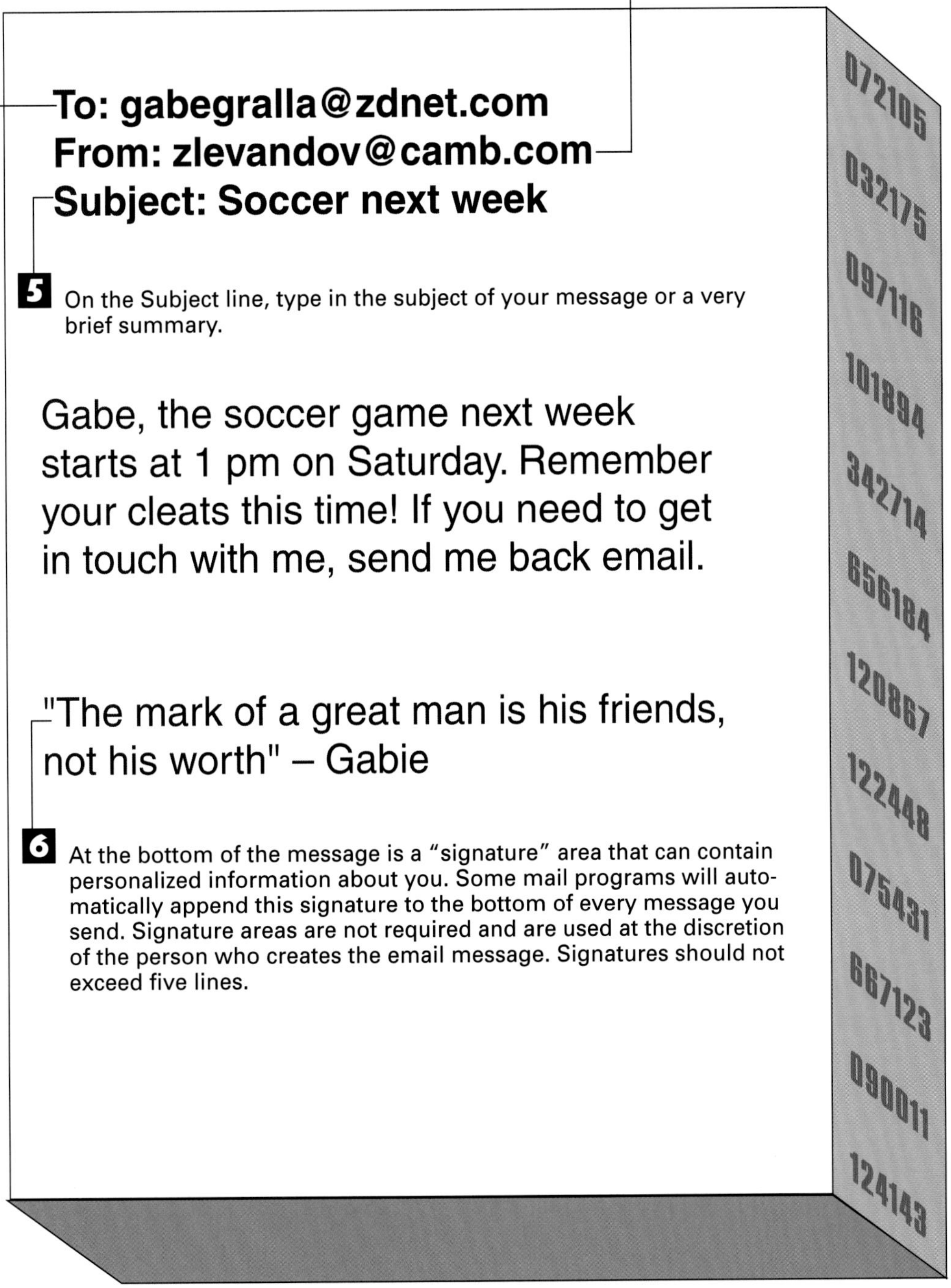

To: gabegralla@zdnet.com
From: zlevandov@camb.com
Subject: Soccer next week

5 On the Subject line, type in the subject of your message or a very brief summary.

Gabe, the soccer game next week starts at 1 pm on Saturday. Remember your cleats this time! If you need to get in touch with me, send me back email.

"The mark of a great man is his friends, not his worth" – Gabie

6 At the bottom of the message is a "signature" area that can contain personalized information about you. Some mail programs will automatically append this signature to the bottom of every message you send. Signature areas are not required and are used at the discretion of the person who creates the email message. Signatures should not exceed five lines.

072105
032175
097116
101894
342714
656184
120867
122448
075431
667123
090011
124143

How Email Is Delivered over the Internet

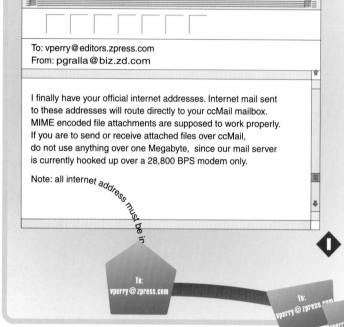

1 After you create and send an email message, it is sent as a stream of packets using the Internet's TCP/IP protocol. Each packet bears the address of the destination.

2 Routers on the Internet look at the addresses in each packet and send the packets on the best path to get there. Many factors go into how the packets are routed, including the traffic volume on different backbones. Each packet may take a different route, so the mail packets may arrive at the destination out of order.

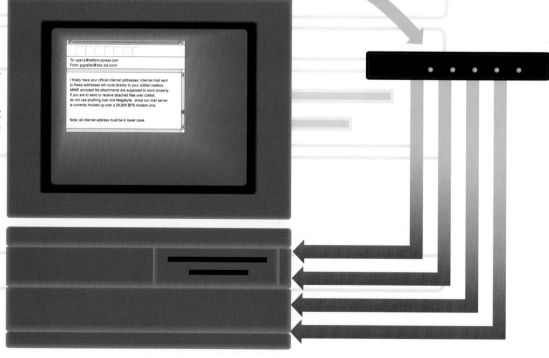

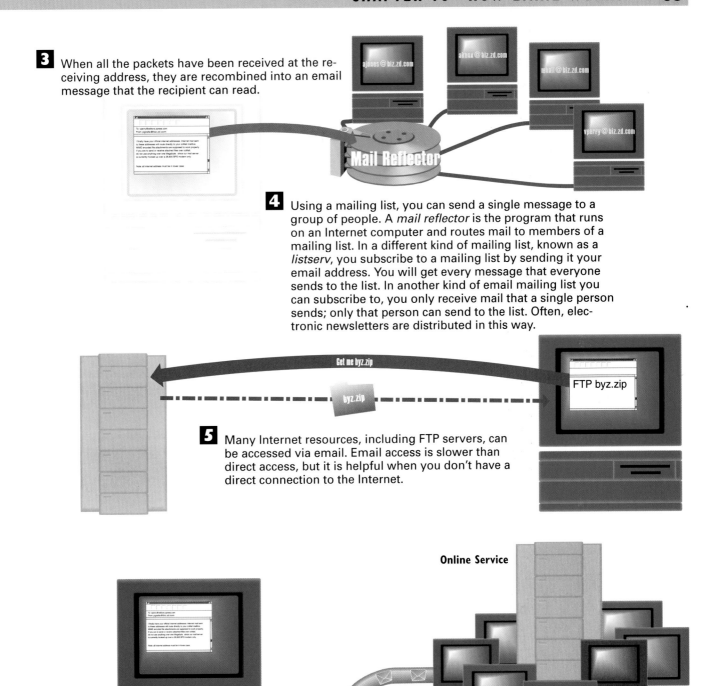

3 When all the packets have been received at the receiving address, they are recombined into an email message that the recipient can read.

4 Using a mailing list, you can send a single message to a group of people. A *mail reflector* is the program that runs on an Internet computer and routes mail to members of a mailing list. In a different kind of mailing list, known as a *listserv*, you subscribe to a mailing list by sending it your email address. You will get every message that everyone sends to the list. In another kind of email mailing list you can subscribe to, you only receive mail that a single person sends; only that person can send to the list. Often, electronic newsletters are distributed in this way.

5 Many Internet resources, including FTP servers, can be accessed via email. Email access is slower than direct access, but it is helpful when you don't have a direct connection to the Internet.

6 Using the Internet, email can be exchanged among all the major online services, computer bulletin boards, and other networks. From the Internet, you can send email to any of those networks—and from any of those networks, mail can be sent to the Internet. When mail is sent from one of those networks to another, it often must pass through the Internet as a way of routing the mail.

How Email Software Works

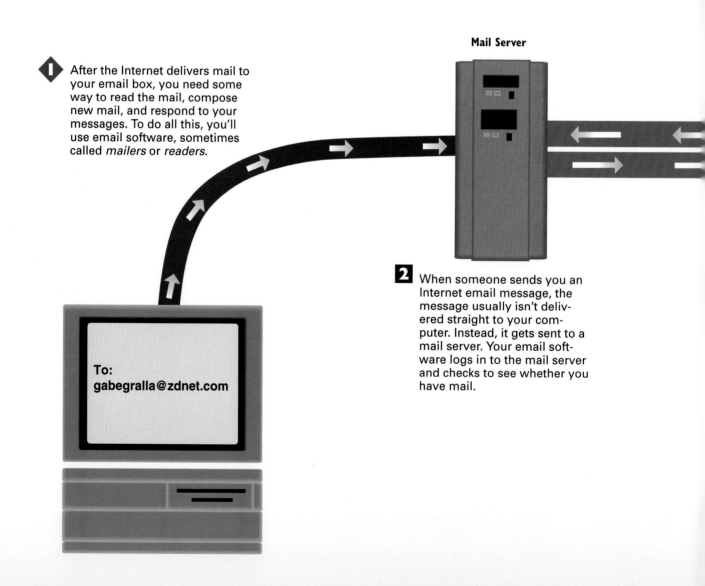

1 After the Internet delivers mail to your email box, you need some way to read the mail, compose new mail, and respond to your messages. To do all this, you'll use email software, sometimes called *mailers* or *readers*.

Mail Server

2 When someone sends you an Internet email message, the message usually isn't delivered straight to your computer. Instead, it gets sent to a mail server. Your email software logs in to the mail server and checks to see whether you have mail.

To:
gabegralla@zdnet.com

3 If you have new mail, you'll see a list of your new mail messages when you log in to the server. You'll often see the name of the sender, the subject of the message, and the date and time that the message was sent.

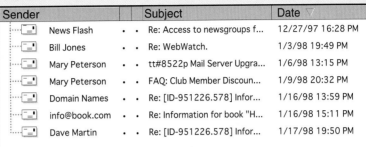

Sender		Subject	Date
News Flash	• •	Re: Access to newsgroups f...	12/27/97 16:28 PM
Bill Jones	• •	Re: WebWatch.	1/3/98 19:49 PM
Mary Peterson	• •	tt#8522p Mail Server Upgra...	1/6/98 13:15 PM
Mary Peterson	• •	FAQ: Club Member Discoun...	1/9/98 20:32 PM
Domain Names	• •	Re: [ID-951226.578] Infor...	1/16/98 13:59 PM
info@book.com	• •	Re: Information for book "H...	1/16/98 15:11 PM
Dave Martin	• •	Re: [ID-951226.578] Infor...	1/17/98 19:50 PM

Do I have mail?

Here it is.

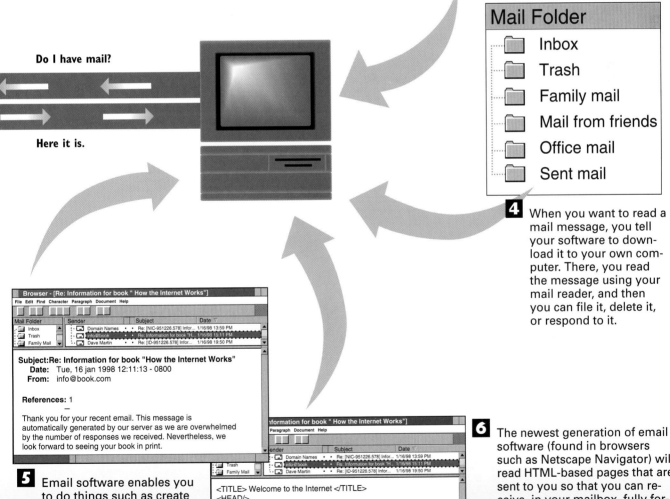

Mail Folder

- Inbox
- Trash
- Family mail
- Mail from friends
- Office mail
- Sent mail

4 When you want to read a mail message, you tell your software to download it to your own computer. There, you read the message using your mail reader, and then you can file it, delete it, or respond to it.

Browser - [Re: Information for book " How the Internet Works"]

File Edit Find Character Paragraph Document Help

Mail Folder	Sender	Subject	Date
Inbox	Domain Names • •	Re: [NIC-951226.578] Infor...	1/16/98 13:59 PM
Trash	info@book	Re: Information for book "H...	1/16/98 15:11 PM
Family Mail	Dave Martin • •	Re: [ID-951226.578] Infor...	1/16/98 19:50 PM

Subject:Re: Information for book "How the Internet Works"
   Date: Tue, 16 jan 1998 12:11:13 - 0800
   From: info@book.com

References: 1

Thank you for your recent email. This message is automatically generated by our server as we are overwhelmed by the number of responses we received. Nevertheless, we look forward to seeing your book in print.

5 Email software enables you to do things such as create folders for storing mail, search through your messages, keep an address book of people to whom you send mail, create group mailing lists, create and add a signature file, and more.

nformation for book " How the Internet Works"]

Paragraph Document Help

ender	Subject	Date
	Re: [NIC-951226.578] Infor...	1/16/98 13:59 PM
Trash	info@book	Re: Information for book "H...	1/16/98 15:11 PM
Family Mail	Dave Martin • •	Re: [ID-951226.578] Infor...	1/16/98 19:50 PM

```
<TITLE> Welcome to the Internet </TITLE>
<HEAD/>
<Body BGCOLOR="#ffffff" LINK ="#0000ff" VLINK="#ff0000"
ALINK="#ff0000
TEXT='#000000"
<MAP NAME="mainmap">
AREA COORDS="0,0,73,24"
HREF="http://guide.escape.com/?h">AREA COORDS="0,0,73,24"
AREA COORDS="142,0,208,24"
HREF="http://guide.bbentsol/comprod/at_work/index.html">
```

6 The newest generation of email software (found in browsers such as Netscape Navigator) will read HTML-based pages that are sent to you so that you can receive, in your mailbox, fully formatted Web pages. When you click the links in them, your browser will launch and visit the page it is linked to.

How a Mailing List Works

1 Mailing lists are a way for groups of people to have public discussions via email. After you join a mailing list, every message you write to the list can be read by everyone on the list.

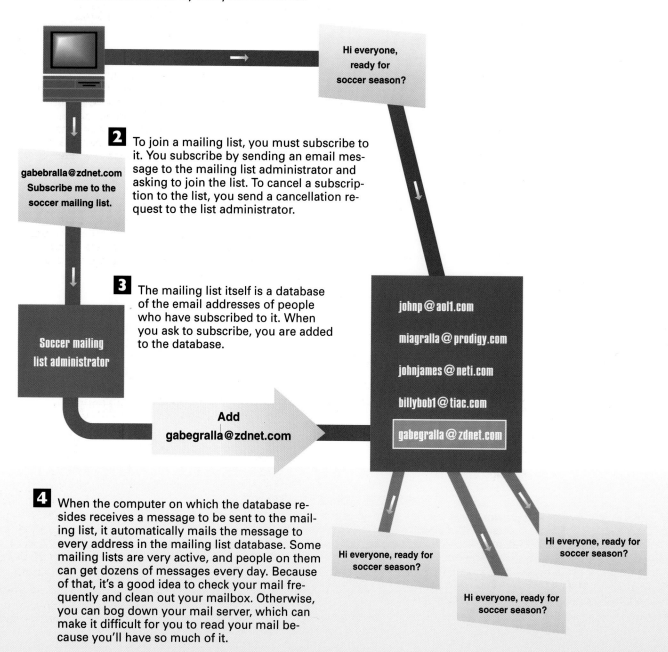

Hi everyone, ready for soccer season?

gabebralla@zdnet.com Subscribe me to the soccer mailing list.

2 To join a mailing list, you must subscribe to it. You subscribe by sending an email message to the mailing list administrator and asking to join the list. To cancel a subscription to the list, you send a cancellation request to the list administrator.

3 The mailing list itself is a database of the email addresses of people who have subscribed to it. When you ask to subscribe, you are added to the database.

Soccer mailing list administrator

Add gabegralla@zdnet.com

johnp@aol1.com

miagralla@prodigy.com

johnjames@neti.com

billybob1@tiac.com

gabegralla@zdnet.com

4 When the computer on which the database resides receives a message to be sent to the mailing list, it automatically mails the message to every address in the mailing list database. Some mailing lists are very active, and people on them can get dozens of messages every day. Because of that, it's a good idea to check your mail frequently and clean out your mailbox. Otherwise, you can bog down your mail server, which can make it difficult for you to read your mail because you'll have so much of it.

Hi everyone, ready for soccer season?

Hi everyone, ready for soccer season?

Hi everyone, ready for soccer season?

How Email Is Sent Between Networks

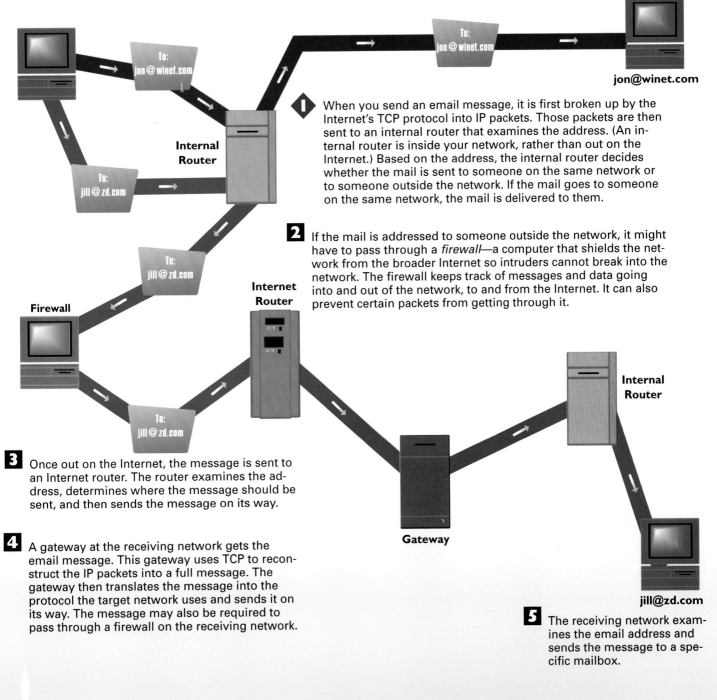

jon@winet.com

1 When you send an email message, it is first broken up by the Internet's TCP protocol into IP packets. Those packets are then sent to an internal router that examines the address. (An internal router is inside your network, rather than out on the Internet.) Based on the address, the internal router decides whether the mail is sent to someone on the same network or to someone outside the network. If the mail goes to someone on the same network, the mail is delivered to them.

2 If the mail is addressed to someone outside the network, it might have to pass through a *firewall*—a computer that shields the network from the broader Internet so intruders cannot break into the network. The firewall keeps track of messages and data going into and out of the network, to and from the Internet. It can also prevent certain packets from getting through it.

3 Once out on the Internet, the message is sent to an Internet router. The router examines the address, determines where the message should be sent, and then sends the message on its way.

4 A gateway at the receiving network gets the email message. This gateway uses TCP to reconstruct the IP packets into a full message. The gateway then translates the message into the protocol the target network uses and sends it on its way. The message may also be required to pass through a firewall on the receiving network.

5 The receiving network examines the email address and sends the message to a specific mailbox.

Internal Router

Firewall

Internet Router

Gateway

Internal Router

jill@zd.com

To: jon@winet.com

To: jill@zd.com

To: jill@zd.com

To: jill@zd.com

How White Page Directories (LDAP) Work

Millions of people have email addresses on the Internet, but it's always been difficult to find an email address if you know only a name. The Lightweight Directory Access Protocol (LDAP) makes creating White Page-style directories easier, so it's now possible to look up people's addresses if you know only their name.

2 Like much other Internet technology, LDAP works on a client/server model. The client runs on a local computer. Many kinds of clients are available for many kinds of computers. To find someone's email address, you run the client on your computer and type in the name of the person whose email address you want to find.

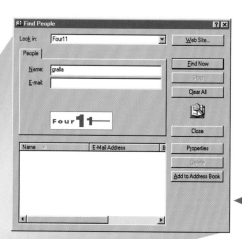

HERE ARE THE RESULTS

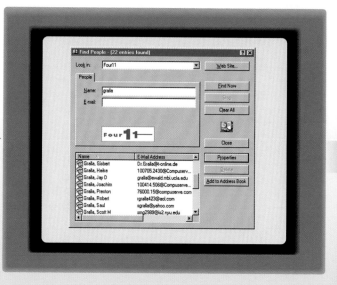

7 The client receives the results and displays them on the local computer.

An LDAP directory is a database that follows LDAP rules and protocols for organizing its information. It is located on an Internet server. A company or business maintains the server and is responsible for keeping the information on it up-to-date by adding new names, deleting old names, and updating existing names.

3 Before sending the request itself, the client sends an LDAP command, called the BindRequest, to the server. Basically, this is a command telling the server that the client wants to make a request.

BINDREQUEST

4 The server answers with a command called the BindResponse, telling the client that it can go ahead and make a request.

BINDRESPONSE

FIND "GRALLA"

5 The client then sends the request to the server, sending a person's name and asking for his or her email address.

Lightweight Directory Access Protocol (LDAP)

Name		Address
Allan Scott	• •	a_scott@lantern.com
Bill Jones	• •	BOJ@pol.net
Mary Peterson	• •	Brandywine@rocketmail.com
Crash Corrigan	• •	Crash_98@mailexcite.com
Stephen Adams	• •	s_adams_98@yahoo.com
Jenna MacCimbri	• •	CGF@Zamora.net
Dave Martin	• •	Martini@olive.com
Flash Flannagan	• •	FF_100@access.com
Carolyn Jones	• •	morticia@noctem.net
Carl Magnus	• •	aachen@imperator.com
Darlena Morraine	• •	DCM@blonde.net
Clutch Cargo	• •	CC_cartoon@tvland.com
Patricia Douglas	• •	p_ddouglas@yahoo.com

6 The LDAP directory performs a search and finds the email address or addresses in its database. It sends the results to the client.

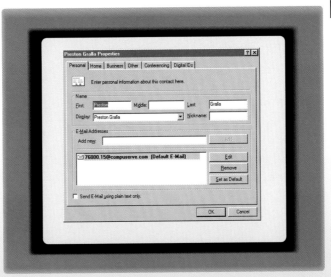

8 Depending on the software you're using, you can now add the name and email address to your local address book, or you can immediately send an email to the person.

CHAPTER

17

Email Spam and Blocking

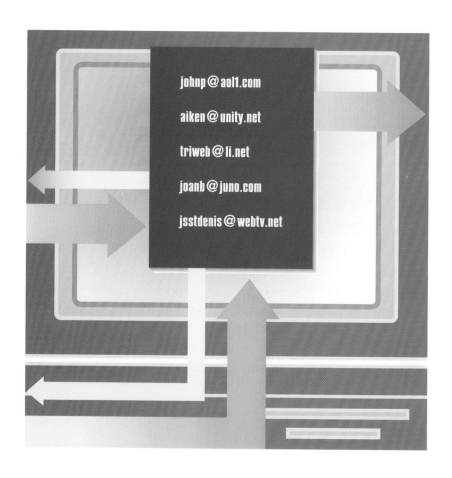

ONE of the most contentious issues to surface on the Internet in the last few years has to do with what Internet users call "Spam." Spam is unsolicited junk email that commercial companies send out, asking you to buy their goods and services. At times it may contain inducements to visit the seller's site. The email usually contains a phone number to call, an address to send money to, or a Web site to visit to buy the goods and services.

The term "Spam" comes from a Monty Python skit in which every item on a menu contained Spam luncheon meat. It was originally used to refer to unsolicited postings for commercial products or services on Usenet, especially when they were cross-posted to several newsgroups.

Spam may seem like a minor annoyance, but the truth is, it can cause major problems. Spam floods the Internet with unwanted mail, which can lead to delayed or lost mail. It clogs the Internet pipeline, making other information slower to send. It wastes time for those who have to go through their email boxes deleting unsolicited mail, especially when they pay for their email service by the hour. Additionally, it's fairly common for Spammers to hide their real email addresses by forging other people's names onto the From or Sender header of an email message. So, those people whose names were forged may be the target of angry mail. This makes it difficult for Webmasters and mail administrators to filter Spam messages by From address or domain name. Sometimes Spammers even use other people's servers to deliver their bulk email; in essence, forcing someone else to pay the costs of the Spammer's mail delivery.

In some ways, Spam is not very different from traditional junk mail. Spammers buy or compile massive lists of email addresses, in the same way that junk mailers buy or compile U.S. Postal addresses. The Spammer then uses special software to send a solicitation to every person on the list—not uncommonly, tens of thousands of pieces of email in a single Spam mailing. To hide their true identity, Spammers forge names onto the headers of email messages, and even "relay" their Spam to another mail server on the Internet, so that it is impossible to find out where the mail comes from. Often, a user will request to be taken off the list by replying to email addresses that the Spammers provide. However, this verifies the user's address and he or she will get even more Spam.

A variety of ways have been devised to block Spam, including having email filters on email software ignore any mail from known Spammers. This doesn't always work well, however, because Spammers often change or forge their email addresses. There are also calls for the courts or Congress to take action. Congress has considered several laws, including one that would ban Spam entirely, in the same way that junk faxes were banned several years ago. Until then, try doing an Internet search for Web sites that will help you download and install software to help filter your email and stop Spam.

How Email Spam Is Sent

1 *Spam* is a term used to describe unsolicited email sent to you, often by commercial firms that attempt to sell you goods and services. Spam is sent out as bulk email, often to lists of 10,000 or more people at once. It's inexpensive to send, so its use has exploded on the Internet to the point where it is common for someone to get several dozen of these messages in a single day. Spam has become enough of an annoyance to warrant calls to ban it outright.

05/21	CONTINENTAL.COM	URGENT MESSAGE
05/21	Ct@mailaol.co	Classmeister 5.0 + Special Offer (com/msg)
05/21	OIL.PATCH.MARKET	E-MAIL LIST FOR SALE GETS RESULTS QUICKLY
05/22	4063986@us.net	~~~ Cable Television Descrambler - Easy To Make !!!
05/22	seanpage@infocom	Business Offer!!!
05/25	TheCreditMan@big	You Are Guaranteed Credit!
05/25	Jill the coy one	4 Million Email Addresses For Sale
05/26	dospub@www.usa.c	publish at home
05/27	Unknown@unknown	This is awesome!
05/27	56369130@swbell.	WANT REVENGE - Get It Right Here - FREE SAMPLES !!!
05/28	To Embrace	A Surprise Birthday Party And Gift For YOU :-)))))
05/29	kat @hol.gr	adults only
05/29	connect@internet	Qualify For Survey Sweepstakes Win $25!

Bulk Email List

2 To send out unsolicited bulk email, a Spammer first needs to get a list of email addresses. Often, Spammers buy the lists from companies that compile them. These companies use automated software robots to get the email addresses. The robots get the lists from a number of sources. One way is to go into Usenet newsgroups and harvest email addresses by looking inside every message, which usually has in it the email address of the person who posted it.

johnp @ aol1.com

aiken @ unity.net

triweb @ li.net

joanb @ juno.com

jsstdenis @ webtv.net

Get Email Addresses

ADD: aiken@unity.net
triweb@li.net

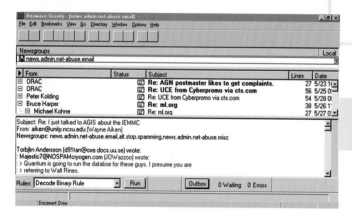

Usenet Newsgroups

3 Email addresses can also be harvested from email directories on the Web sites that allow people to look up others' email addresses. Software robots can go into the directory and grab every address in the directory. Robots also can go into chat areas, such as those on America Online, and gather email addresses.

Get Email Addresses

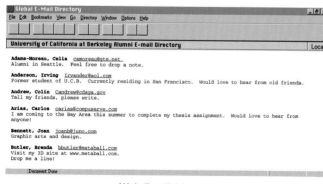

Web Email Directory

ADD: aiken@unity.net
triweb@li.net

4 The Spammer either buys the resulting email list or compiles one of his or her own. The Spammer uses the list, along with bulk mailing software, and sends a Spam message to every person on the list. In the message may be a return address, Web site, or phone number where the reciever can get more information about the goods and services being sold.

5 Some Spammers will include in the email a return address where someone who no longer wants to receive Spam can send a message and be taken off the Spam list. When the remove message is received, a robot automatically takes the person off the list. However, Spammers rarely do this because most people would opt not to be on the Spam lists.

Remove Me

Bulk Emailer

johnp@aol1.com

aiken@unity.net

triweb@li.net

joanb@juno.com

jsstdenis@webtv.net

SPAM

Spam

SPAM

SPAM

Spam

Mail Server

SPAM

From Nowhereman
Sender Nobody
Subject "Free cash

6 Spammers realize that Spam offends most people, so the Spammers go to great lengths to hide their true email addresses. As one way of hiding their real email addresses, they "forge" parts of the message header in the email address such as the From, Sender, and Reply fields so it appears that the email has come from someone other than the Spammer. Doing this is sometimes called *Spamouflauge*.

Mail Server

7 As a further way of hiding their true addressers, Spammers relay their bulk Spam to a server that is not associated with them and then have that server send out the bulk Spam. Sometimes Spammers have the bulk Spam relayed among several different servers to make it even more difficult to trace who really sent the mail.

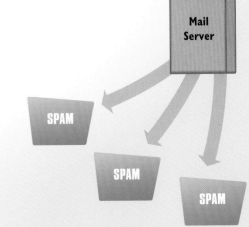

SPAM

SPAM

SPAM

How Email Spam Is Blocked

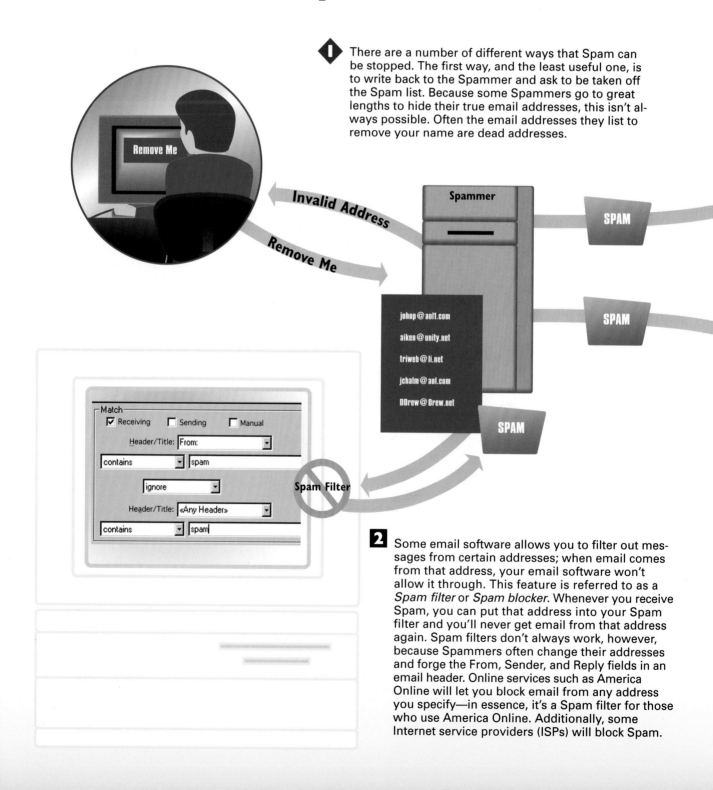

1 There are a number of different ways that Spam can be stopped. The first way, and the least useful one, is to write back to the Spammer and ask to be taken off the Spam list. Because some Spammers go to great lengths to hide their true email addresses, this isn't always possible. Often the email addresses they list to remove your name are dead addresses.

Remove Me

Invalid Address

Remove Me

Spammer

SPAM

SPAM

johnp @ aol1.com

aiken @ unity.net

triweb @ li.net

jchalm @ aol.com

DDrew @ Drew.net

SPAM

Spam Filter

Match
- ☑ Receiving   ☐ Sending   ☐ Manual
- Header/Title: From:
- contains | spam
- ignore
- Header/Title: «Any Header»
- contains | spam

2 Some email software allows you to filter out messages from certain addresses; when email comes from that address, your email software won't allow it through. This feature is referred to as a *Spam filter* or *Spam blocker*. Whenever you receive Spam, you can put that address into your Spam filter and you'll never get email from that address again. Spam filters don't always work, however, because Spammers often change their addresses and forge the From, Sender, and Reply fields in an email header. Online services such as America Online will let you block email from any address you specify—in essence, it's a Spam filter for those who use America Online. Additionally, some Internet service providers (ISPs) will block Spam.

3 ISPs and online service such as America Online can block Spammers from sending bulk mail to their subscribers. A router examines all incoming mail to the ISP or online service. The router has been told that when email comes from certain addresses, to block mail from getting into the network. These addresses are put in a routing table that can be changed whenever new Spammers are found.

Routing Table

ISP Router

Spam Filter

Bounced SPAM

4 Because Spammers often change their addresses, using routing tables won't always work. Online services and ISPs have gone to court to ban Spammers from sending email to their customers. Although the law remains murky, in a number of instances, the courts have decided in favor of online services and the ISPs, and have banned Spammers from sending mail through them.

5 A number of laws and schemes have been proposed to regulate or outlaw Spam. In one plan, every piece of Spam would have to contain a specific piece of information in the message header, identifying it as unsolicited email. In this way, people could set their Spam filters to block every single piece of Spam, filtering out that piece of information. Some laws have been proposed that would outlaw Spam entirely, in the same way that junk faxes were banned.

IAMSPAM

6 One way to prevent being Spammed is to make sure that your email address isn't added to Spam lists. To do this, when posting to Usenet newsgroups, edit your header so that it doesn't contain your email address. You should also notify email directories that you'd like to be taken off their lists. In this way your email address won't be harvested by robots, and you should get less Spam.

Usenet

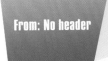

From: No header

CHAPTER

18

How Usenet Newsgroups Work

USENET, the world's biggest electronic discussion forum, provides a way for messages to be sent among computers across the entire Internet. People from all over the world participate in discussions on thousands of topics in specific areas of interest called *newsgroups*.

There are at least 20 different major hierarchies of newsgroups, such as recreation (identified by the letters "rec") and computers (identified by the letters "comp"). Within these major hierarchies are subcategories (such as rec.arts) and further subcategories (such as rec.arts.books). Individual newsgroups can cover anything from movies to parenting, ecology, sports teams, clip art, and news about Usenet itself. Not all Internet sites carry all newsgroups. An administrator at each site decides which newsgroups to carry.

To participate in newsgroups, you'll need special software to read and respond to them. There are readers for PC, Macintosh, and UNIX computers. Online services such as CompuServe and America Online have their own proprietary software that lets you participate in newsgroups.

A good newsgroup reader will let you view the ongoing discussions as threads. *Threads* are ongoing conversations that are grouped by topic. So, for example, in the rec.arts.books newsgroup there may be many different threads going on at one time, each discussing a different book.

Many newsgroups have a list of Frequently Asked Questions, or FAQs (pronounced "facks"), associated with them. These FAQs answer common questions about the newsgroup. It's a good idea to read the FAQ before submitting questions to the newsgroup as a whole.

You participate in newsgroups by reading the messages and responding to them. There are moderated and unmoderated newsgroups. In a *moderated newsgroup*, each message goes to a human moderator. The moderator looks at the messages, making sure they're appropriate for the group. If they are appropriate, the messages are posted. All messages sent to an *unmoderated newsgroup* are automatically posted.

When messages are posted, Usenet servers distribute them to other sites that carry the newsgroup. A site usually carries only the most current messages; otherwise, they would soon run out of storage space. Some sites *archive*, or store, old discussions.

A convenient way to check newsgroups is to subscribe to those that interest you. That way, whenever you check the Usenet server, new messages in your subscribed newsgroup will be delivered to you. You can also cancel your subscription to a newsgroup if you are no longer interested in it. You can read newsgroups without subscribing to them; in that case, you'll have to manually ask to read specific newsgroups instead of having it done automatically for you.

Binary files such as pictures and multimedia can be posted in newsgroups. These files must be specially encoded in order for them to be posted. To view them, you'll have to transfer them to your computer and then unencode them with special software. A common encoding scheme used on newsgroups is called uuencode.

How Usenet Works

1 Usenet is a global bulletin board and discussion area. It collects messages about many thousands of different topics into newsgroups, which are freewheeling discussion areas in which anyone can participate. Newsgroups can be found on many host computers across the Internet. There are thousands of newsgroups that cover just about every topic you've ever imagined and many you probably haven't thought of.

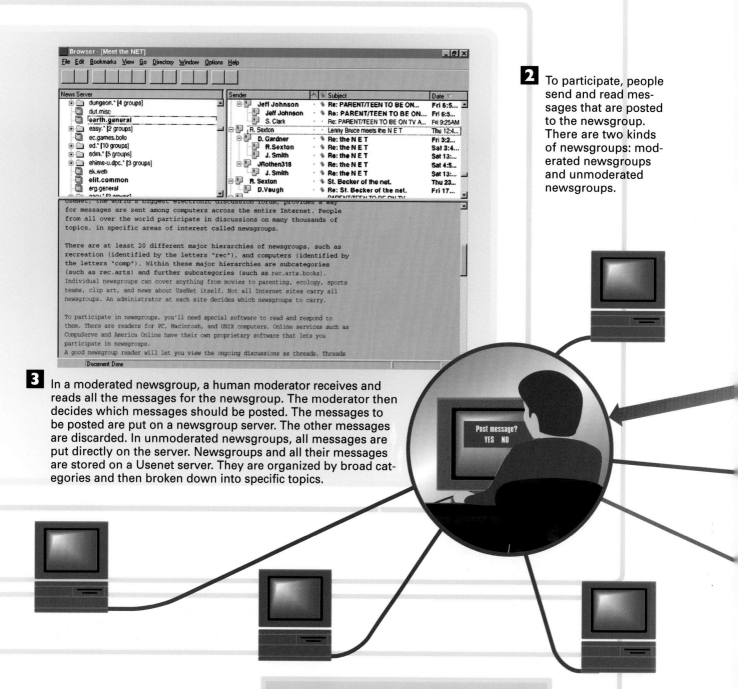

2 To participate, people send and read messages that are posted to the newsgroup. There are two kinds of newsgroups: moderated newsgroups and unmoderated newsgroups.

3 In a moderated newsgroup, a human moderator receives and reads all the messages for the newsgroup. The moderator then decides which messages should be posted. The messages to be posted are put on a newsgroup server. The other messages are discarded. In unmoderated newsgroups, all messages are put directly on the server. Newsgroups and all their messages are stored on a Usenet server. They are organized by broad categories and then broken down into specific topics.

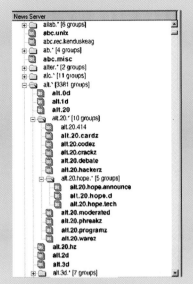

6 Newsgroup reader software lets you read messages and respond to newsgroups. The software gives you ways to manage your newsgroups by also allowing you to subscribe to newsgroups, which means that new messages will automatically be delivered to you when you check the server. You'll also be able to cancel your subscription.

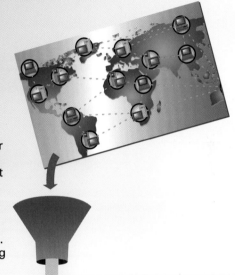

5 Pictures, multimedia files, and even executable programs can be posted in newsgroups for other people to see and use. However, because of the technology used in newsgroups, those files must be specially encoded to be posted. To view, play, or use the files, you'll have to first transfer them to your own computer and then unencode them with special software. A common encoding scheme used on newsgroups is called uuencode. There are versions of this encoding and decoding program that work on PC, Macintosh, and UNIX computers. MIME is another encoding scheme.

"Check out this picture"

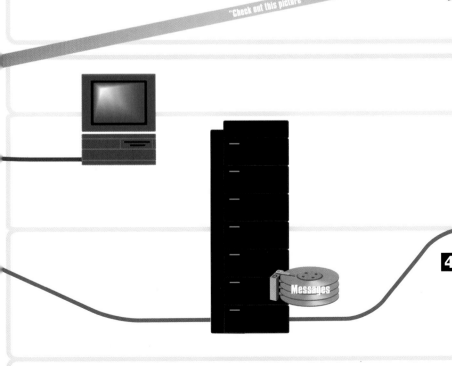

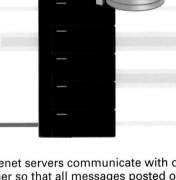

4 Usenet servers communicate with one another so that all messages posted on one server are duplicated on the other servers. While there are many Usenet servers, not all servers carry all newsgroups. Each site decides which newsgroups to carry.

Understanding the Hierarchy of Usenet Newsgroups

1 There are thousands of Usenet newsgroups. They are divided into hierarchies of topics to make it easier for you to find the particular newsgroups you want to participate in. Not all sites carry all newsgroups. System administrators decide which newsgroups to carry at their site. Online services, as well as Internet providers that give direct connections to the Internet, allow access to Usenet newsgroups.

2 In the hierarchy of Usenet newsgroups, the major topic (such as "rec" for recreation) comes first, followed by a subtopic (such as rec.arts). That subtopic can be further subdivided (such as rec.arts.books) and then subdivided even further, if need be. Pictured in this illustration are many of the major newsgroup topics, but they are only a very tiny percentage of the thousands of newsgroups available. New newsgroups are constantly being created and old ones are constantly being eliminated. You can get a list of Internet newsgroups by using your newsgroup client software and asking that it give you a complete, up-to-date list.

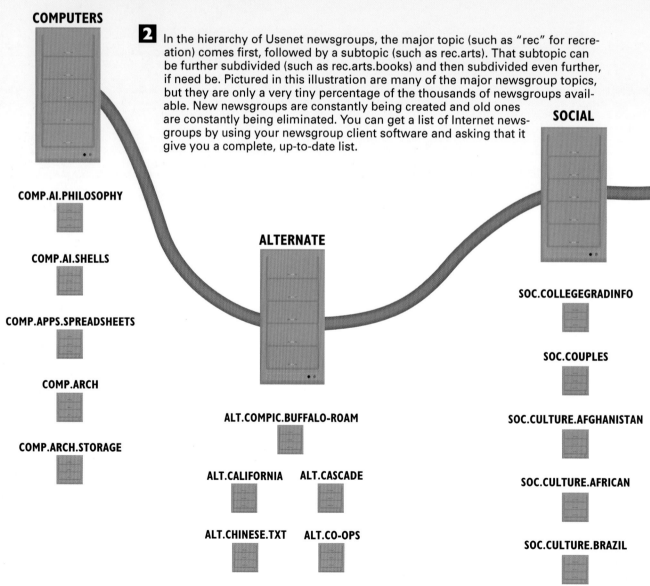

COMPUTERS

COMP.AI.PHILOSOPHY

COMP.AI.SHELLS

COMP.APPS.SPREADSHEETS

COMP.ARCH

COMP.ARCH.STORAGE

ALTERNATE

ALT.COMPIC.BUFFALO-ROAM

ALT.CALIFORNIA   ALT.CASCADE

ALT.CHINESE.TXT   ALT.CO-OPS

SOCIAL

SOC.COLLEGEGRADINFO

SOC.COUPLES

SOC.CULTURE.AFGHANISTAN

SOC.CULTURE.AFRICAN

SOC.CULTURE.BRAZIL

3 You can often identify the newsgroup by its name. Major Usenet topics include "comp" for discussions of computer-related topics; "soc" for discussions of societal topics; "sci" for discussions of scientific topics; "news" for discussions about newsgroups; "rec" for discussions of recreation topics; and "alt" for discussions of alternate topics, among others. So, for example, the rec.arts.books newsgroup carries discussions about books.

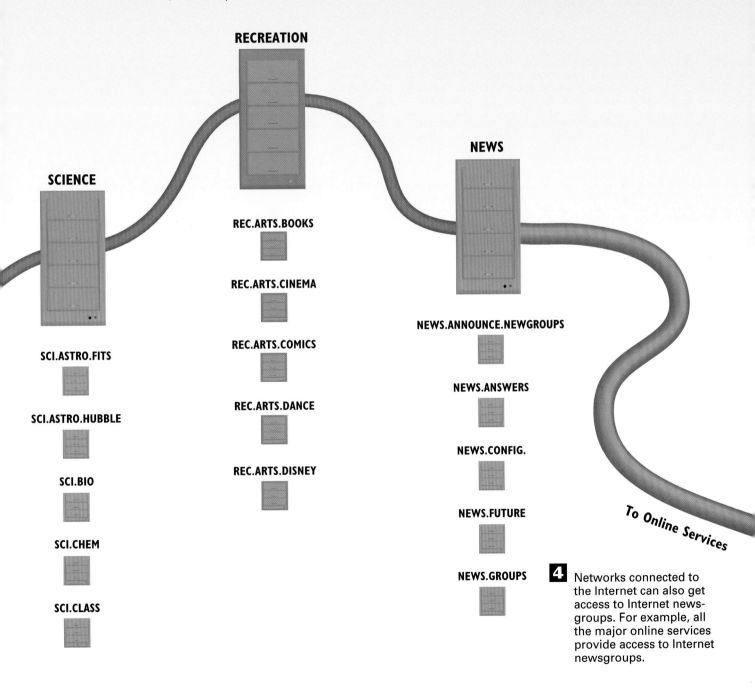

RECREATION

SCIENCE

NEWS

REC.ARTS.BOOKS

REC.ARTS.CINEMA

REC.ARTS.COMICS

REC.ARTS.DANCE

REC.ARTS.DISNEY

SCI.ASTRO.FITS

SCI.ASTRO.HUBBLE

SCI.BIO

SCI.CHEM

SCI.CLASS

NEWS.ANNOUNCE.NEWGROUPS

NEWS.ANSWERS

NEWS.CONFIG.

NEWS.FUTURE

NEWS.GROUPS

To Online Services

4 Networks connected to the Internet can also get access to Internet news-groups. For example, all the major online services provide access to Internet newsgroups.

CHAPTER

19

How Internet Chat and Instant Messaging Work

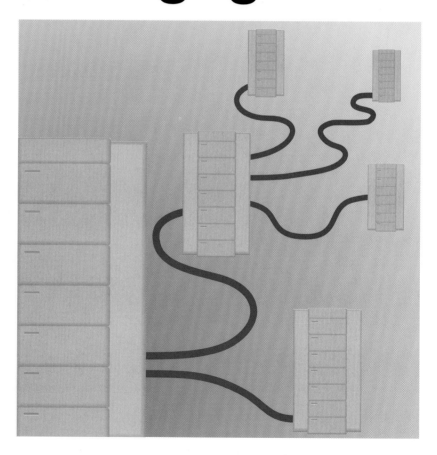

ONE of the most immediate ways to communicate with others via the Internet is to participate in live "chat." Chat doesn't refer to people actually talking to each other and hearing each other's voices. Instead, it means that you hold live keyboard "conversations" with other people on the Internet—that is, you type words on your computer and other people on the Internet can see those words on their computers immediately, and vice versa. You can hold chats with many people simultaneously all over the world.

A number of ways are available to chat on the Internet, but one of the most popular ones is called *IRC*, or *Internet Relay Chat*. Every day, thousands of people all over the world hold conversations on many topics via IRC. Each different topic is called a "channel." When you join a channel, you can see what other people on the channel type on their keyboards. In turn, everyone in the channel can see whatever you type on your keyboard. You can also hold individual side conversations with someone. Channels live on different servers around the world. Some servers have only a few channels, and others have many of them.

IRC has facilitated communications during natural disasters, wars, and other crises. In 1993, for example, during the attempted Communist coup in Russia when Russian legislators barricaded themselves inside the Parliament building, an IRC "news channel" was set up for relaying real-time, first-person accounts of the events taking place.

IRC follows a client/server model, which means that both client and server software are required in order to use it. Many IRC clients are available for many kinds of computers, so whether you have a PC, a Macintosh, or a UNIX workstation, you'll be able to use IRC.

Your IRC client communicates with an IRC server on the Internet. You log on to a server using the client and pick a channel on which you want to chat. When you type words on your keyboard, they are sent to your server. Your server is part of a global IRC server network. Your server sends your message to other servers, which, in turn, send your messages to people who are part of your channel. They can then see and respond to your message.

You can chat on the Internet in other ways, as well. Many Web sites, for example, use proprietary chat software that doesn't use the IRC protocol, but enables you to chat when you're on the site.

Another kind of chat is called *instant messaging*. In instant messaging, you communicate privately, one-on-one, with another person. You can create special lists so that you're informed when your "buddies" come online ready to chat, and they're informed when you come online.

How IRC Works

1 IRC (Internet Relay Chat) is a way for people all over the world to "chat" with one another by using their keyboards. The typed words are instantly relayed to computers all over the world, where recipients can read them. This process happens in real-time, which means everyone sees the words as people type them.

2 IRC runs on a client/server model, which means that to use it, you need client software on your computer. Many IRC clients are available for PCs, Macintoshes, UNIX workstations, and other kinds of computers.

3 When you want to chat, you make a connection to the Internet and then start your client software. Next, you need to log on to an IRC server located on the Internet. Many IRC servers are located all over the world. They are connected together in a network so that they can send messages to one another. The servers are connected in a spanning tree fashion, in which each server is connected to several others, but all the servers are not directly connected to one another.

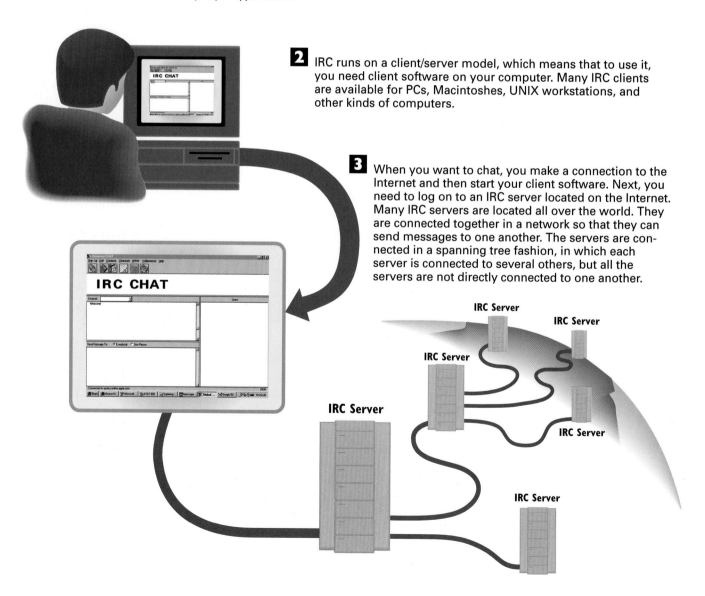

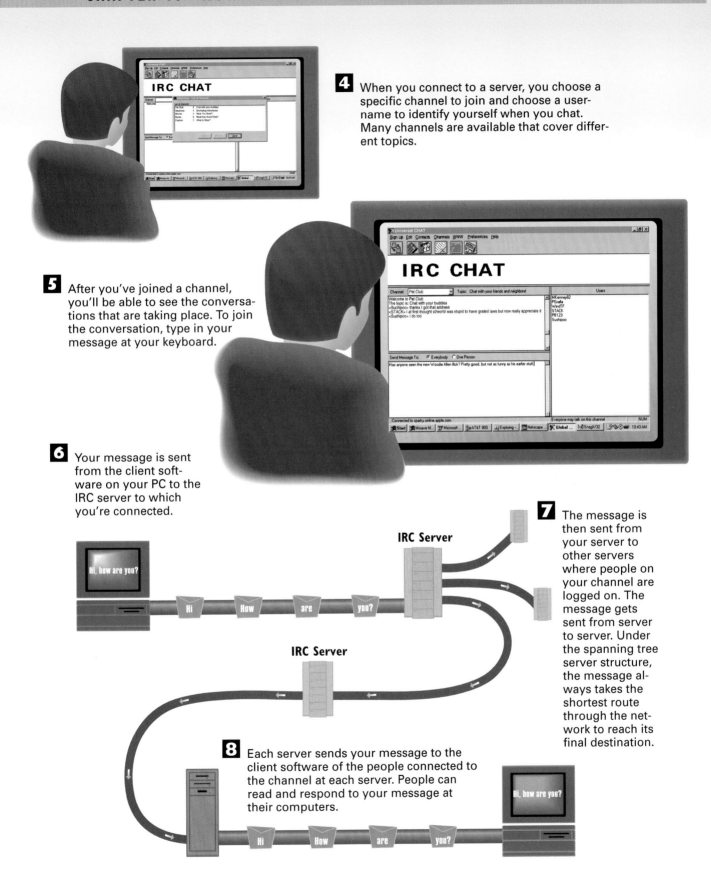

4 When you connect to a server, you choose a specific channel to join and choose a username to identify yourself when you chat. Many channels are available that cover different topics.

5 After you've joined a channel, you'll be able to see the conversations that are taking place. To join the conversation, type in your message at your keyboard.

6 Your message is sent from the client software on your PC to the IRC server to which you're connected.

7 The message is then sent from your server to other servers where people on your channel are logged on. The message gets sent from server to server. Under the spanning tree server structure, the message always takes the shortest route through the network to reach its final destination.

8 Each server sends your message to the client software of the people connected to the channel at each server. People can read and respond to your message at their computers.

IRC Server

IRC Server

How Instant Messaging Works

People can send instant messages—one-to-one, private communications—to one another on the Internet in many ways. The various instant messaging systems don't work with one another. Pictured here is one of the most popular instant messaging systems—America Online's Instant Messenger on the Internet. Yahoo! Pager works similarly, and is popular as well.

LOG IN

CLOSE CONNECTION

1 The Internet version of America Online's Instant Messenger (AIM) runs as a piece of client software on your computer. To use it, you must be connected to the Internet. When you run the software, it opens up a TCP connection to an Instant Messenger login server. The software sends your screen name and password over the connection to log you into the server.

2 The server checks the screen name and password. If they're correct, the login server instructs the Instant Messenger software to close the connection to the login server and to open up a new connection to a different AIM server—the one that will handle your instant message session. This connection uses a special communications protocol that allows for AIM functionality.

4 When you establish a connection with the AIM server, your client software sends a list of your buddies to the server. The server checks to see if any of the buddies are online—and it continues to do that for as long as you run the software on your computer. If you change the list of buddies during your session, that information is sent to the server as well so that it can keep track of new buddies or ignore buddies that you've deleted from your list.

3 Instant Message software includes "buddy list" capabilities. That means you keep a list of people you'd like to send instant messages to, and when they come online, you are notified so that you can send instant messages to and receive instant messages from them. You create a buddy list in your AIM software by adding your buddies' screen names to it.

"Are my buddies here?"

COOL LIZARD IS ONLINE

"Hi, Mia! Are you interested in getting together sometime next week?"

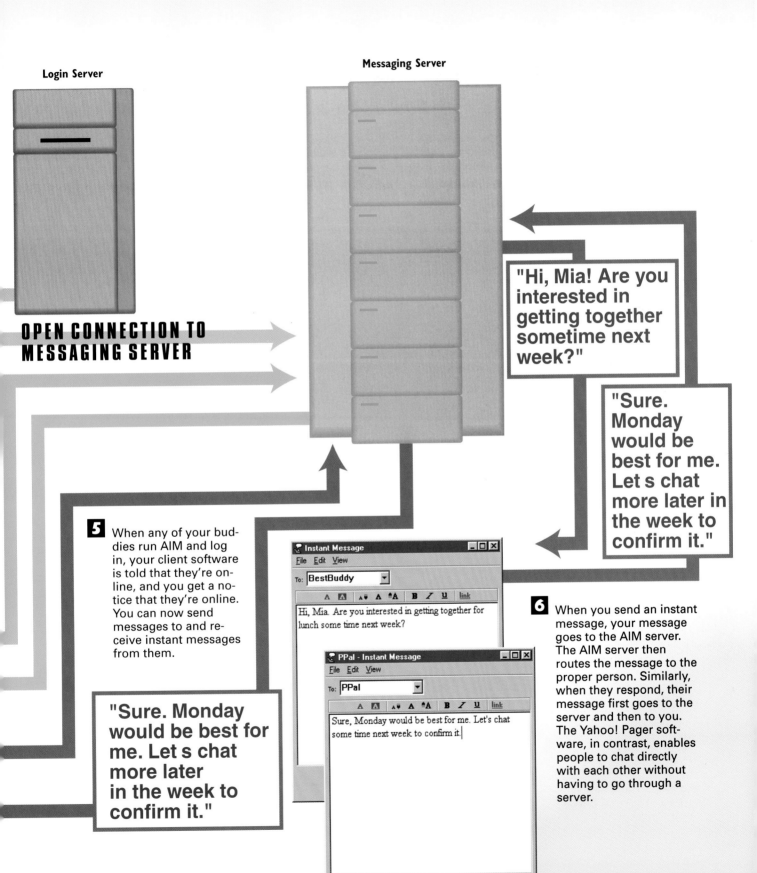

Login Server

Messaging Server

OPEN CONNECTION TO
MESSAGING SERVER

"Hi, Mia! Are you interested in getting together sometime next week?"

"Sure. Monday would be best for me. Let s chat more later in the week to confirm it."

5 When any of your buddies run AIM and log in, your client software is told that they're online, and you get a notice that they're online. You can now send messages to and receive instant messages from them.

"Sure. Monday would be best for me. Let s chat more later in the week to confirm it."

Instant Message
File Edit View
To: BestBuddy
A A A▼ A ▲A B Z U link
Hi, Mia. Are you interested in getting together for lunch some time next week?

PPal - Instant Message
File Edit View
To: PPal
A A A▼ A ▲A B Z U link
Sure, Monday would be best for me. Let's chat some time next week to confirm it.

6 When you send an instant message, your message goes to the AIM server. The AIM server then routes the message to the proper person. Similarly, when they respond, their message first goes to the server and then to you. The Yahoo! Pager software, in contrast, enables people to chat directly with each other without having to go through a server.

CHAPTER

20

Making Phone Calls on the Internet

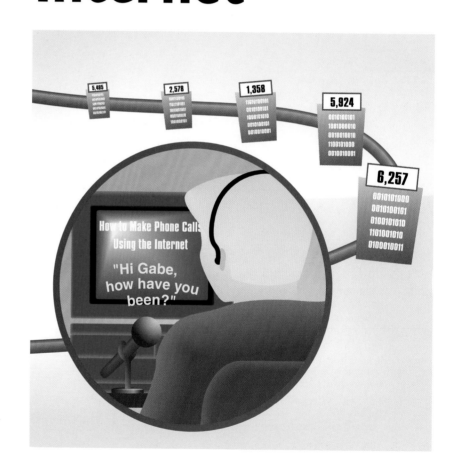

THE Internet has pioneered many new ways to communicate, such as email, live chat, and newsgroups. But it can be used to enable some old-fashioned communications as well: You can make telephone calls using the Internet. When you do so, the sound of your voice and that of the person you're talking to are broken down into packets. Those packets are delivered using the Internet's TCP/IP protocols.

You can make telephone calls over the Internet in two ways. In the first way, you use your computer and special hardware and software to make calls, so that you communicate through your PC. In the second way, often referred to as Internet telephony, you make a phone call as you normally do on your telephone, except your call is routed over the Internet rather than through the normal phone service. This usually cuts the cost to you of making long-distance phone calls.

The revolutionary part of using the Internet to make phone calls from your PC is the price: it's free. You pay only for your Internet connection, as if you were browsing the Web or sending email. You don't actually have to pay for the phone call itself. In addition, you can make calls anywhere in the world. However, you will only be able to make telephone calls to and receive calls from someone who has an Internet address, so you won't be able to replace your telephone by using the Internet. A number of different competing products enable you to talk over the Internet, but as yet, they don't communicate with one another. No standard way of making Internet telephone calls exists, so you'll be able to talk only to people who use the exact same software you do for making and receiving phone calls.

Many different schemes and software packages will enable you to make phone calls from your PC over the Internet. You don't actually use your telephone with any of them. Instead, you speak into a microphone attached to your computer and listen through speakers and a sound card.

Although each company's software works somewhat differently, in general, they use similar ways of enabling people to make phone calls over the Internet. To make a phone call, first you'll have to know someone's Internet address. (You can consult directories that function like telephone books to get this information.) After you find the person's Internet address, you can connect to them by running special software and then by double-clicking their name. (The person on the other end must be running the same software you are using.) A message goes out to them over the Internet to see if they're available to talk.

When you make phone calls over the Internet using your normal phone, things work differently. You make the call as you would any other phone call. After you make the call, however, your voice will be digitized and converted into IP packets, and then delivered using the same TCP/IP technology as the rest of the Internet uses. On the other end of the call, the digitized voice data is converted and can be listened to over the phone.

How to Make Phone Calls Using Your PC and the Internet

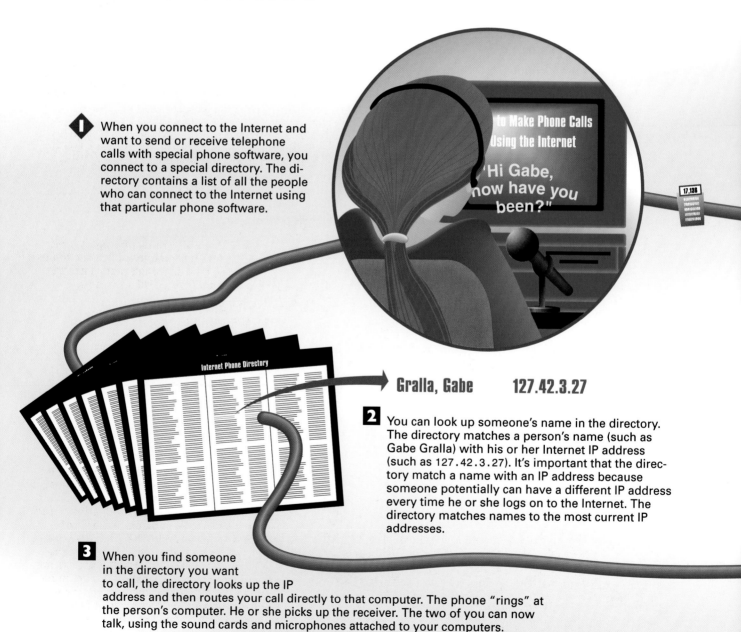

1 When you connect to the Internet and want to send or receive telephone calls with special phone software, you connect to a special directory. The directory contains a list of all the people who can connect to the Internet using that particular phone software.

Internet Phone Directory

Gralla, Gabe   127.42.3.27

2 You can look up someone's name in the directory. The directory matches a person's name (such as Gabe Gralla) with his or her Internet IP address (such as 127.42.3.27). It's important that the directory match a name with an IP address because someone potentially can have a different IP address every time he or she logs on to the Internet. The directory matches names to the most current IP addresses.

3 When you find someone in the directory you want to call, the directory looks up the IP address and then routes your call directly to that computer. The phone "rings" at the person's computer. He or she picks up the receiver. The two of you can now talk, using the sound cards and microphones attached to your computers.

"Hi Gabe, how have you been?"

4 When you talk into the microphone, software turns your voice into binary data files that computers can read. It also compresses the voice data to make it smaller and able to be sent over the Internet more quickly. Normally, voice files are very large, and without compression, they would be too large to quickly send over the Internet.

5 The software also determines the speed of the Internet connection. If the connection is a high-speed connection, it creates voice files of high quality. If it's a lower-speed connection, it creates files of a lesser sound quality because at lower speeds it would take too long to send voice files, even after they had been compressed.

HI GABE, HOW HAVE YOU BEEN?

28,800bps

H I G A B E , H O W H A

14,400bps

6 The software breaks up the voice files into a series of packets to be sent over the Internet using the Internet's TCP/IP protocols.

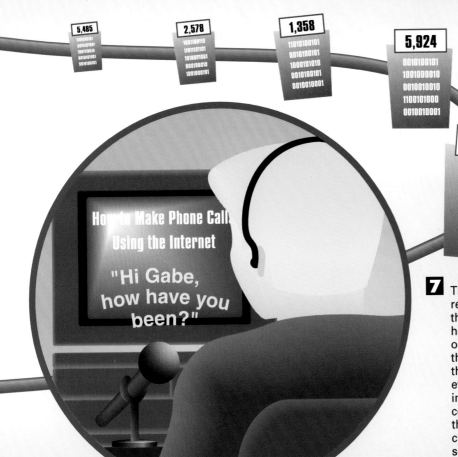

"Hi Gabe, how have you been?"

How to Make Phone Calls Using the Internet

7 The packets are sent to the receiver. On the receiving computer, software decompresses the packets so they can be played and heard. Sometimes packets will arrive out of order on the receiving end, so some of them will be missing. When that happens, the software, based on the received packets, is able to estimate what the sounds are in the missing packet that has yet to be received. When the missing packet arrives, the software knows that it has already re-created what that packet would have sounded like. The software will then discard the packet.

How Internet Telephony Works

Hi, Mia. How about lunch next Tuesday?

 2 The first part of the call goes over the normal Public Switched Telephone Network (PSTN), as does any other call; at this point, it is no different in any way.

1 When you make a phone call using IP telephony, you use a normal telephone, not a computer. Depending on the IP telephony service you use, you may have to dial in a special code first, as a way of routing the call to an IP telephony service.

IP Voice Gateway

Hi, Mia. How about lunch next Tuesday?

IP (Internet Protocol) Telephony refers to telephone calls that are made over normal telephones but are delivered, in part, through the Internet instead of solely through a voice network, commonly called the Public Switched Telephone Network, or PSTN. Because the calls are routed through the Internet, they can be delivered at less cost than normal phone calls. But the voice quality may not be as good as calls delivered over the normal phone network.

PUBLIC SWITCHED TELEPHONE NETWORK

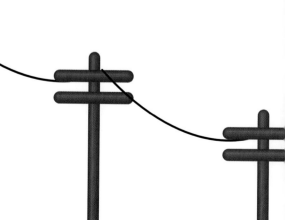

3 The call is sent to a special IP voice gateway. This gateway—a server and server software—may be located at the branch of the telephone company, or may instead be in a different location. The gateway converts the voice signal to digital data and compresses it. It compresses it because the data files of an uncompressed voice call could be too large to deliver in a timely fashion across the Internet.

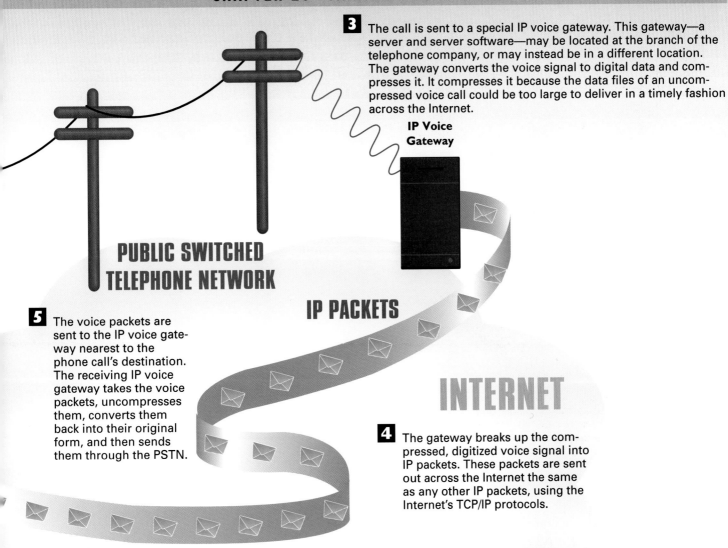

IP Voice Gateway

PUBLIC SWITCHED TELEPHONE NETWORK

IP PACKETS

5 The voice packets are sent to the IP voice gateway nearest to the phone call's destination. The receiving IP voice gateway takes the voice packets, uncompresses them, converts them back into their original form, and then sends them through the PSTN.

INTERNET

4 The gateway breaks up the compressed, digitized voice signal into IP packets. These packets are sent out across the Internet the same as any other IP packets, using the Internet's TCP/IP protocols.

6 The call travels on the PSTN the same as any other telephone call. The person receiving the call picks up the phone and talks, the same as with any other telephone conversation. When the receiving person speaks into the phone, the voice is sent back through the PSTN to the IP voice gateway and across the Internet in the same way that the call was initially made.

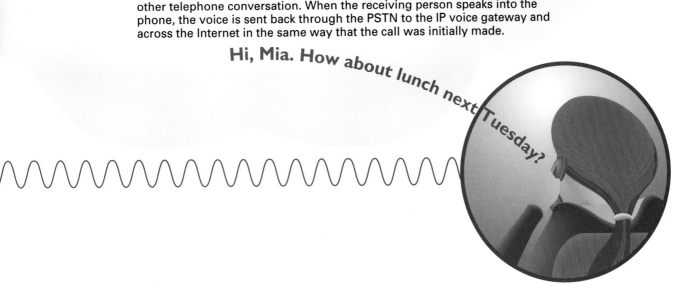

Hi, Mia. How about lunch next Tuesday?

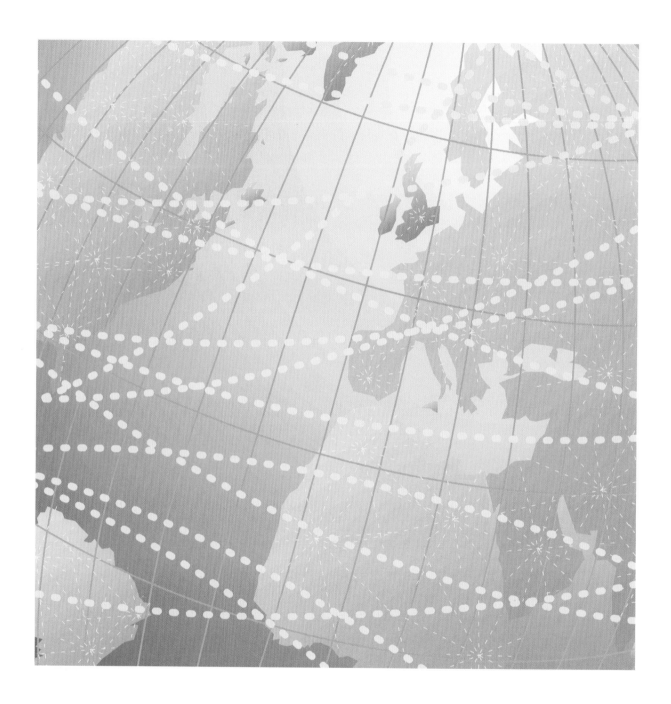

P A R T

COMMON INTERNET TOOLS

AN enormous amount of information and entertainment is available on the Internet, but how do you access it? Although using the Internet gets easier every day, it's still not quite as simple as turning on your television or reading your daily newspaper.

The solution is to use a variety of Internet tools. These tools enable you to tap into the colossal resources of the Internet. Some of these resources, such as the World Wide Web, are quite well known. Others, such as FTP (file transfer protocol) are used quite often—and sometimes people use them without even knowing it. Still others, such as Telnet, are not nearly as popular, although they are still useful. Many of these Internet tools predate the Web, but they are still useful today.

For many people, the term "Internet" really means the World Wide Web, but as this section of the book will show, a world exists well beyond the Web. Turn to Part 6, "How the World Wide Web Works," for information about the Web—the fastest growing and most visible part of the Internet.

The Web, of course, is only one part of the Internet. A lot more information is available on the Internet than that found via the Web. However, just as you need a browser to use the Web, you'll need special client software—what we can generically call Internet tools—to get at these other parts of the Internet. In this section, we'll look at how the most common and useful Internet tools work. And we'll also look at how Internet search engines work. Chapter 21, "How Gophers Work," describes how to use gophers. *Gophers* were one of the first attempts to corral the enormous amount of information available on the Internet. They help solve a major problem with the Internet—so much information is available that it can be difficult to find what you want. Gophers work on a simple menuing system and enable you to access information no matter where it's found, without having to remember to launch other Internet resources such as FTP or Telnet. Some of the ideas first introduced in gophers were later taken up by the World Wide Web.

Chapter 22, "How Telnet Works," covers one of the older Internet technologies, and one that is still in widespread use—Telnet. *Telnet* enables you to take over the resources of a distant computer while sitting at your own computer. What you type on your keyboard is sent across the Internet to the distant computer, the commands are carried out by the distant computer, and the results of your commands are sent to your own computer screen. It appears as if you're sitting at the distant computer's keyboard. Telnet is used in many ways, notably by libraries making their catalogs available over the Internet. When you log into a distant computer using Telnet, you often use a menuing system.

In Chapter 23, "FTP and Downloading Files," we'll cover one of the most popular uses of the Internet—downloading files. Generally, files are downloaded from the Internet using FTP, the Internet protocol. Not only will we look at how FTP works, but also at how files are compressed and decompressed on the Internet. A compressed file will take less time to be sent over the Internet to your computer. You may not know it, but many times when you're on a Web site and download a file, you're actually using the FTP protocol.

Finally, in Chapter 24, "Searching the Internet," we'll look at Internet search engines. The Internet contains such a vast amount of information that it's often impossible to find exactly what you want. *Search engines* look through the entire Internet—not only Web pages, but other sites such as newsgroups—and find information you're looking for, based on keywords that you type.

21

How Gophers Work

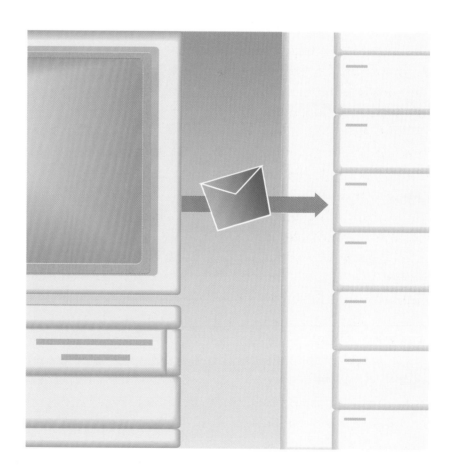

TO a certain extent, the Internet has been a victim of its success. There is such an enormous amount of information on it that it's often difficult to find what you want.

This problem led to the development of a software program called an Internet Gopher. A Gopher organizes information in a logical fashion to lead you to files, Internet resources, data, and anything else you might search for on the Internet. Gophers were the first client software programs to allow access to many types of protocols and servers from within one client.

Because Gophers make it easy to access many types of information, they helped fuel the Internet's growth. Because they are easy to build, they set in motion a wave of publishing on the Internet. Gophers are not used as frequently now as they were in the early days, however, largely due to the explosion of the World Wide Web.

There are many Gophers located on the Internet. Organizations and universities generally create Gophers, often for internal use by employees or students. Most of the Gophers you'll come across are created and maintained by universities, and have been set up as a way to make it easier for students to tap into the resources of the university and the Internet. Although the Gophers were created by the university or an organization, they are often made available to anyone on the Internet.

Gophers work in a client/server model. You run a Gopher client on your own computer. The client sends requests to a Gopher server located on the Internet. The server sends back the information to the client, which displays the information on your computer screen. There are Gopher clients available for PCs, Macintoshes, and UNIX computers. Online services also have Gopher client software built into them.

Gophers are organized in a tree-like menu fashion. When you first engage a Gopher, you'll be greeted with the Gopher's main menu, called the *root gopher*. From this menu you choose items that interest you. Frequently, those items will be other menus, called submenus. Keep burrowing down through menus until you reach the information you want.

Gophers can link you to many types of Internet resources. The information you request often doesn't reside on the Gopher. Instead, the Gopher points you to other locations on the Internet. Gophers can lead you to text files, binary files, logins to remote computers, graphics files, multimedia files, WAIS database searches, other Gophers, and more.

What's helpful about Gophers is that you won't need to know which kind of Internet resource is required to get the information—a Gopher takes care of it for you. For example, if you request a file through a Gopher, the Gopher will automatically send it through FTP to your computer; you don't need to launch FTP software. (See Chapter 23, "FTP and Downloading Files," for details on FTP.)

Lastly, if the Gopher leads you to log on to a remote computer, the Gopher will do it for you; you won't need to launch a separate Telnet session. (Telnet is the topic of the next chapter.)

How Gophers Work

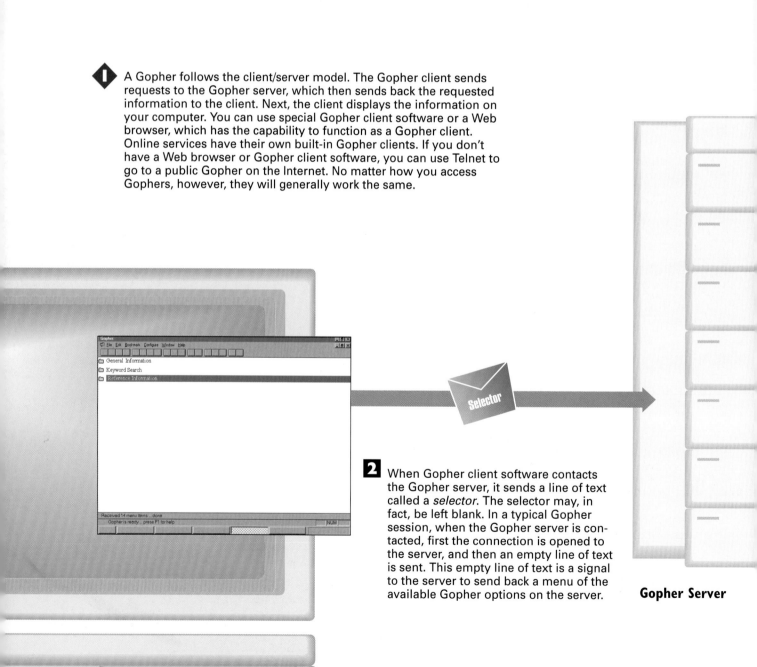

1 A Gopher follows the client/server model. The Gopher client sends requests to the Gopher server, which then sends back the requested information to the client. Next, the client displays the information on your computer. You can use special Gopher client software or a Web browser, which has the capability to function as a Gopher client. Online services have their own built-in Gopher clients. If you don't have a Web browser or Gopher client software, you can use Telnet to go to a public Gopher on the Internet. No matter how you access Gophers, however, they will generally work the same.

Selector

2 When Gopher client software contacts the Gopher server, it sends a line of text called a *selector*. The selector may, in fact, be left blank. In a typical Gopher session, when the Gopher server is contacted, first the connection is opened to the server, and then an empty line of text is sent. This empty line of text is a signal to the server to send back a menu of the available Gopher options on the server.

Gopher Server

User Display String

Selector String

3 The server sends a series of lines back to the client, each of which ends with a carriage return and line feed. Each line is made up of a series of components separated by tab characters—a number; text called a *user display string* that the Gopher user will see in a menu; a selector string that will be sent to the Gopher server to retrieve a document or a directory; the domain name of the host that has the document or directory; and a port number, which tells the Gopher client and server how to connect over the TCP/IP connection.

0 ↵ About this gopher ↵ dog.mbu.edu ↵ 70

1 ↵ Places around town ↵ town. mbu.edu ↵ 70

1 ↵ Latest news ↵ news.mbu.edu ↵ 70

1 ↵ Other resources ↵ other.mbu.edu ↵ 70

8 ↵ Library of Congress ↵ locis.loc.gov ↵ 70

4 The Gopher client displays only the user display string of each line. All the user display lines taken together make up the Gopher menu that you'll see.

Gopher

About this gopher
Places around town
Latest news
Other resources
Library of Congress

8 ↵ Library of Congress ↵ locis.loc.gov ↵ 70

5 When you choose an item from the Gopher menu, the entire string—not just the string you see—is sent from the client back to the Gopher server. The number at the beginning of the string tells the server what kind of resource is being requested. A 0 means the item is a file; a 1 means the item is a directory; a 5 or a 9 means the item is a binary file; a 7 means a search will be launched; and an 8 points to a Telnet session.

Use Telnet on Library of Congress Info System

L O C I S : LIBRARY OF CONGRESS INFORMATION SYSTEM

To make a choice; type a number, then press ENTER

1 Library of Congress Catalog   4   Braille and Audio
2 Federal Legislation   5   Organizations
3 Copyright Information   6   Foreign Law

7 Searching Hours and Basic Search Commands
8 Documentation and Classes
9 Library of Congress General Information
10 Library of Congress Fast Facts
11 * * Announcements * *

12 Comments and Logoff
   Choice:

6 Using the selector string, the domain name, and the port number, in addition to the number at the beginning of the string, the server retrieves the information requested by the client. If the information requested was a directory, the Gopher server will send a series of lines, each of which displays a menu option, just as was done when the server was first requested.

7 If the information requested was a search, the client software will be sent data allowing for a search.

8 If the information requested is a file or binary document, that file or document will be sent. Often, the information requested will be on a different server than the Gopher server. In that event, the Gopher server will contact the other server and have the requested material sent to the Gopher client. The Gopher client can now read or otherwise use the material.

CHAPTER

22

How Telnet Works

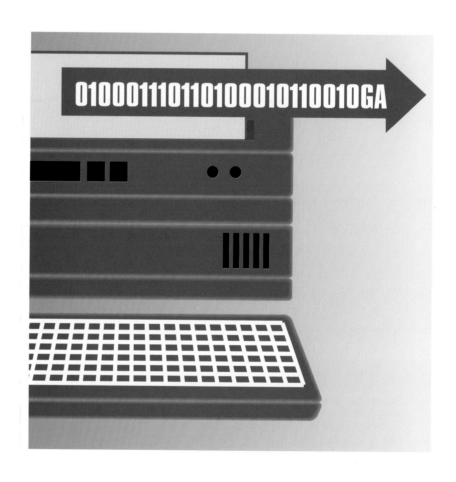

ONE of the more remarkable features of the Internet is the way it lets you use the resources of a distant computer somewhere else in the world. From your own home or office, you can log onto another computer, issue commands just as if you were at that computer's keyboard, and then gain access to all the computer's resources. You do this with an Internet resource called Telnet. Telnet follows a client/server model, which means that you run a piece of software on your own PC (the client) to use the resources of a distant server computer. This distant computer is called the *host*.

The host allows many different clients to access its resources at the same time; it isn't devoted to a single user. To use Telnet and the host's resources, you'll need to know the address of the Internet host whose resources you want to access.

When you use Telnet, before you can take over the resources of a host computer you'll typically have to log onto the host. Often, you can use the name "guest" to log on. Some systems require that you also give information about yourself, such as your name and address. And some may require that you choose a username and a password that you will use the next time you log in.

You can access many hosts on the Internet by using Telnet. They are all different computers, so many of them don't work or look alike. For example, some might be UNIX-based systems, some might be NT-based computers, some might be Macintoshes, as well as a variety of other computers, and they all work and look different from one another. As a way to make things easier, many hosts use a menuing system that gives you access to their resources. Also, when you connect using Telnet, you'll have to use terminal emulation; in essence you make sure your keyboard and monitor function as the host expects. The most common terminal emulation is the VT-100 emulation, so if you use Telnet software, that's a safe emulation to use.

Telnet clients are available for all the major operating systems, including UNIX, Macintosh, and all versions of Windows. If you use an Internet shell account instead of a SLIP/PPP connection, you'll typically use a Telnet client by simply typing the word "Telnet" followed by the Internet address of the computer you want to access. For example, if you wanted to gain access to a computer run by the federal government called Fed World that lets you access a great deal of government information, you'd type "Telnet fedworld.gov". A Windows- or Macintosh-based Telnet client is easier to use than a DOS- or UNIX-based Telnet client because the former will remember hostnames for you. With clients, you can often keep an address book of hostnames so you can easily revisit them.

How Telnet Works

1 To use Telnet, you need to know the Internet address of the host whose resources you want to use; your Telnet client contacts the host, using its Internet address.

Fedworld.gov

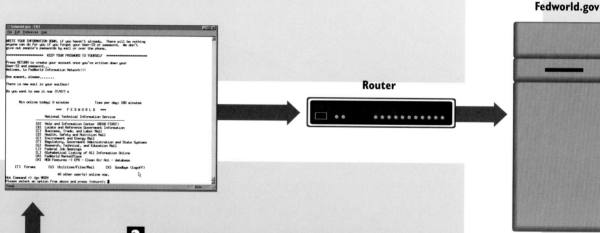

Router

2 When you contact the host, the distant computer and your computer negotiate how they will communicate with each other. They decide which terminal emulation will be used. Terminal emulation determines how your keyboard will transmit information to the distant computer and how information will be displayed on your screen. It determines, for example, things such as how certain keys like the backspace key will work. VT-100 is the most common type of terminal emulation.

Network Virtual Terminal

Printer

Keyboard

Network Virtual Terminal

Printer

Keyboard

3 When a client and a server communicate, they use the Telnet protocol. The Telnet protocol assumes that each end of the connection—the client and the server—is a Network Virtual Terminal (NVT). Each NVT has a virtual "printer" and a virtual "keyboard." The keyboard sends data from one NVT to the other. When you type text on your keyboard, you're using the NVT keyboard. The printer is not really a printer at all—it receives and displays the data on the computer screen. When a distant Telnet connection sends you data and you display it on your screen, it is the printer that displays the information.

4 Typed text in a Telnet session accumulates in a buffer on your computer. When a complete line of data is ready for transmission, or when you give a command to transmit data (such as pressing the Enter key), the data is sent across the Internet from your NVT keyboard. Along with the data is the host's IP address, which makes sure the packet is sent to the proper location.

Printer

Keyboard

Printer

Keyboard

5 Your IP address is also sent, so that information can be routed back to you. Additionally, specific Telnet commands are sent that the other NVT will use to decide what to do with the data, or how to respond to the data. For example, when data is sent from one NVT to another, and certain information must be sent back to the originating NVT for a process to proceed, the Telnet Go Ahead (GA) command is sent.

6 The Telnet host receives the data you've sent. It processes the data and returns to your screen (your NVT "printer") the results of using the data or running the command on a distant computer. So, for example, if you type a series of keys with the letters "dir" and press Enter, the distant computer will carry out the dir command. That computer will also return to your screen the dir command and send the results of running that command on the distant computer.

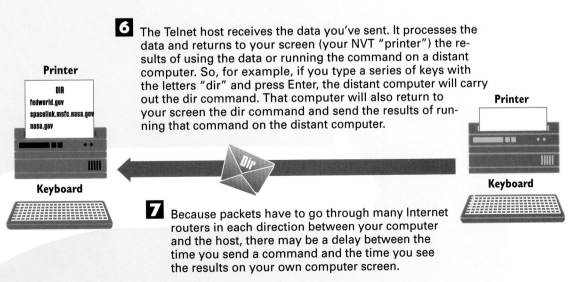

Printer

DIR
fedworld.gov
spacelink.msfc.nasa.gov
nasa.gov

Keyboard

Printer

Keyboard

7 Because packets have to go through many Internet routers in each direction between your computer and the host, there may be a delay between the time you send a command and the time you see the results on your own computer screen.

CHAPTER

23

FTP and Downloading Files

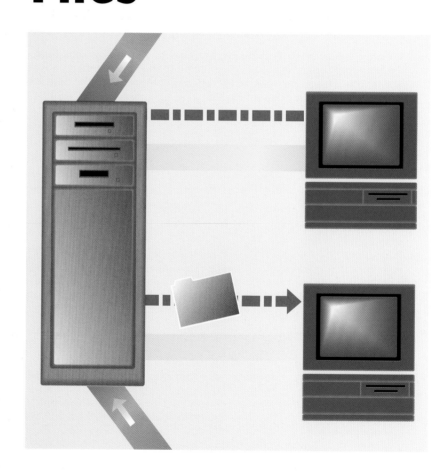

ONE of the most popular uses of the Internet is to download files—that is, transfer files from a computer on the Internet to your computer. These files can be of many types: programs that you can run on your own computer; graphics you can view; sounds and music you can listen to; or text files that you can read. Many tens of thousands of files are downloaded every day on the Internet. Most of those files are downloaded using the Internet's File Transfer Protocol, commonly referred to as FTP. FTP can also be used to upload files from your computer to another computer on the Internet.

FTP, like many Internet resources, works on a client/server model. You run FTP client software on your computer to connect to an FTP server on the Internet. On the FTP server, a program called an FTP daemon (pronounced "demon") allows you to download and upload files.

To log on to an FTP site and download files, an account number (or username) and a password must be typed in before the daemon will allow you to enter. Some sites allow anyone to enter and download files—but an account number (or username) and password must still be entered. Often, to get in, you use "anonymous" as your username and your email address as your password. Because of this, these sites are often referred to as anonymous FTP sites. Some FTP sites are private, only allowing certain people with the proper account number and password to enter.

FTP is fairly simple to use. When you log on to an FTP site, you can browse through the available files by changing directories and you can see a listing of all the files available in each directory. When you see a file you want to download, you use your client software to instruct the FTP server to send you the file.

As the World Wide Web gains popularity, downloading software is becoming even easier. You can use your Web browser and click on links to files; behind the scenes, FTP is often still downloading the files. FTP remains the most popular way to download files from the Web and the Internet. The HTTP protocol of the Web can be used for downloading files from the Web, but it's not as efficient as FTP, so it isn't used as frequently.

One problem with downloading files over the Internet is that some files are so large it can take a tremendous amount of time to download them, especially if the connection is made via modem. Even at 28,800bps, downloading files can be slow. As a way to speed up file transfers and save space on the FTP server, files are commonly compressed—shrunk in size using special compression software. Many different methods are used to compress files. Depending on the file type, files are usually compressed from 10 to 50%. After the files have been downloaded, you'll need to run the compression software on your own computer to decompress the files so you can use them.

How an FTP Session Works

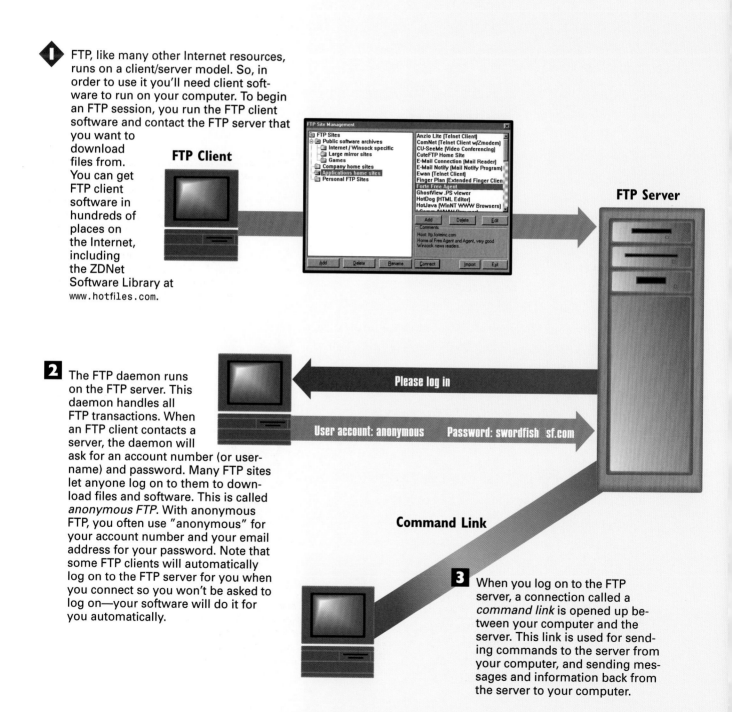

1 FTP, like many other Internet resources, runs on a client/server model. So, in order to use it you'll need client software to run on your computer. To begin an FTP session, you run the FTP client software and contact the FTP server that you want to download files from. You can get FTP client software in hundreds of places on the Internet, including the ZDNet Software Library at www.hotfiles.com.

FTP Client

FTP Server

Please log in

User account: anonymous   Password: swordfish sf.com

2 The FTP daemon runs on the FTP server. This daemon handles all FTP transactions. When an FTP client contacts a server, the daemon will ask for an account number (or username) and password. Many FTP sites let anyone log on to them to download files and software. This is called *anonymous FTP*. With anonymous FTP, you often use "anonymous" for your account number and your email address for your password. Note that some FTP clients will automatically log on to the FTP server for you when you connect so you won't be asked to log on—your software will do it for you automatically.

Command Link

3 When you log on to the FTP server, a connection called a *command link* is opened up between your computer and the server. This link is used for sending commands to the server from your computer, and sending messages and information back from the server to your computer.

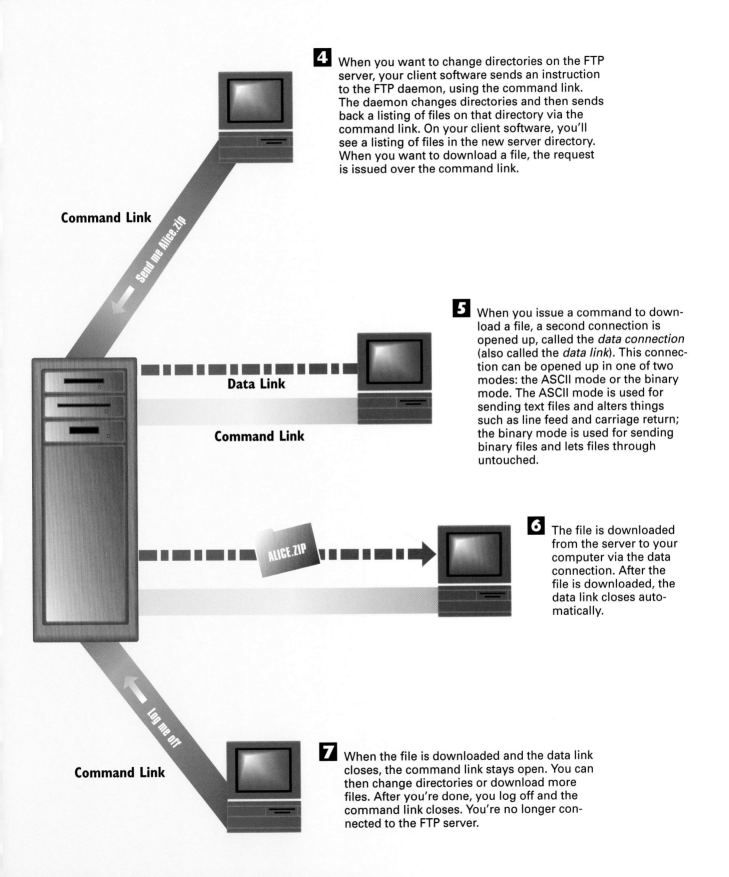

4 When you want to change directories on the FTP server, your client software sends an instruction to the FTP daemon, using the command link. The daemon changes directories and then sends back a listing of files on that directory via the command link. On your client software, you'll see a listing of files in the new server directory. When you want to download a file, the request is issued over the command link.

Command Link

Send me Alice.zip

Data Link

Command Link

5 When you issue a command to download a file, a second connection is opened up, called the *data connection* (also called the *data link*). This connection can be opened up in one of two modes: the ASCII mode or the binary mode. The ASCII mode is used for sending text files and alters things such as line feed and carriage return; the binary mode is used for sending binary files and lets files through untouched.

ALICE.ZIP

6 The file is downloaded from the server to your computer via the data connection. After the file is downloaded, the data link closes automatically.

Log me off

Command Link

7 When the file is downloaded and the data link closes, the command link stays open. You can then change directories or download more files. After you're done, you log off and the command link closes. You're no longer connected to the FTP server.

How File Compression Works

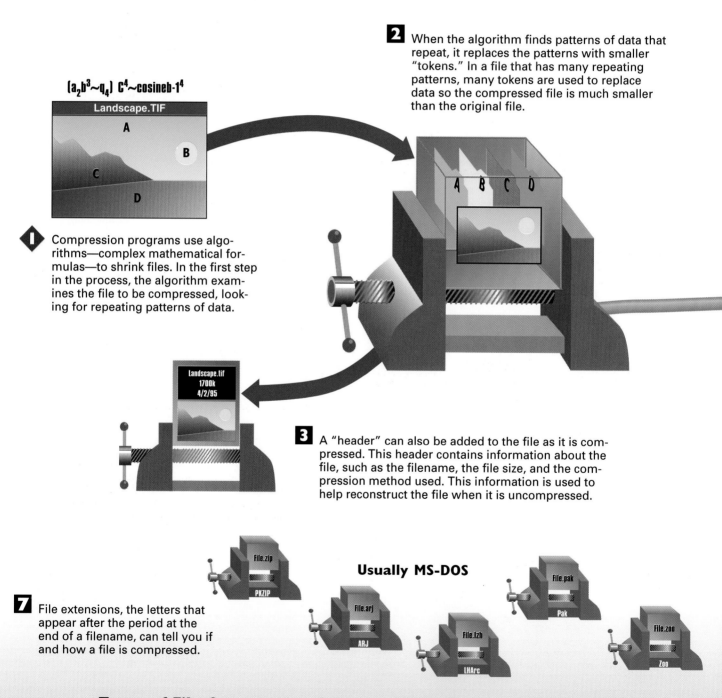

$(a_2b^3{\sim}q_4)\ C^4{\sim}cosineb{-}1^4$

Landscape.TIF

A
B
C
D

1 Compression programs use algorithms—complex mathematical formulas—to shrink files. In the first step in the process, the algorithm examines the file to be compressed, looking for repeating patterns of data.

2 When the algorithm finds patterns of data that repeat, it replaces the patterns with smaller "tokens." In a file that has many repeating patterns, many tokens are used to replace data so the compressed file is much smaller than the original file.

Landscape.tif
1700k
4/2/95

3 A "header" can also be added to the file as it is compressed. This header contains information about the file, such as the filename, the file size, and the compression method used. This information is used to help reconstruct the file when it is uncompressed.

Usually MS-DOS

File.zip
PKZIP

File.arj
ARJ

File.lzh
LHArc

File.pak
Pak

File.zoo
Zoo

7 File extensions, the letters that appear after the period at the end of a filename, can tell you if and how a file is compressed.

Types of File-Compression Schemes You'll Find on the Internet

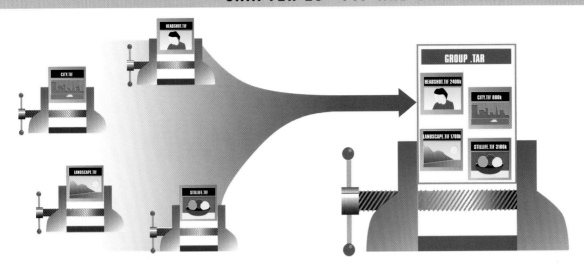

4 Some compression software, such as PKZIP for the PC, can also archive files, combining several compressed files. The UNIX command TAR can also combine many files into a single archive.

5 When you want to use a compressed file you find on the Internet, transfer it over the Internet to your computer.

$(a_2b^3{\sim}q_4)\ C^4{\sim}cosineb\text{-}1^4$

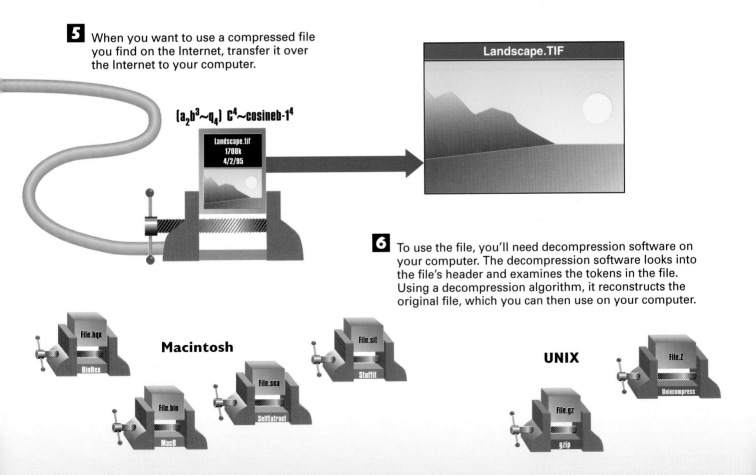

6 To use the file, you'll need decompression software on your computer. The decompression software looks into the file's header and examines the tokens in the file. Using a decompression algorithm, it reconstructs the original file, which you can then use on your computer.

CHAPTER 24

Searching the Internet

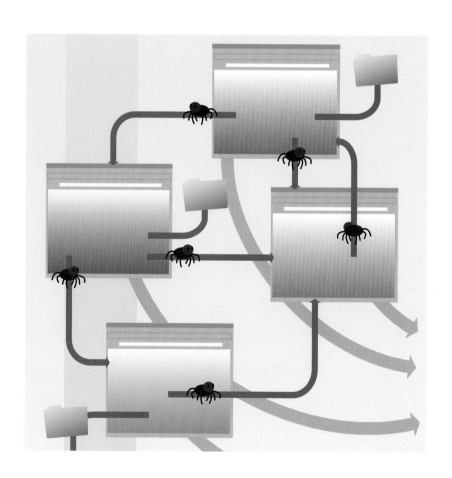

SO much information is available on the Internet, but there is so little organization to the Internet that it can seem impossible to find the information or documents you want. A number of solutions have sprung up to solve the problem. The two most popular ones are indexes and search engines.

Indexes present a highly structured way to find information. They enable you to browse through information by categories, such as arts, computers, entertainment, sports, and so on. In a Web browser, you click a category, and you are then presented with a series of subcategories. Under sports, for example, you'll find baseball, basketball, football, hockey, and soccer. Depending on the size of the index, several layers of subcategories may be available. When you get to the subcategory you're interested in, you'll be presented with a list of relevant documents. To get to those documents, you click the links to them. Yahoo! (`http://www.yahoo.com/`) is the largest and most popular index on the Internet. Yahoo! and other indexes also enable you to search by typing words that describe the information you're looking for. You then get a set of search results—links to documents that match your search. To get the information, you click a link.

Another popular way of finding information is to use *search engines,* also called *search tools* and sometimes called *Web crawlers* or *spiders.* Search engines operate differently from indexes. They are essentially massive databases that cover wide swaths of the Internet. Search engines don't present information in a hierarchical fashion. Instead, you search through them as you would a database, by typing keywords that describe the information you want.

Many popular Internet search engines exist, including Lycos, Excite, and AltaVista. Although the specifics of how they operate differ somewhat, generally they are all composed of three parts: at least one spider, which crawls across the Internet gathering information; a database, which contains all the information the spiders gather; and a search tool, which people use to search through the database. Search engines are constantly updated to present the most up-to-date information, and they hold enormous amounts of information. Search engines extract and index information differently. Some index every word they find in a document, for example, and others index only the key 100 words in each document. Some index the size of the document; some index the title, headings, subheadings, and so on.

Additionally, each search engine returns results in a different way. Some weigh the results to show the relevance of the documents; some show the first several sentences of the document; and some show the title of the document as well as the URL.

Many search engines and indexes are on the Internet, each with its own strengths and weaknesses. To cast the widest possible net when looking for information, you'd like to search as many of them as you can. The problem is that doing so is too time-consuming. So a type of software called meta-search software has been developed. With this software, you type a search on your own computer. The software then submits the search to many Internet search engines and indexes simultaneously, compiles the results for you, and then delivers the results to your computer. To visit any resulting site, just click the link, the same as if you were on an index or search engine site.

How Internet Search Engines Work

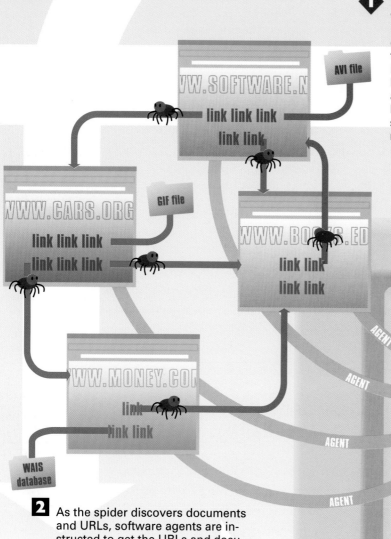

1 Each search engine uses a crawler or spider with its own set of rules guiding how documents are gathered. Some follow every link on every home page that they find and then, in turn, examine every link on each of those new home pages, and so on. Some spiders ignore links that lead to graphics files, sound files, and animation files. Some ignore links to certain Internet resources such as WAIS databases, and some are instructed to look primarily for the most popular home pages.

2 As the spider discovers documents and URLs, software agents are instructed to get the URLs and documents and send information about them to indexing software.

INDEXING SOFTWARE

And/Or/Not/End/Cancel [End]

Searching for #3 AND #4
Press any key to interrupt processing

Set number 6 resulted in 569 references found in 88 citations

Command/HELP/BYE [View 6]: c

First Set number (1-6) to Combine/List/BYE {CANCEL}: 5

And/Or/Not/End/Cancel [And]: or

Next Set number (1-6) to Combine/List/BYE [CANCEL]: 6

And/Or/Not/End/Cancel [End]:

Searching for #5 AND #6
Press any key to interrupt processing

Set number 7 resulted in 748 references found in 118 citations

Command/HELP/BYE [View 7]

SET NUMBER	CITATIONS	SEARCH HITS	SET CRITERIA
1	911	2269	Subject - Arts
2	7150	14448	Abstract - Computers
3	1031	4421	Abstract - Entertainment
4	49486	109752	Subject - Sports
5	31	179	#1 AND #2
6	88	569	#3 AND #4
7	118	748	#5 OR #6

6 When you click a link to one of the documents that interest you, you're sent straight to that document. The document itself is not in the database or on the search engine site.

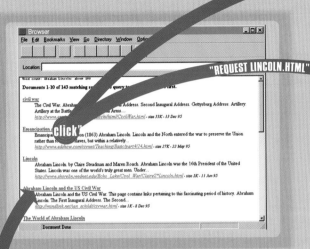

"REQUEST LINCOLN.HTML"

5 The database is searched, based on the criteria you've set. Results are returned in HTML pages. Each search engine returns results in a different way. Some weigh the results to show how relevant the document is to your search; some show the URL, as well as the first several sentences of the document; and some show the title of the document and the URL.

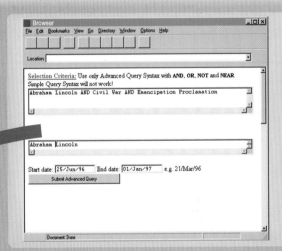

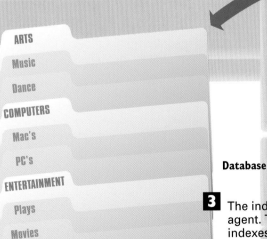

ARTS
Music
Dance
COMPUTERS
Mac's
PC's
ENTERTAINMENT
Plays
Movies
SPORTS
Basketball
Soccer

Database

4 When you visit a search engine and want to search the Internet for information, you'll type words on a Web page that describe the information you want to find. Depending on the search engine, more than just keywords can be used. For example, you can search by date and other criteria with some search engines.

3 The indexing software receives the documents and URLs from the agent. The software extracts information from the documents and indexes it by putting the information into a database. Each search engine extracts and indexes different kinds of information. Some index every word in each document, for example, but others index only the key 100 words in each; some index the size of the document and the number of words in it; some index the title, headings and subheadings, and so on. The kind of index built will determine what kind of searching can be done with the search engine and how the information will be displayed.

How Meta-search Software Works

Meta-search software is software that sits on your computer and enables you to search through many Internet search engines simultaneously and to view and use the results. You can browse through the results on your computer and click those pages that you want to visit. This illustration shows how one such piece of meta-search software, called Copernic, works.

2 The meta-search software sends many "agents" simultaneously—depending on the speed of your connection, usually from 4 to 8, but it can be as many as 32 different agents. Each agent contacts one or more search engines or indexes, such as Yahoo!, Lycos, or Excite.

Preston's Picks

http://www.hotfiles.com/home.html
http://www.hotfiles.com/index.html
http://www.hotfiles.com/prespick/presmain.html

Preston's Picks

http://www.hotfiles.com/index.html
http://www.hotfiles.com/prespick/presmain.htm

I When you want to search for something on the Internet, you type descriptive words or a search term into the meta-search software.

Query

? Enter your search word(s) or phrase:

Preston's Picks

Meta-Search Software

5 The agent sends the results back to the meta-search software. After the agent sends its report back to the meta-search software, it goes to another search engine and submits a search in that engine's proper syntax, and then again sends the results back to the meta-search software.

Preston's Picks

http://www.hotfiles.com/home.html
http://www.hotfiles.com/index.html
http://www.hotfiles.com/prespick/0498/pc.html

6 The meta-search software takes all the results from all the search engines and examines them for duplicate results. If it finds duplicate results, it deletes them. It then displays the results of the search, ranking each "hit" by the likelihood that it contains the information you requested. It figures out the ranking by examining the title of the site found, the header information in the site, and the words on the site.

Preston's Picks

http://www.hotfiles.com/prespick/0498/pc.html
http://www.hotfiles.com/prespick/.../pres0498.
http://www.hotfiles.com/prespick/pres1097/pc.

		Title	Address	Rank	Hit Count	Date Found
	☐	ZDNet Software Library - Top Rated Home & ...	http://www.hotfiles.com/home.html	8	2	5/8/98 4:16:10 I
		write(""); Home & Education options Make the grade in math. You need not be a believer to appreciate Bible's poetry and parables.				
	☐	ZDNet Software Library - Top Rated Shareware	http://www.hotfiles.com/index.html	2	3	5/8/98 4:16:10 I
		.leftnav2 { color: #FFFF00; } .leftnav { color: white; } = 3.0) {btype=1;} else if (browser_name == Microsoft Internet Explorer && browser_version = 3.0) {btype=1;} // popup window //interURL = url; if (btype==1) { var ApplyWindow = window. Our collection of top-rated b...				
	☐	Preston's Picks for April	http://www.hotfiles.com/prespick/0498/more.html	4	3	5/8/98 4:16:10 I
		More Free Files on ZDNet There are lots more places in the ZDNet Software Library and on ZDNet with collections of free files. ... - Vinson Clair Bushnell RE: Doug Gibson Regarding.				
	☐	Preston's Picks for April	http://www.hotfiles.com/prespick/0498/pc.html	5	1	5/8/98 4:16:10 I
		It also lets you create playlists of your files, so that you can in essence put together your own multimedia album. .. - Chris Wilson Fakalofa, Kia ora, Preston, ... - Sione My sympathies to owners of Win.				
	☐	Preston's Picks for April	http://www.hotfiles.com/prespick/.../pres0498.html	6	2	5/8/98 4:16:10 I
		var cleargif_date=(new Date()), .. - Preston Gralla Clyde: We use cookies for our ... - Preston Gralla Just wanted to say THANKS for ... - Larry D. Stauffer Hey Clyde, you should have thr.				
	☐	ZDNet Software Library - Preston's Picks for	http://www.hotfiles.com/prespick/pres1097.html	6	3	10/06/97
		ZDNet Software Library - Preston's Picks for October Join for FREE! Editors' Picks / Preston's Picks Downloads Internet Explorer 4....				
	■	ZDNet Software Library - Preston's Picks	http://www.hotfiles.com/prespick/presmain.html	1	5	5/8/98 4:16:10 I
		Preston Gralla, ZDNet's "shareware guru," is executive editor of software for ZDNet. Each month, Preston selects his favorite new shareware programs from the ZDNet Software Library, giving you a chance to download the very best we have to offer.				

3 The agents are intelligent enough to know how each search engine functions—for example, whether a particular engine allows for Boolean searches (searching by using AND, OR and other variables). The agents also know the exact syntax that each engine requires. The agents put the search terms in the proper syntax required at each specific search engine and submit the search—they don't have to fill out forms, as users normally do at search engines.

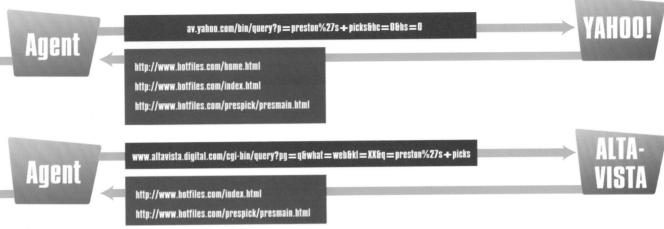

Agent → av.yahoo.com/bin/query?p=preston%27s+picks&hc=0&hs=0 → YAHOO!

http://www.hotfiles.com/home.html
http://www.hotfiles.com/index.html
http://www.hotfiles.com/prespick/presmain.html

Agent → www.altavista.digital.com/cgi-bin/query?pg=q&what=web&kl=XX&q=preston%27s+picks → ALTA-VISTA

http://www.hotfiles.com/index.html
http://www.hotfiles.com/prespick/presmain.html

4 The search engines report the results of the search to each agent. The results typically include the URL of each site that matches the search, and often a summary of information found on the site, the date the site was last updated, and other data.

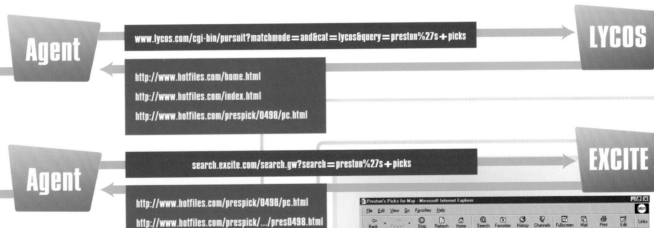

Agent → www.lycos.com/cgi-bin/pursuit?matchmode=and&cat=lycos&query=preston%27s+picks → LYCOS

http://www.hotfiles.com/home.html
http://www.hotfiles.com/index.html
http://www.hotfiles.com/prespick/0498/pc.html

Agent → search.excite.com/search.gw?search=preston%27s+picks → EXCITE

http://www.hotfiles.com/prespick/0498/pc.html
http://www.hotfiles.com/prespick/.../pres0498.html
http://www.hotfiles.com/prespick/pres1097/pc.html

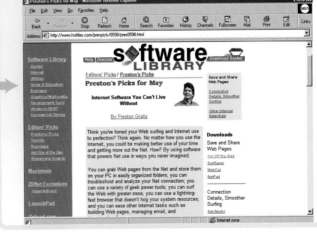

7 You browse through the results in the meta-search software. When you see a page you're interested in, you double-click it. You'll then be sent to that site.

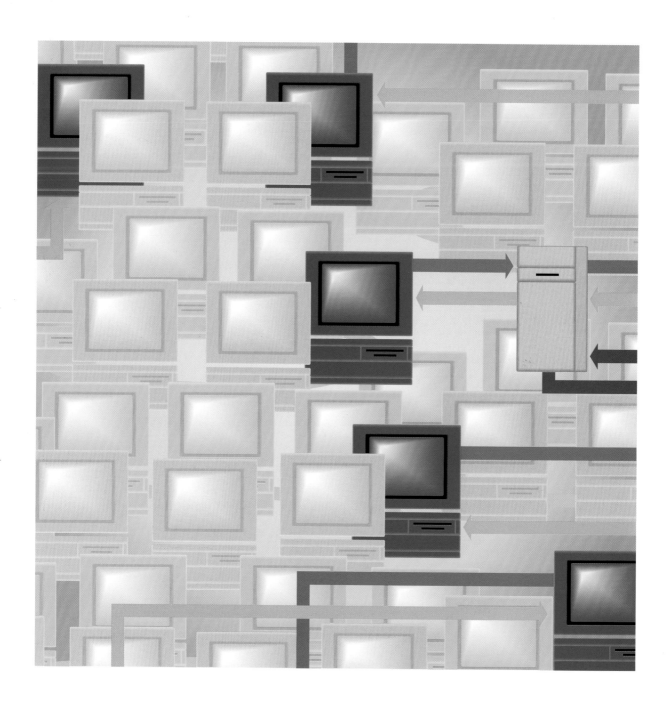

P A R T

HOW THE WORLD WIDE WEB WORKS

WHEN many people use the word "Internet," they are really talking about the World Wide Web. The Web is the most interesting, the most innovative, the most visible, and the fastest growing part of the Internet. To a great degree, the explosive growth of the Web has been what's fueled the enormous amount of interest in the Internet in the past several years. When people refer to "surfing the Net," they're usually talking about using the World Wide Web.

This section of the book looks in great detail at how the World Wide Web works, from basic technologies such as how Web pages work, to more advanced features such as imagemaps, and the way that the Web is becoming increasingly integrated directly into your computer. We'll learn what the Web comprises, how a Web browser works, and thoroughly investigate URLs (uniform resource locators), as well as many other aspects of the Web and Web browsers.

Chapter 25, "How Web Pages Work," examines the most basic part of the Web. It starts by covering the general technology of the Web and describes how the Web works. Web pages are, in essence, multimedia publications that can include music, audio, video and animation, as well as graphics and text. Web pages are connected via hypertext that enables you to jump from any page to any other page, and to graphics, binary files, multimedia files, and other Internet resources. To jump from one page to another, or to another resource, you merely click a hypertext link.

The chapter details how all that works and looks at the client/server model of the Web. It shows what happens behind the scenes when you type a URL into your browser—how that information gets routed properly so that you visit the Web site that interests you. The chapter also delves into how Web pages are organized on a site and how an entire Web site works as a unit to deliver its information to you.

Chapter 26, "How Web Browsers Work," examines browsers. *Web browsers* are pieces of software that interpret the language of the Web, Hypertext Markup Language (HTML), and then display those results on your computer. The chapter begins by delving into how browsers do that job.

Browsers, however, now go far beyond merely allowing you to visit the Web. Both Netscape Communicator and Internet Explorer have grown to become full-blown application suites. Communicator, for example, includes the Navigator browser along with many other programs for communicating with others on the Internet. It includes a news reader, an email package, conferencing and whiteboard software, and even a powerful editing tool that enables you to create and publish your own Web pages.

Browsers also increasingly blur the distinction between the Internet and your own computer, as we'll see in Chapter 26. Internet Explorer allows your Windows desktop to be HTML-enabled, which means you can have hyperlinks directly on your desktop to bring you to the Web. Even more significantly, it enables components created on the desktop to take information from the Internet automatically and put it on your PC; a real-time stock ticker is an example of this.

As mentioned earlier, HTML is the language of the Web. Chapter 27, "How Markup Languages Work," explains how HTML forms the building blocks for creating Web pages. The language is an essential set of directions that tells your browser how to display and manage a Web document. The chapter shows in detail how all that works.

Chapter 28, "How Hypertext Works," looks at hyperlinks, which set the Web apart from most other portions of the Internet. This chapter describes the various ways that documents can link to each other on the Web and explains concepts such as relative links and absolute links.

Chapter 29, "How URLs Work," looks in great detail at *URLs*, the addresses you type into your browser to visit a Web site. We'll look at the underlying structure of a URL and gain a better understanding of how a URL is put together and what it can tell you about the site you're visiting. We'll also see precisely how URLs help retrieve documents from the Web.

Chapter 30, "How Imagemaps and Interactive Forms Work," looks at two technologies you use every day on the Web without realizing it: imagemaps and interactive forms. *Imagemaps* aren't maps in a traditional sense. Instead, they're graphics with URLs embedded inside them. When you click one part of the graphic, you'll be sent to one site, and when you click another, you'll be sent to a different site. An imagemap could be a picture of a house, for example, and when you clicked the living room, you'd be sent to an entertainment site; when you clicked on a home office, you'd be sent to a business site.

Interactive forms are the forms you fill out on the Web for doing things such as registering at a site or sending information about yourself before you're allowed to download a particular piece of software free of charge.

Chapter 31, "How Web Host Servers Work," looks at Web server software. As I mentioned before, the Web works on a client/server model. Your Web browser (the client) contacts the Web server. This chapter explains how Web server software interacts with your browser to deliver Web content to you.

Finally, Chapter 32, "How Web Sites Work with Databases," looks at databases. Databases are used on the Web for many things. Web indexes and search sites such as Yahoo! are, in essence, databases that interact with the Web.

CHAPTER

25

How Web Pages Work

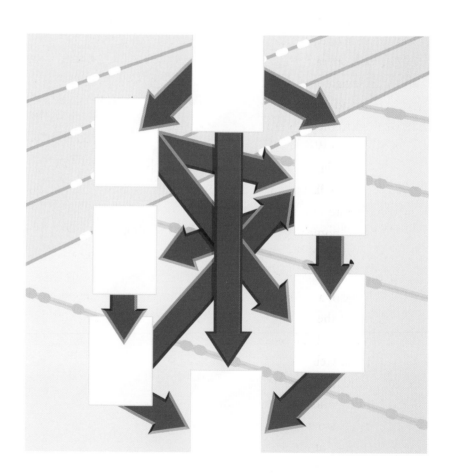

THE World Wide Web is the fastest growing, and in many ways, the most exciting and intriguing part of the Internet. When people refer to "surfing the Net," more often than not they're talking about using the World Wide Web.

As its name implies, the World Wide Web is a globally connected network. The Web contains many things, but what makes it so fascinating to so many are the Web "pages" that incorporate text, graphics, sound, animation, and other multimedia elements. In essence, each page is an interactive multimedia publication that can include videos and music as well as graphics and text.

Pages are connected to each other using *hypertext* that allows you to move from any page to any other page, and to graphics, binary files, multimedia files, as well as any Internet resource. To jump from one page to another, click on a hypertext link.

The Web operates on a client/server model. You run Web client browser software such as Netscape Navigator or Microsoft's Internet Explorer on your computer. That client contacts a Web server and requests information or resources. The Web server locates and then sends the information to the Web browser, which displays the results.

Pages on the Web are built using a markup language called HTML (Hypertext Markup Language). The language contains commands that tell your browser how to display text, graphics, and multimedia files. It also contains commands for linking the page to other pages, and to other Internet resources.

The term "home page" is often used to refer to the first, or top, page in a collection of pages that make up a Web site. This is to distinguish it from the many pages collected together as a single "package" of sorts that often make up Web sites. The home page is like a magazine cover or the front page of a newspaper. Usually, it acts as an introduction to the site, explaining its purpose and describing the information found on other pages throughout the site. In this way, the home page often acts as the table of contents for the rest of the site.

In general, Web sites use three kinds of organizational structures to organize their pages. In a *tree structure*, a pyramid or outline format makes it easy for users to navigate through the site and find the information they want. In a *linear structure*, one page leads to the next, which then leads to the next, and so on, in a straight line. Finally, in a *random structure*, pages are connected to each other, seemingly at random.

The last illustration in this chapter shows how someone might build his or her own pages using an HTML editor. Once you create your pages, you use FTP software to post them onto a small portion of a Web server. You can either rent the server space from a local ISP or set up your own Web server.

How the World Wide Web Works

1 The World Wide Web is the fastest growing and most innovative part of the Internet. When you browse the Web, you view multimedia pages composed of text, graphics, sound, and video. The Web uses hypertext links that allow you to jump from one place to another on the Web. The language that allows you to use hypertext links and to view Web pages is called Hypertext Markup Language, more commonly known as HTML.

2 The Web works on a client/server model in which client software—known as a Web browser—runs on a local computer. The server software runs on a Web host. To use the Web, you first make an Internet connection, and then launch your Web browser.

3 In a Web browser, you type the URL for a location you want to visit or click on a link that will send you to the desired location. The names for Web locations are URLs (uniform resource locators). Your Web browser sends the URL request using HTTP (Hypertext Transfer Protocol), which defines the way the Web browser and the Web server communicate with one another.

7 When the server finds the requested home page, document, or object, it sends that home page, document, or object back to the Web browser client. The information is then displayed on the computer screen in the Web browser. When the page is sent from the server, the HTTP connection is closed and can be reopened.

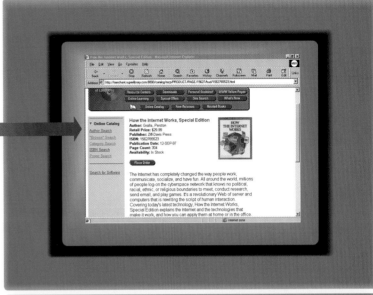

6 The Web server receives the request using the HTTP protocol. It is told which specific document is being requested.

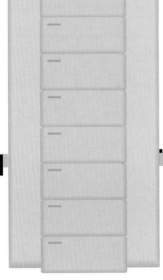

5 The request is sent to the Internet. Internet routers examine the request to determine which server to send the request to. The information just to the right of the http:// in the URL tells the Internet on which Web server the requested information can be found. Routers send the request to that Web server.

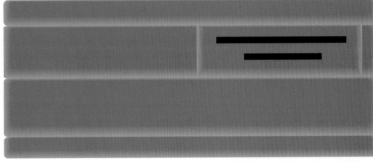

4 URLs contain several parts. The first part—the http://—details which Internet protocol to use. The second part—the part that usually has a www in it—sometimes tells what kind of Internet resource is being contacted. The third part—such as zdnet.com—can vary in length and identifies the Web server to be contacted. The final part identifies a specific directory on the server and a home page, document, or other Internet object.

How Web Pages Are Organized on a Web Site

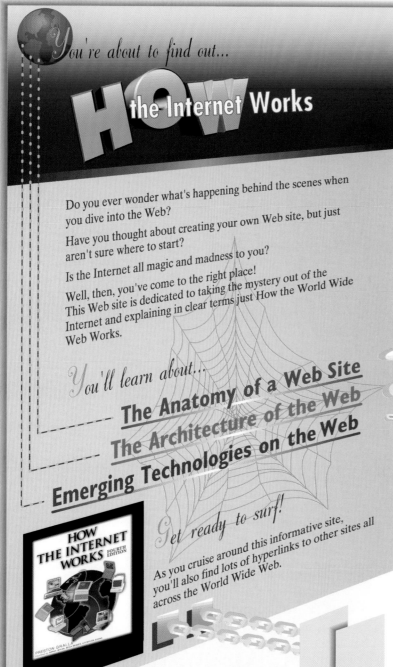

You're about to find out...

the Internet Works

Do you ever wonder what's happening behind the scenes when you dive into the Web?

Have you thought about creating your own Web site, but just aren't sure where to start?

Is the Internet all magic and madness to you?

Well, then, you've come to the right place! This Web site is dedicated to taking the mystery out of the Internet and explaining in clear terms just How the World Wide Web Works.

You'll learn about...

The Anatomy of a Web Site
The Architecture of the Web
Emerging Technologies on the Web

Get ready to surf!

As you cruise around this informative site, you'll also find lots of hyperlinks to other sites all across the World Wide Web.

HOW THE INTERNET WORKS FOURTH EDITION

PRESTON GRALLA

1 The home page is the first or top page of any Web site. A site can be just one page, or can comprise dozens or even hundreds of pages. In the latter case, the home page acts as a table of contents to organize the site and help users find information available on the site.

2 Underlined or highlighted hyperlink text is often embedded in the home page. The hyperlinks serve to connect the top page with other pages throughout the site.

3 Related documents residing together on a Web host computer make up a Web site. However, a single server can host multiple Web sites, each contained in a separate area or directory, much like a hard drive can accommodate multiple directories. Some Web sites are so large and heavily trafficked that they cannot fit on a single server and require multiple servers.

4 Good Web design principles suggest that pages throughout a site link back to the home page. This approach allows users to always find their way back to the top of a site to navigate in other directions.

Tree

5 Documents within a site can be linked to any other document in the site—and even to documents on other sites. Most Web sites, however, are designed in a pyramid or outline structure that gives users a visual model to understand how information is arranged, and indicates how to find and navigate through the site's documents.

6 Web sites are typically organized in one of three ways. The first is an outline or tree structure, which arranges information hierarchically, moving from general information to more specific data.

Linear

The Anatomy of a Web Site

The Architecture of the Web

Emerging Technologies on the Web

7 The second organizational method is linear, in which one page leads to the next, which leads to the next one, and so on.

Random

8 The third organizational structure is really a lack of structure, in which pages are connected to one another seemingly at random. (It's this last structure, though, that makes it clear why the Web is called the Web.)

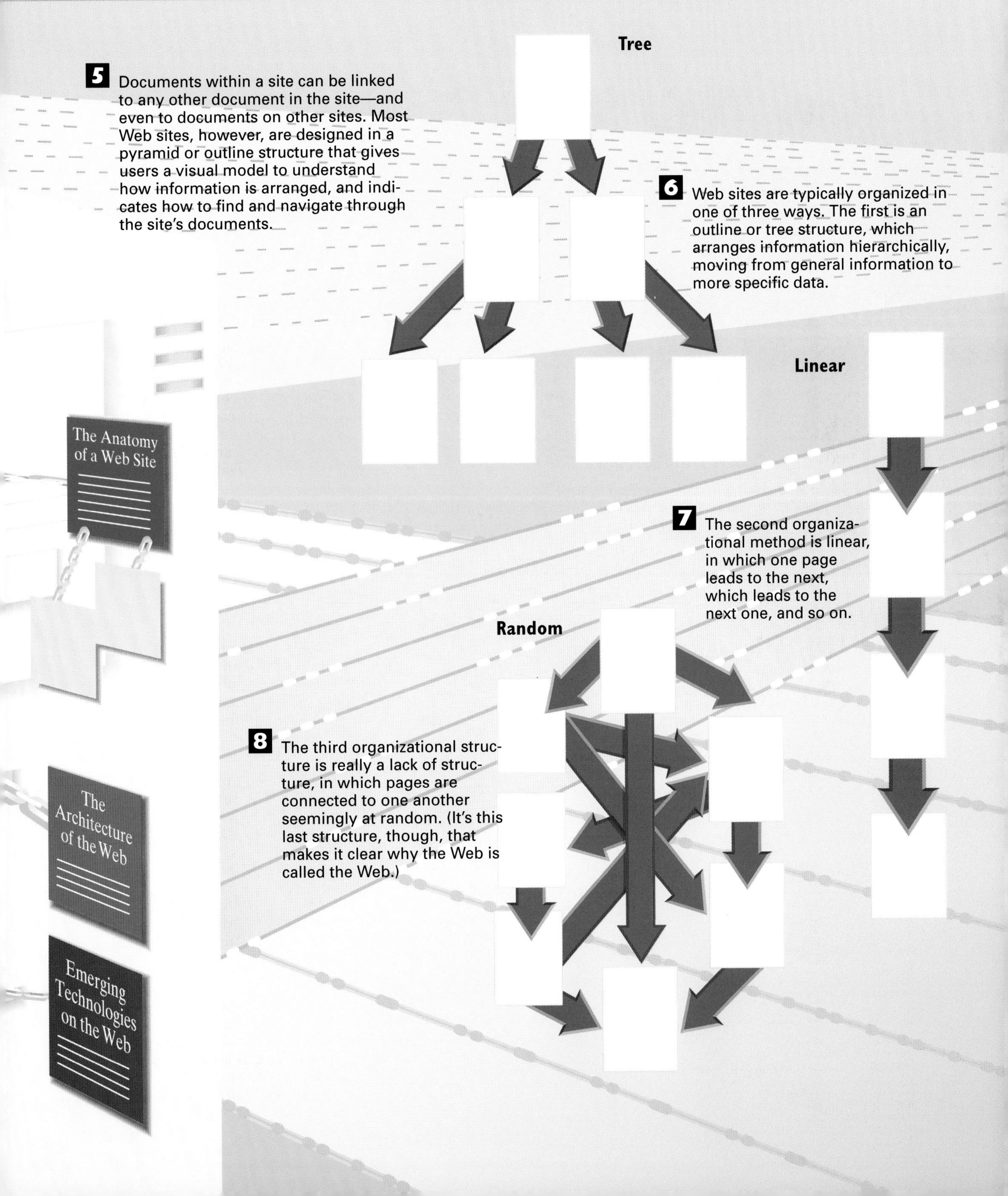

How Web Sites Work

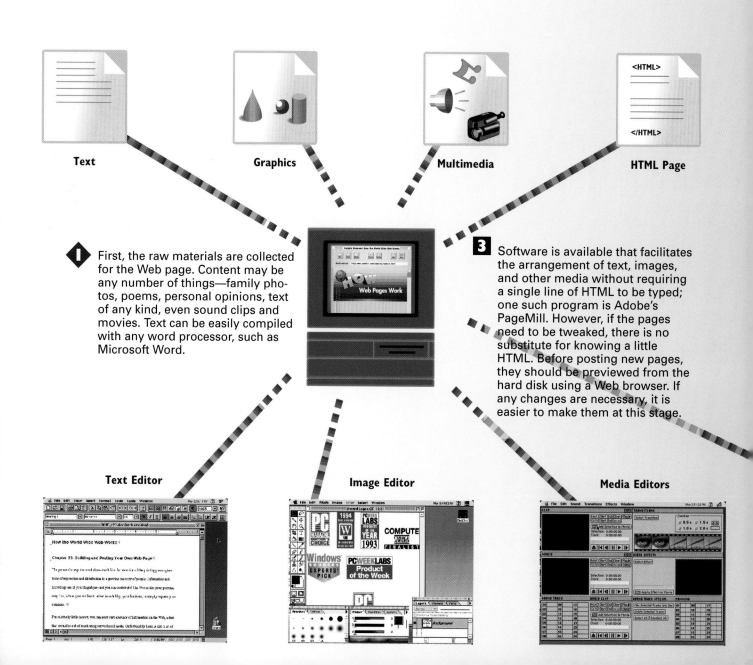

Text

Graphics

Multimedia

HTML Page

1 First, the raw materials are collected for the Web page. Content may be any number of things—family photos, poems, personal opinions, text of any kind, even sound clips and movies. Text can be easily compiled with any word processor, such as Microsoft Word.

3 Software is available that facilitates the arrangement of text, images, and other media without requiring a single line of HTML to be typed; one such program is Adobe's PageMill. However, if the pages need to be tweaked, there is no substitute for knowing a little HTML. Before posting new pages, they should be previewed from the hard disk using a Web browser. If any changes are necessary, it is easier to make them at this stage.

Text Editor

Image Editor

Media Editors

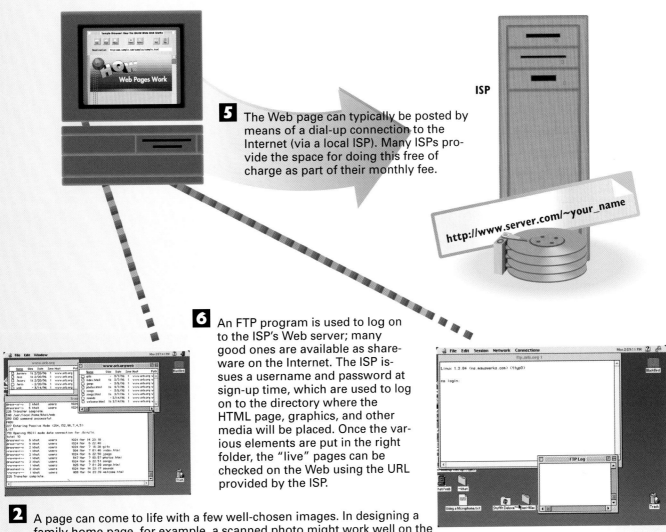

5 The Web page can typically be posted by means of a dial-up connection to the Internet (via a local ISP). Many ISPs provide the space for doing this free of charge as part of their monthly fee.

ISP

http://www.server.com/~your_name

6 An FTP program is used to log on to the ISP's Web server; many good ones are available as shareware on the Internet. The ISP issues a username and password at sign-up time, which are used to log on to the directory where the HTML page, graphics, and other media will be placed. Once the various elements are put in the right folder, the "live" pages can be checked on the Web using the URL provided by the ISP.

2 A page can come to life with a few well-chosen images. In designing a family home page, for example, a scanned photo might work well on the Web page. Icons or colored bullets spruce up a text list, and navigational icons such as arrows or pointers let a user move logically around the site. A whole range of shareware image editors is available on the Internet. The most full-featured commercial image editor is Photoshop by Adobe. Photoshop is a professional-grade program that allows you to modify, create, or resize virtually any digital image.

HTML Editor

4 If you want to add other media to your pages—such as digitized sound, music, or video—you will need access to the digital files, or you can digitize them yourself with additional computer hardware. When you are dealing with media with large file sizes—like a 4MB movie—it will take users a very long time to download the file. During editing, try to trim all the fat out of video and audio clips. Also try to scale back the length and resolution of audio and video to decrease file size.

CHAPTER
26

How Web Browsers Work

LIKE much of the Internet, the World Wide Web operates on a client/server model. You run a Web client on your computer—called a Web browser—such as Netscape Communicator, or Microsoft's Internet Explorer. That client contacts a Web server and requests information or resources. The Web server locates and then sends the information to the Web browser, which displays the results.

When Web browsers contact servers, they're asking to view pages built with Hypertext Markup Language (HTML). They interpret those pages and display them on your computer. They also can display applications, programs, animations, and similar material created with programming languages such as Java and ActiveX, and scripting languages such as JavaScript.

Sometimes, home pages contain links to files that the Web browser can't play or display, such as sound or animation files. In that case, you'll need a plug-in or a helper application. You configure your Web browser to use the helper application or plug-in whenever it encounters a sound or animation file that the browser can't run or play.

Over the years, Web browsers have become increasingly sophisticated. Browsers have now become full-blown software suites that can do everything from videoconferencing to letting you create and publish HTML pages. They have also begun to blur the line between your local computer and the Internet—in essence, they can make your computer and the Internet function as a single computer system.

Toward this end of bringing the Internet more directly into computers, Microsoft has integrated Web browsing and the Internet directly into the operating system. For example, with Internet Explorer 4.0 and above, and with Windows 98, the Windows desktop can be HTML-based. This means Web links can be directly embedded into the desktop. So, for example, you can have links to your favorite Web pages right on the desktop. And even applications such as word processors now have Web capabilities built into them, such as being able to browse the Web, or build home pages. Even more significantly, using technology that Microsoft calls Active Desktop, Internet-based *desktop components* can live on the desktop. These components can be things such as stock tickers, which deliver live Web content directly to the desktop. You don't need to go fire up your Web browser to get the information; it's delivered straight to your Windows desktop without your having to do anything.

Both Microsoft and Netscape have also built entire suites of software around their browsers. Netscape, for example, calls its suite Netscape Communicator. Communicator includes modules for reading newsgroups; for reading, sending and managing Internet mail; for audio conferencing; for collaborative work on *whiteboard applications* in which people can view and mark up the same documents simultaneously; and more. These enhancements will help usher in an era of collaborative computing. Not only will the Internet be used to transmit and receive information, but it will also alter the way we do business and help us communicate more effectively.

How a Web Browser Works

1 Web browsers consist of client software that runs on your computer and displays home pages on the Web. There are clients for PC, Macintosh, and UNIX computers.

2 A Web browser displays information on your computer by interpreting the Hypertext Markup Language (HTML) that is used to build home pages on the Web. Home pages usually display graphics, sound, and multimedia files, as well as links to other pages, files that can be downloaded, and other Internet resources.

<HTML> **3**

<HEAD>
<TITLE>
</HEAD>

The coding in the HTML files tells your browser how to display the text, graphics, links, and multimedia files on the home page. The HTML file that your browser loads to display the home page doesn't actually have the graphics, sound, multimedia files, and other resources on it. Instead, it contains HTML references to those graphics and files. Your browser uses those references to find the files on the server and then display them on the home page.

<BODY>
<P> Do you ever wonder what's happening behind the screens when you dive into the Web?

<H3> You'll learn about:

<A HREF="URL"> Go TO URL</A>

4 The Web browser also interprets HTML tags as links to other Web sites, or to other Web resources, such as graphics, multimedia files, newsgroups, or files to download. Depending on the link, it will perform different actions. For example, if the HTML code specifies the link as another home page, the browser will retrieve the URL specified in the HTML file when the user clicks on the underlined link on the page. If the HTML code specifies a file to be downloaded, the browser will download the file to your computer.

<P> <IMG SRC="BOOK.GIF"

<H2> Get ready to surf!

<P> As you cruise around this informative site, you'll also find lots of hyperlinks to other sites all across the World Wide Web.

</BODY>
<HTML>

NOTE There are many kinds of files on the Internet that Web browsers cannot display. In particular, this pertains to many kinds of multimedia files such as sound, video, and animation files. Still, there are often references to these kinds of files on Web pages. To view or play these files, you'll need what are called "helper applications" and plug-ins. You must configure your Web browser to launch these helper applications and plug-ins whenever you click on an object that needs them in order to be viewed. Helper applications and plug-ins can also be used for displaying virtual reality pages, for chatting on the Internet, and for doing other Internet tasks.

NOTE The meanings of tags are easily decipherable. Every HTML tag, or instruction, is surrounded by a less-than and a greater-than sign—<P>. Often tags appear in pairs, the beginning tag and the ending tag. They are identical except for a simple slash in the end tag. So a paragraph of text will frequently be surrounded by tags like this: <P> Paragraph of text.</P>. Also, tags are not case sensitive. <P> equals <p>.

How Netscape Communicator Works

1 Netscape Communicator is a complete suite of Internet applications, not merely a Web browser. Any individual component can be run alone, or it can be run in concert with other components.

2 The centerpiece of Communicator is Netscape Navigator, the Web browser component.

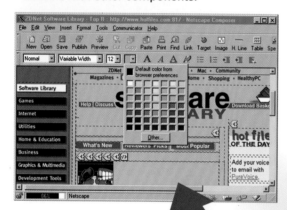

7 Communicator also includes an HTML editor that allows you to edit, create, and post HTML to the Web.

Netscape Communicator

Web Server

6 The Netcaster component of Communicator allows for push technology to send information to you over the Internet, and for "subscriptions" to Web sites. This saves time and allows information to be read offline while you're not connected to the Internet.

3 Netscape Conference is the workgroup and multimedia communications component of Communicator, used primarily on intranets. It allows people to hold group conference calls from their computers, as well as view and use shared files and documents together. This is called a *whiteboard* application.

Conference

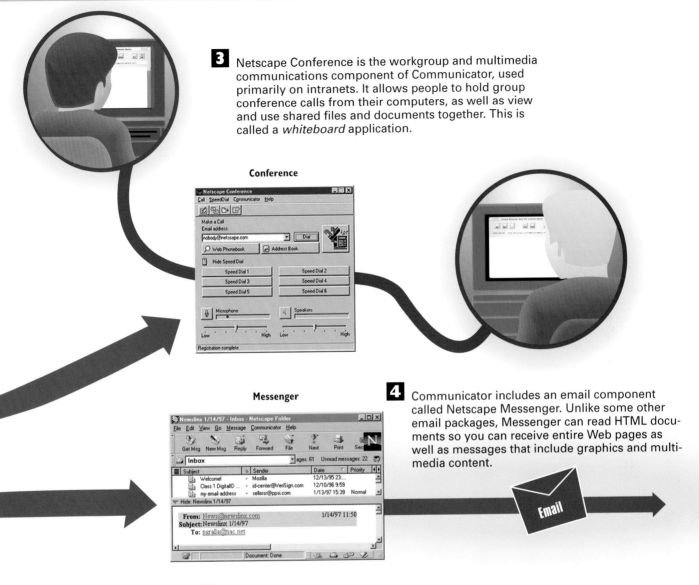

Messenger

4 Communicator includes an email component called Netscape Messenger. Unlike some other email packages, Messenger can read HTML documents so you can receive entire Web pages as well as messages that include graphics and multimedia content.

Email

5 Two other Communicator components allow for reading newsgroups and online discussions on the Internet. A Usenet newsgroup reader gives access to Usenet, whereas software called Collabra allows for intranet-based discussions.

Usenet

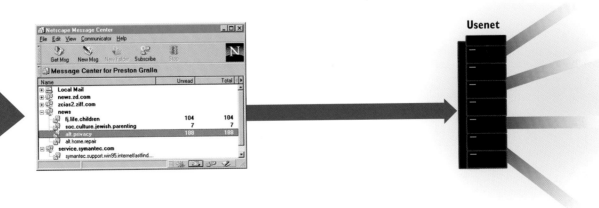

How Internet Explorer Integrates into Windows

1 Internet Explorer 4.0 and above—and Windows 98—blur the distinction between your computer and the Internet. This change has a great impact on Web browsing. The Active Desktop is primarily responsible for this enhancement.

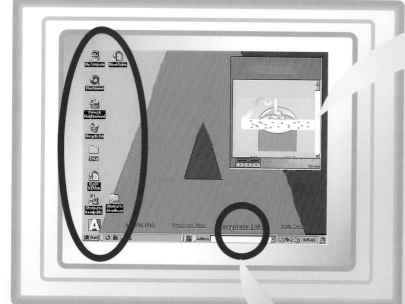

2 The Active Desktop is built with several layers. One layer, the background, allows your normal Windows 95 background to function as an HTML page instead of wallpaper or a color. So, for example, Web links could be placed on the background of your desktop. When you click on the link, it launches Internet Explorer and sends you to the Web site.

3 On top of the background HTML layer is the icon layer. The icons are the same shortcuts that exist in Windows. When icons are clicked upon, they launch a program or a file, open a folder, or do anything else that icons normally do in Windows.

3 *Desktop components* can be placed on this background HTML layer. Desktop components are HTML frames that contain HTML-based content, sites, and applications. For example, a desktop component may be a stock ticker that displays constantly changing stock prices.

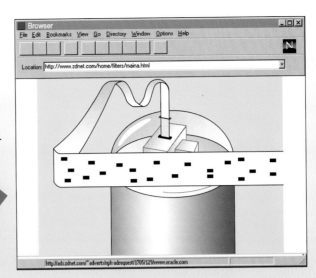

4 A desktop component, such as a stock ticker, can actually be a Web page or component that exists on the Internet. The Active Desktop contacts the Web server hosting the page, downloads it to your local PC, and then displays it within the desktop component frame, resizing the component or page to fit into the frame.

6 Another way Internet Explorer 4.0 and above and Windows 98 integrate your local PC with the Internet is by allowing you to browse the contents of your computer while you're using your browser on the Internet. When you type the drive letter of your computer (such as C:), you will be able to see the folder structure of your computer from within Internet Explorer.

7 You can then launch any document by double-clicking it, just as you would normally do in Windows. You'll read the document in your normal application, not within Internet Explorer.

27 How Markup Languages Work

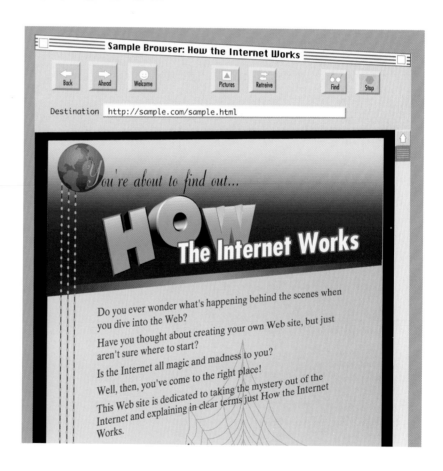

MARKUP languages are the road signs of a Web page. They are sets of directions that tell the browser software how to display and manage a Web document, much like written music scores are instructions that tell a musician how to play a particular song. These instructions (called *tags* or *markups*) are embedded in the source document that creates the Web page.

Tags reference graphic images located in separate files, and they instruct the browser to retrieve and display these images within the page. Tags can also tell a browser to connect a user to another file or URL when he or she clicks an active hyperlink. So each Web page has everything it needs to be displayed on any computer with a browser that can interpret the markup language.

Your original text will probably have headings, multiple paragraphs, and some simple formatting. A Web browser will not understand all these layout instructions because the original text isn't formatted with HTML, the language of the Web (discussed later in this chapter). Paragraphs, carriage returns, indents, and multiple spaces will be shown instead as a single space if no HTML markup is added.

Markup languages should not be confused with programming languages, such as C+ or Pascal. Programming languages are used to write complex applications, such as word processors or spreadsheets. Markup languages, in contrast, are much simpler and describe the way that information should be displayed—for example, by defining when text should be boldface. In markup languages, tags are embedded within documents to describe how the documents should be formatted and displayed.

Hypertext Markup Language (HTML) is the markup language of the Web. It defines the format of a Web document and enables hypertext links to be embedded in the document. You can use any text editor or word processor to add HTML tags to an ASCII text document, although a number of shareware and commercially available HTML editors can assist Web page authors as well.

The Web evolves daily, and HTML also expands and changes along with it. The newest changes to HTML are a group of technologies, which together are termed *Dynamic HTML* or DHTML. These technologies allow HTML to be more than a static language, and they enable HTML to perform animations and become more interactive and flexible. It may take awhile for this technology to catch on, but when it does, it should change the way everyone uses the Web.

Perhaps the best way to get a feel for HTML is to look at text as it is displayed on your screen and text that is "marked up" using HTML. Turn the page for an example of this.

How HTML Works

1 To display Web pages in any browser, you need to add HTML tags to your original text. This process is called *tagging*.

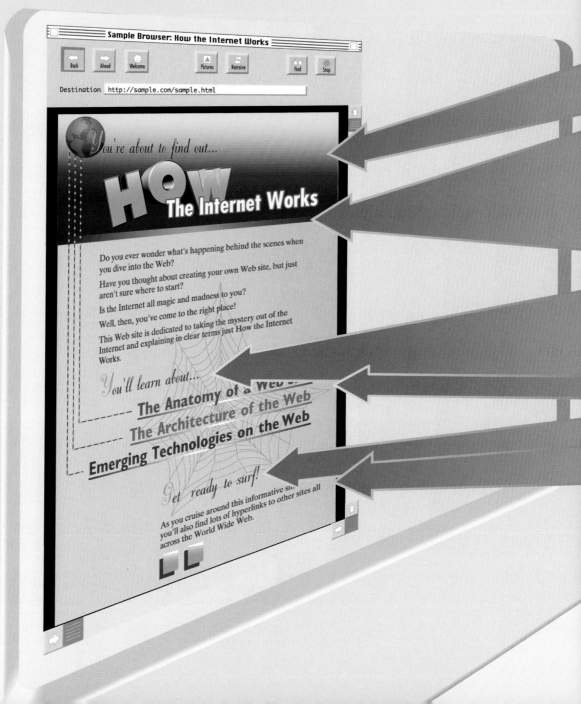

2 Use HTML to give your text structure. All HTML files begin and end with the HTML tags. Headings are marked as such, as are paragraphs, line breaks, block quotes, and special character emphasis. Any carriage returns or indentations within the source text do not affect the browser's display of the page. HTML tags need to be put in if they are to be displayed in a browser.

3 The finished HTML document will be the source page for any browser on any computer. This simplicity of HTML makes cross-platform compatibility easy and reliable. The more complex and specialized the HTML tagging, the longer it will take to download and display the document.

Display text "How the Internet Works"

```
<HTML>
<HEAD>
<TITLE>Sample Browser: How The Internet Works</TITLE>
</HEAD>
```

Display text "Do you ever wonder..."

```
<BODY background= "Spider.GIF">
<IMG SRC = "top.gif">
<P>
<BLOCKQUOTE>
Do you ever wonder what's happening behind the scenes when you dive into the Web?
<P>
Have you thought about creating your own Web site, but just aren't sure where to
start?
<P>
Is the Internet all magic and madness to you?
<P>
Well, then, you've come to the right place!
<P>
This web site is dedicated to taking the mystery out of the Internet and explaining in
clear terms just How the Internet Works.
```

Display text "You'll learn about. . ."

```
<H1> You'll learn about...</H1>
<BLOCKQUOTE>
<A HREF = "anatomy.html">The Anatomy of a Web Site</A>
<P>
<A HREF = "architecture.html">The Architecture of the Web</A>
<P>
<A HREF = "emerging.html">Emerging Technologies on the Web</A>
</BLOCKQUOTE>
</BLOCKQUOTE>
```

Create a link to this site

```
<IMG SRC = "footer.gif" ALIGN=LEFT>
```

Display text "Get ready to surf!"

```
<BLOCKQUOTE>
<H2> Get ready to surf!</H2>
```

Display text "As you cruise..."

```
As you cruise around this informative site, you'll also find lots of hyperlinks to other
sites all across the World Wide Web.
</BLOCKQUOTE>

</BODY>
</HTML>
```

4 Most Web browsers will enable your document to retain its structural integrity when you display, or *parse,* it. Headings will appear in a larger font size than text within paragraphs, for example, and block quotes will be uniformly indented. However, the look may vary from browser to browser. Note that browsers determine the exact font, size, and color. Also be aware that the relative importance of the elements is always kept intact.

How Dynamic HTML Works

1 Dynamic HTML (DHTML) differs from traditional HTML in that it enables Web pages to be changed on-the-fly, after they've been downloaded. In plain HTML, once a page is downloaded, it is static and can be changed only when a user takes an action of some kind. But DHTML, for example, could cause an animation of a rocket to fly across your browser window several seconds after the page has been downloaded—without you doing anything.

Web Server   **Web Page**

2 DHTML does its work without having to contact the server after the page downloads, which means that it can perform some interactive functions more quickly than other technologies that have to contact the server. The instructions for performing the commands are in the HTML commands that are in the page itself.

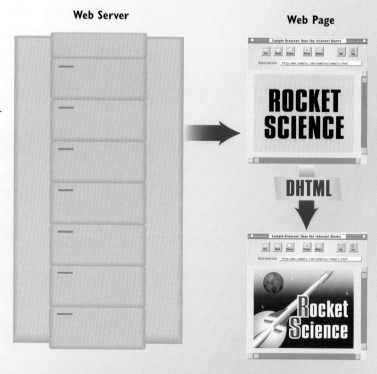

3 Although DHTML is often referred to as if it is a single technology, it is, in fact, a general term used for a group of technologies that can work together or by themselves to change a Web page after the page has been downloaded to your computer. These technologies are the Document Object Model (DOM), Cascading Style Sheets (CSS), and client-side scripting languages, such as JavaScript.

Elements of DHTML   **Plain HTML**   **DHTML**

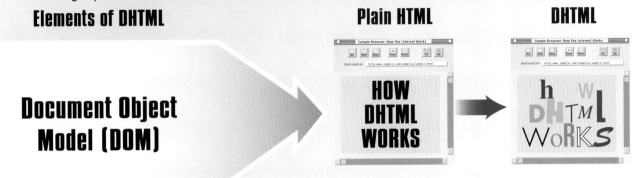

Document Object Model (DOM)

4 The *DOM* defines every object and element on a Web page and enables those objects to be manipulated or accessed. This includes fonts, graphics, tables, and visual elements, as well as elements you can't necessarily see, such as the browser's version number and the current date and time. Without DOM, all the elements on a page are static. So on the simplest level, DHTML could use the DOM to change the font of every letter, individually, on a Web page.

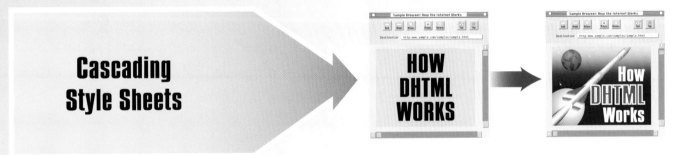

Cascading Style Sheets

5 *Cascading Style Sheets* are, in essence, templates that apply formatting and style information to the elements of a Web page. They're called cascading because any single page can have more than one style sheet associated with it. Additionally, Cascading Style Sheets enable images to overlap one another. This enables animations to be created easily on a page.

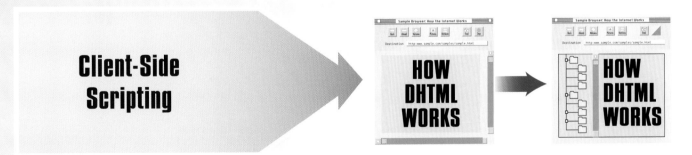

Client-Side Scripting

6 *Client-side scripting languages* perform much of the work of DHTML. These languages access the DOM and manipulate its elements, and they do the same to Cascading Style Sheets. They perform the actions of DHTML. So a script, for example, could turn a word a different color when a mouse moves across it, or it could create easy-to-use collapsible navigation on every page on a Web site.

CHAPTER

28

How Hypertext Works

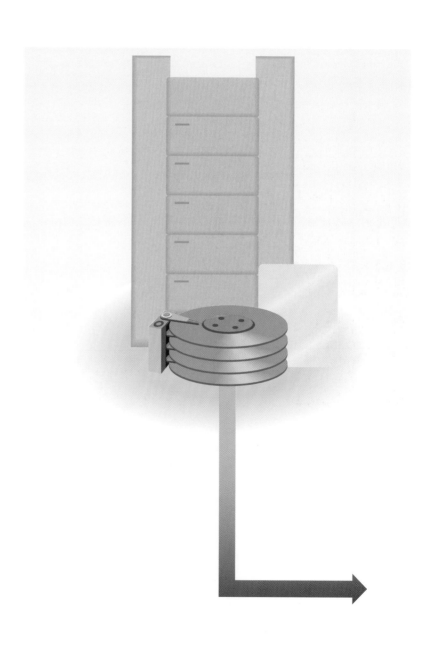

IN the late 1960s, a computer scientist named Ted Nelson introduced hypertext, a concept that lays the foundation for the World Wide Web and its connections between documents, or pages.

Nelson wanted to create a new way of exploring information. He wanted to provide the reader with a spontaneous means of accessing more and more in-depth information about something that sparked the reader's interest when reading text on the page. Rather than reading a document from beginning to end, digesting the material in a sequential order, the reader could highlight a word and receive more information on the meaning of that word, for example.

Nelson imagined that you could read the United States Constitution, come across the term "electoral college," and then open another document that explained how the electoral college works. From that document, you might open another document that listed the votes of the electoral college from its founding to the present. From there, you might choose to open a document about William Jefferson Clinton, then another about the First Cat, Socks, then another about the care and feeding of felines, and so forth. Ultimately, you could find a subject that wasn't even remotely connected to the Constitution, but which you would find interesting or entertaining.

This hypertext concept was obviously on Tim Berners-Lee's mind when he began thinking about how researchers could share their work across the Internet. He envisioned a system where a document could be linked to other documents, enabling researchers to easily find more and related information simply by following a link from one document on the network to another.

Typically, hypertext consists of a hyperlink that appears onscreen as a highlighted word, icon, or graphic. By moving a mouse cursor over the item, or object, and clicking on it, you easily navigate to additional information. On the Web, that information can be located at any other place on the Web, be it on the same host server or one across the globe. A linked object can be various media, such as text (linking from one character to a whole document, for example), a graphical button (such as direction arrows that move from page to page), or still images (photos, icons, or a comic strip), for example. The documents and objects that are being linked to can be on the same site as the original document, or in an entirely different document.

Hypertext links are embedded into a Web document using HTML, Hypertext Markup Language. A text link usually appears on the screen as an underlined word or phrase and is sometimes rendered in a different color from other text, depending on how your Web browser interprets the HTML codes. When you place the mouse cursor on this underlined text and click the mouse button, you initiate a request by the browser for a new Web page or—if the text references an internal link to information in the same document—direct your browser to scroll to another, specific point within the same document.

Images or icons can also act as hyperlinks. When you move the mouse cursor over the icon or graphic and click the mouse button, you launch the request to retrieve the linked information.

How Hyperlinks Work

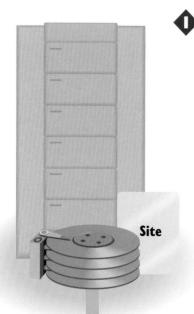

1 The "hyperlinking" begins when you first retrieve a Web page from a remote Web server. Target links within the page move you quickly from one part of the page to the next.

Site

CHAPTER **28** How Hypertext Works

You're about to find out...

HOW the Internet Works

Part 6: How the World Wide Web Works

Chapter 25: How Web Pages Work
Chapter 26: How Web Browsers Work
Chapter 27: How Markup Languages Work
Chapter 28: How Hypertext Works
Chapter 29: How Web URLs Work
Chapter 30: How Image Maps and
          Interactive Forms Work
Chapter 31: How Web Host Servers Work
Chapter 32: How Web Sites Work with Databases

Part 7: Advanced Internet Tools

Chapter 33: How Push Technology Works
Chapter 34: How Java, ActiveX, and JavaScript Work
Chapter 35: How Agents Work
Chapter 36: How CGI Scripting Works

`<A HREF = "#TARGET">TARGET LINKS<A/>`

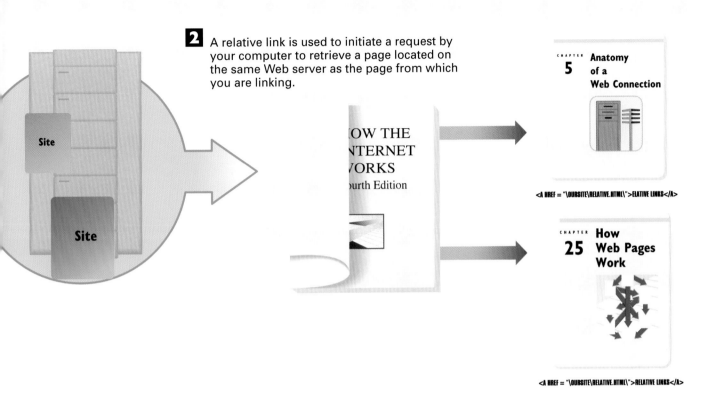

2 A relative link is used to initiate a request by your computer to retrieve a page located on the same Web server as the page from which you are linking.

CHAPTER 5 Anatomy of a Web Connection

<A HREF = "\OURSITE\RELATIVE.HTML\">ELATIVE LINKS</A>

CHAPTER 25 How Web Pages Work

<A HREF = "\OURSITE\RELATIVE.HTML\">RELATIVE LINKS</A>

3 A hyperlink that leads to a completely different Web server uses an absolute link.

<A HREF = "http:\\www.linksite.com\"ABSOLUTE LINKS </A>

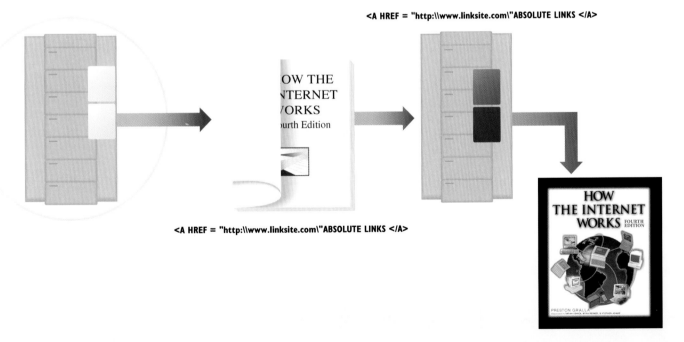

<A HREF = "http:\\www.linksite.com\"ABSOLUTE LINKS </A>

<A HREF = "http:\\www.linksite.com\"ABSOLUTE LINKS </A>

CHAPTER

29

How URLs Work

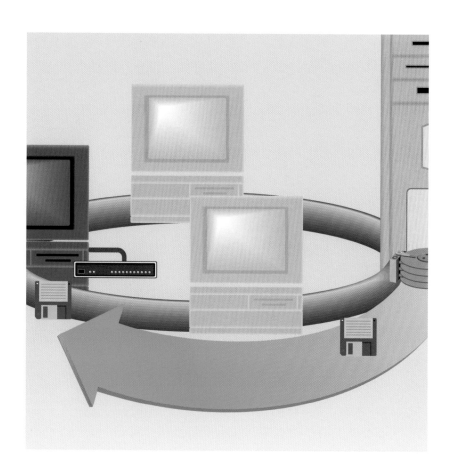

THE Web pages and the hosts that make up the World Wide Web must have unique locations so that your computer can locate and retrieve the pages. The unique identifier for a host is called the IP (Internet Protocol) address and the unique identifier for a page is called the URL, or uniform resource locator. A URL functions much like a postal or email address. Just as postal and email addresses list a name and specific location, a URL, or Web address, indicates where the host computer is located, the location of the Web site on the host, and the name of the Web page and the file type of each document, among other information.

A typical URL looks like this:

```
http://www.zdpress.com/internetworks/index.html/
```

If you were to interpret the instructions in this URL from left to right, it would translate to: "Go to the host computer called zdpress (a commercial business), in a directory called internetworks, and retrieve a hypertext document with the filename index.html." The URL, or address, tells the browser what document to fetch and exactly where to find it on a specific remote host computer somewhere on the Internet.

The first part of the URL indicates what type of transfer protocol will be used to retrieve the specified document. The most common request is for a hypertext document that uses HTTP (Hypertext Transfer Protocol).

The second portion of the URL refers to the specific host computer on which the document resides, which is to be contacted by the browser software. This part of the address is also called the *domain name*. See Chapters 4, "Understanding Internet Addresses and Domains," and 6, "Internet File Types," for more information about domains.

The third part of the URL is the directory on the host computer that contains a specific Web site or multiple Web sites. This is always located after the first single slash in the URL and is essentially the subdirectory on the hard disk that houses the Web site. Subdirectories might also be indicated in this part of the address. For example, if the above URL were changed to

```
http://www.zdpress.com/internetworks/partone/chapters/chapte.html
```

there would be two subdirectories—part one and chapters.

In the above example, the filename is chapte.html. This is always the last portion of the URL. If you see an address without a filename, it is assumed that the filename index.html contains the requested Web page. The default document a Web server will deliver to the client when no other filename is listed is index.html.

The illustration in this chapter shows the process necessary to request and retrieve a Web document. When a request for a document occurs for the first time in a Web-browsing session, the host computer must first be located in order to find the file. After that, the specific subdirectory and document are retrieved.

The Structure of a Web URL

1 The first part of the URL indicates what type of transfer protocol will be used to retrieve the specified document. The most common request is for a hypertext document that uses the HTTP protocol.

3 The third part of the URL is the directory on the host computer that contains a specific Web site. A host computer can house multiple Web sites. This third segment of the address is essentially the root directory that houses the site. Subdirectories might also be indicated in this part of the address.

| Back | Ahead | Welcome | | Pictures | Retrieve | | Find | Stop |

Destination   http://www.sample.com/samples/sample.html

2 The second portion of the URL is the specific host computer on which the document resides, which is to be contacted by the browser software. This part of the address is also called the domain. Domain names end in a suffix that indicates what kind of organization the domain is. For example, .com indicates a commercial business, .edu indicates a college or university, .gov indicates a government office, .mil a military facility, and .org a not-for-profit organization. The suffix can also indicate the country in which the host computer is located. For example, .ca is in Canada and .au is in Australia.

4 The last segment of the URL is the filename of the specific Web page you are requesting. If no filename is indicated, the browser will assume a default page, usually called index.html.

How URLs Help Retrieve Web Documents

1 The Web browser installed on your local computer sends your TCP/IP software a signal that it is ready to request a document. TCP/IP makes a connection with the host TCP/IP software. Once the connection is established, your browser makes a request for a document by sending its URL through the two-way connection maintained by TCP/IP to the server.

2 The HTTP server is the portion of the host computer that runs HTTP server software. TCP/IP makes and maintains the connection this way. The browser can use HTTP to send requests and receive pages through the host's Web server software. This software allows the host to communicate with the client browser, in HTTP, over TCP/IP.

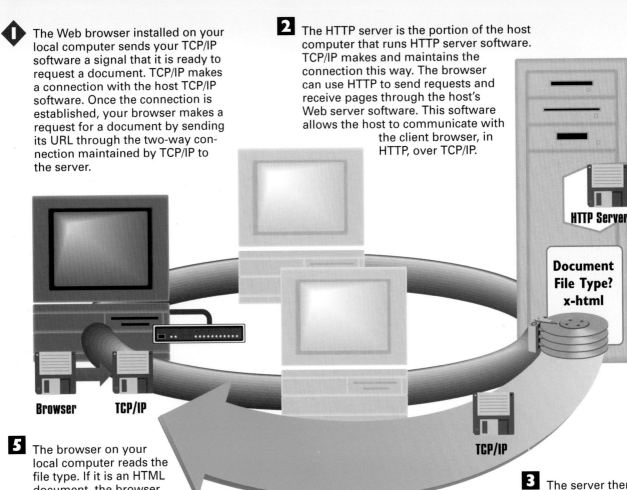

HTTP Server

Document File Type? x-html

Browser   TCP/IP

TCP/IP

5 The browser on your local computer reads the file type. If it is an HTML document, the browser examines the content, breaking it down into meaningful parts. Two general parts include text, which is displayed by the browser word for word; the other part consists of HTML markup information called *tags* that are not displayed, but display formatting information, such as normal text, bold headers, or colored hypertext. The results are displayed on your monitor.

4 If the document is found, the host checks its file type (usually either x-html or x-text) and sends this information to the client with the requested page. When the client receives the page, it first checks the file type. If the type is one it can display, it does so; otherwise, it prompts the user to see if he or she would like to save it to disk or open it using a helper application. The x-html file type is by far the most common one used when transmitting Web pages.

3 The server then receives the transmitted URL and responds in one of three ways. It follows the directory path given in the URL; the server finds the file on its local hard disk and opens it; the server runs a CGI script or it detects an error (such as "file not found") and generates an error document to be sent back to the client.

CHAPTER

30

How Imagemaps and Interactive Forms Work

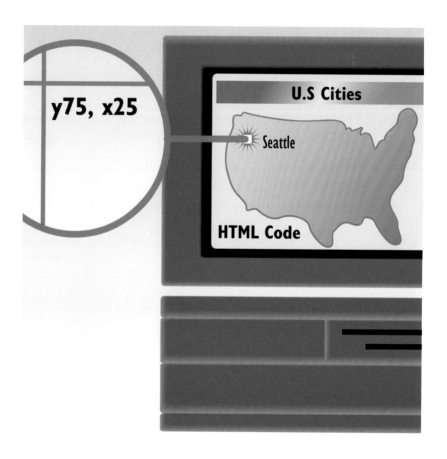

GRAPHICS called imagemaps and functions called interactive forms demonstrate two of the more common and helpful uses of HTML. *Imagemaps* are static images that have been turned into clickable images with various clickable parts. *Interactive forms* are HTML-based pages that you fill out by providing information such as your name, email address, and similar information. Both imagemaps and interactive forms are created using Common Gateway Interface, or CGI, a communications protocol by which a Web server can communicate with other applications. (For more information about how CGI works, turn to Chapter 36, "How CGI Scripting Works.")

Imagemaps may be thought of as fancy hyperlinks. However, instead of a word or entire icon or image linking to another page, an image is divided into different segments, or coordinates, that link to different HTML pages. That is, imagemaps link to another document through a pre-defined "hot" area within an image. As soon as you click your mouse on a hot spot, a CGI script and special imagemap coordinates file with the suffix .map go to work. A CGI application reads the map file to match coordinates of a mouse click with a corresponding URL. For instance, imagine an electronic map of the United States in which you click on Washington, DC. In the HTML code for that page the electronic map is surrounded by a tag and an attribute called ISMAP. The code looks something like this:

```
<A HREF="some.server/maps/clickable.map>
<IMG SRC+"clickable.map" ISMAP>
</A>
```

The x and y coordinates of your mouse click are sent to the server. The coordinates are received by the server and then redirected to a CGI application. The CGI application scans the file for matching coordinates, then forwards the corresponding URL to the server. Lastly, if the Web page resides on the same server, it will deliver that Web page to the client browser. If not, the server returns the URL to the client browser, which in turn sends a request to the correct server for the page. You then see the page about Washington, D.C. begin to load on your browser. Behind the scenes, the server had passed your mouse click coordinates to a CGI application via the CGI. Then the CGI application matched those coordinates to its URL in a .map file. Finally, the URL sent the URL back to the server, which redirected the client browser to the new Web page.

Forms work differently, although they also use CGI. In a form, when you fill in information on a Web page, that information goes to the server for processing. Next, the server redirects the information to a CGI application that is called by the form "submit." (CGI scripts are activated by the server in response to an HTTP request from the client.) Lastly, a CGI application may send form data to another computer program, such as a database, save it to a file, or even generate a unique HTML document in response to the user's request.

How Imagemaps Work

❶ In this map example, the user clicks on Seattle. The coordinates are 75, 25. In the HTML code, the browser recognizes the ISMAP image tag attribute. The mouse click activates the browser to send the x and y coordinates of the click to the server. The location of the "National.map" file is also sent to the server.

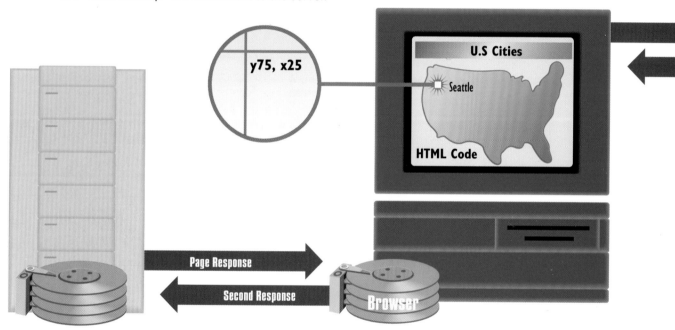

4 The client browser either displays the returned page or (based on the returned URL) sends a request to the correct server for the page.

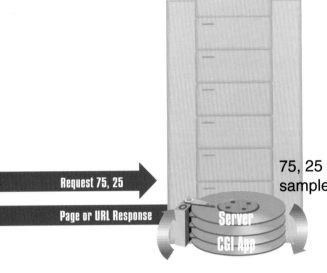

2 The server hands off the coordinate and map file data to a CGI application. The CGI application matches the coordinates to the URL that has been requested by the user by clicking on that portion of the map. This URL is handed back to the server and the server sends the page to the client.

Request 75, 25

Page or URL Response

Server

CGI App

75, 25

samples. ISMAP

3 The Web document is either served up (if it resides on the same server) or the client browser is forwarded the new URL.

How Interactive Forms Work

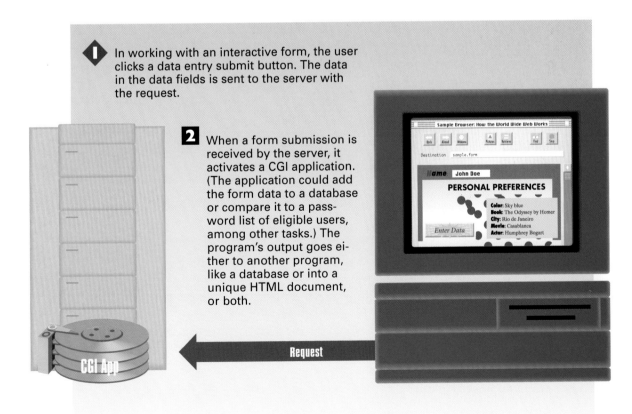

1 In working with an interactive form, the user clicks a data entry submit button. The data in the data fields is sent to the server with the request.

2 When a form submission is received by the server, it activates a CGI application. (The application could add the form data to a database or compare it to a password list of eligible users, among other tasks.) The program's output goes either to another program, like a database or into a unique HTML document, or both.

CGI App

Request

Sample Browser: How the World Wide Web Works

Destination sample.form

Name John Doe

PERSONAL PREFERENCES

Color: Sky blue
Book: The Odyssey by Homer
City: Rio de Janeiro
Movie: Casablanca
Actor: Humphrey Bogart

Enter Data

31

How Web Host Servers Work

TO serve up pages, Web sites need a host—a computer—and server software that runs on the host. The host manages the communications protocols and houses the pages and the related software required to create a Web site on the Internet. The host machine often uses the UNIX, Windows NT, or Macintosh operating systems, which have the TCP/IP protocols built in.

The server software resides on the host and serves up the pages and otherwise acts on the requests sent from the client browser software. The server is not responsible for TCP/IP communications—the host operating system does that—but instead the server handles the HTTP requests and communications with the host operating system.

There are different types of server software (database servers or network servers, for example) that perform different types of services for different types of clients. Specifically, a Web server is an HTTP server and its function is to send information to the client software (typically a browser) using the Hypertext Transfer Protocol.

Usually, the client browser requests that the server return an HTML document. The server receives this request and sends back a response. The top portion of the response includes transmission information and the rest of the response is the HTML file.

A Web server does more than send pages to the browser, however. It passes requests to run CGI (Common Gateway Interface) scripts to the CGI applications. These scripts run external mini-programs, such as a database lookup or interactive forms processing. The server sends the script to the application via CGI and communicates the results of the script back to the browser, if appropriate. Moreover, the server software includes configuration files and utilities to secure and manage the Web site in a variety of ways.

How Web Server Software Works

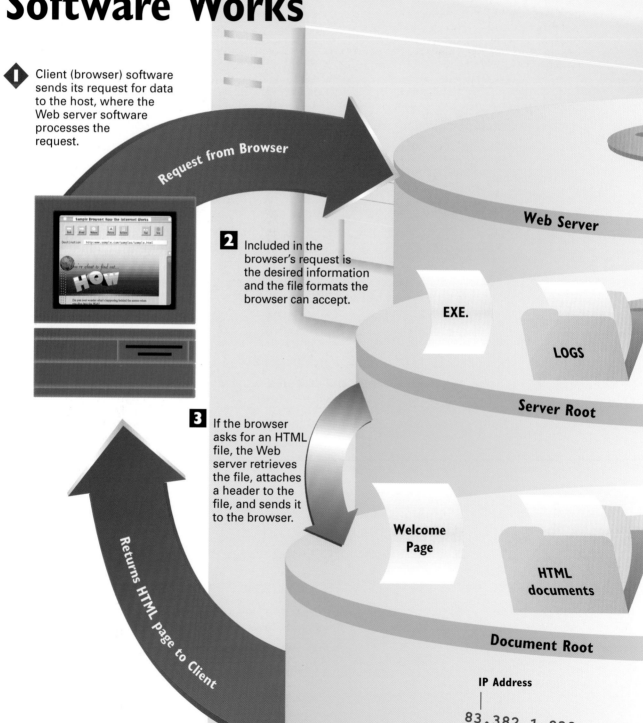

1 Client (browser) software sends its request for data to the host, where the Web server software processes the request.

Request from Browser

2 Included in the browser's request is the desired information and the file formats the browser can accept.

3 If the browser asks for an HTML file, the Web server retrieves the file, attaches a header to the file, and sends it to the browser.

Returns HTML page to Client

Web Server

EXE.

LOGS

Server Root

Welcome Page

HTML documents

Document Root

IP Address

83.382.1.838

4 If the browser has asked for specific database information, the Web server will pass a request through CGI to the application, which performs a database lookup, for example. The CGI script returns the results to the Web server, which in turn attaches a header to the data and sends it to the browser.

NOTE A computer with a single IP address can host several types of servers. This means the address may require a port number to identify the correct server if it is not the IP's default server. Each port is associated with a particular server. Ports are identified by a number from 0 to 65,535, but common server types, such as FTP servers, are given the same number by convention.

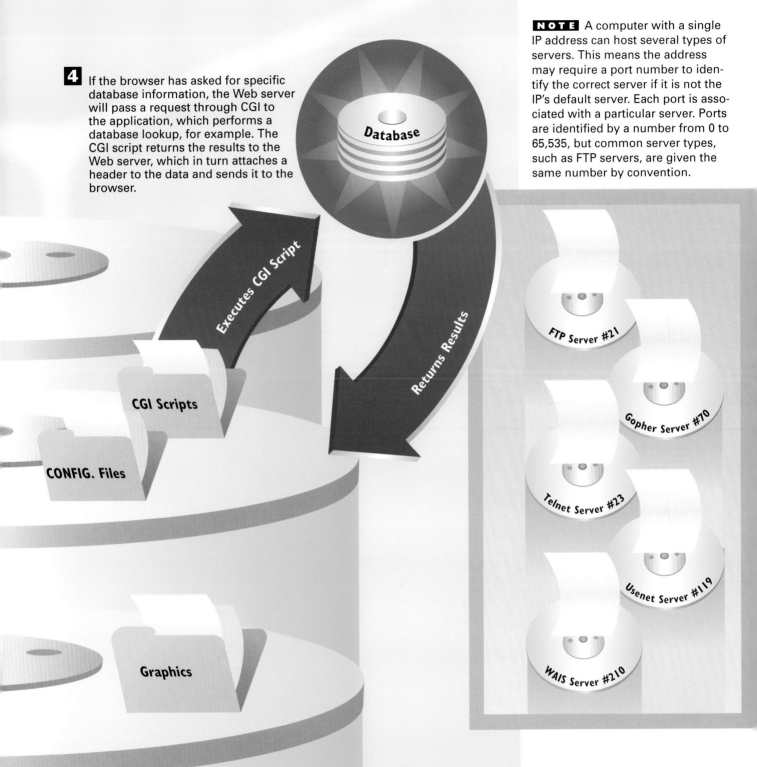

Database

Executes CGI Script

Returns Results

CGI Scripts

CONFIG. Files

Graphics

FTP Server #21

Gopher Server #70

Telnet Server #23

Usenet Server #119

WAIS Server #210

Domain Name

books.zdp.com

NOTE The host computer must have a unique IP address to send and receive information across the Internet. Because raw IP addresses are very intimidating, they are assigned a unique domain name, which is less daunting. The domain name is part of a hierarchical lookup system called the Domain Name System (DNS).

CHAPTER
32

How Web Sites Work with Databases

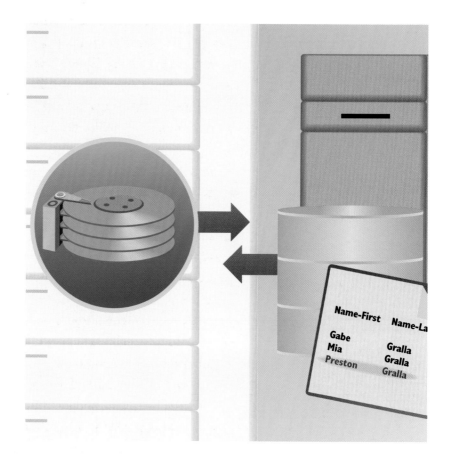

ONE of the most useful applications of the Web is its capability to link a Web site with a database so Web surfers can search for information. In essence, the Web page becomes the front-end for database applications, enabling you to select search criteria and execute even complex searches of a database that resides on the host computer.

A well-known and widely used example of this type of linking between Web sites and databases is the popular Yahoo! Web site. The Yahoo! site serves as a front-end to an extensive database of Web site descriptions, which can be searched according to keywords. The Welcome page includes a search dialog box in which you enter a keyword that represents the subject matter you are looking for. Selecting "Search" from the page sends a request from the browser to the Web server to bring back a list of all Web sites that contain your keyword.

Furthermore, not only can the Web serve up data, it can also collect it. For example, many Web sites ask users to "register" their names, addresses, and other demographic information that is captured and stored in a database.

But how does this all work? You don't have to be a corporate giant—or for that matter even an able programmer—to link your Web site to a database. In fact, linking a Web site to a database can be relatively simple. The database can take just about any form and can be as simple as a FileMaker Pro database, or as complex as an Oracle SQL database. The bridge that brings together Web sites and databases is the Common Gateway Interface (CGI).

On the client side of the database, you see a Web page that includes a form in which you enter your search terms. By executing the search, you launch a CGI script that sends a search command to the Web server in the form of a link to the CGI bin on the Web server. So a search on the Yahoo! site for public relations firms looks like this:

```
http://search.yahoo.com/bin/search?p=public+relations
```

When the Web server receives this URL, it identifies the URL as a trigger for a CGI script (called "script" in this example) and passes it along with the search criteria ("public relations," in this example) to the mini-program using CGI. The CGI script then sends the search to the database, receives the results of the query along with the HTML page created by the database to contain the result, and passes it on to the Web server to be sent back to the client. That's a lot of handing off of requests and data, but typically even a search of a large database is very fast because the majority of UNIX and Windows NT databases—the types most often used—can perform these tasks simultaneously. All of this happens behind the scenes, of course—you won't need to do any kind of database work or scripting yourself. Instead, the Web sites you visit have easy-to-use interfaces that take care of interacting with databases; you'll only have to type in what you're looking for.

How the Web Works with Databases

The search begins on a Web page that includes a form field to accept search terms and HTML codes to execute a CGI script. The browser may pass the data to the Web server in a query string. The *query string* contains the name of the CGI script in a directory called cgi-bin. This directory is followed by a subdirectory that includes the search terms, often separated by a question mark or slashes. The HTML code for an extra path might look like this: <a href="cgi-bin/search?preston+gralla/">.

`<a href="cgi-bin/search?preston+gralla">`

HTTP Response

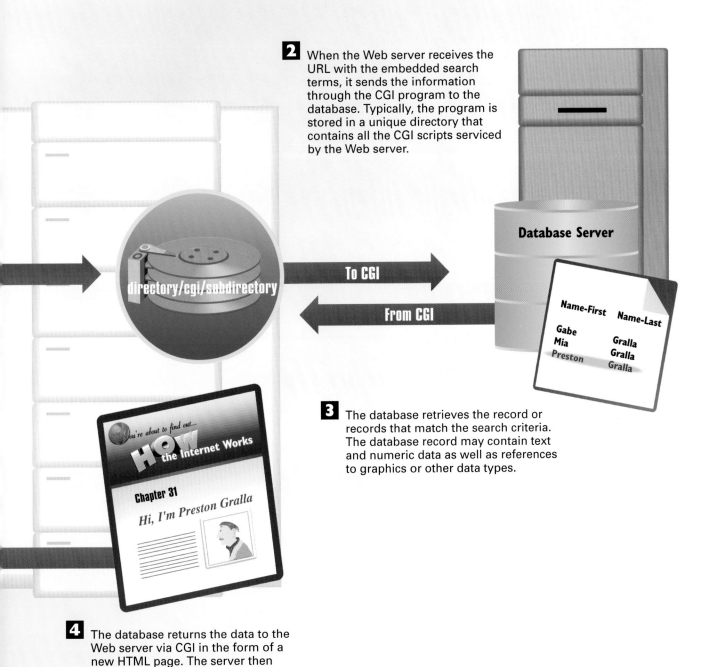

2 When the Web server receives the URL with the embedded search terms, it sends the information through the CGI program to the database. Typically, the program is stored in a unique directory that contains all the CGI scripts serviced by the Web server.

directory/cgi/subdirectory

To CGI

From CGI

Database Server

Name-First	Name-Last
Gabe	Gralla
Mia	Gralla
Preston	Gralla

3 The database retrieves the record or records that match the search criteria. The database record may contain text and numeric data as well as references to graphics or other data types.

You're about to find out...

HOW the Internet Works

Chapter 31

Hi, I'm Preston Gralla

4 The database returns the data to the Web server via CGI in the form of a new HTML page. The server then sends the page back to the client browser as a new HTML page.

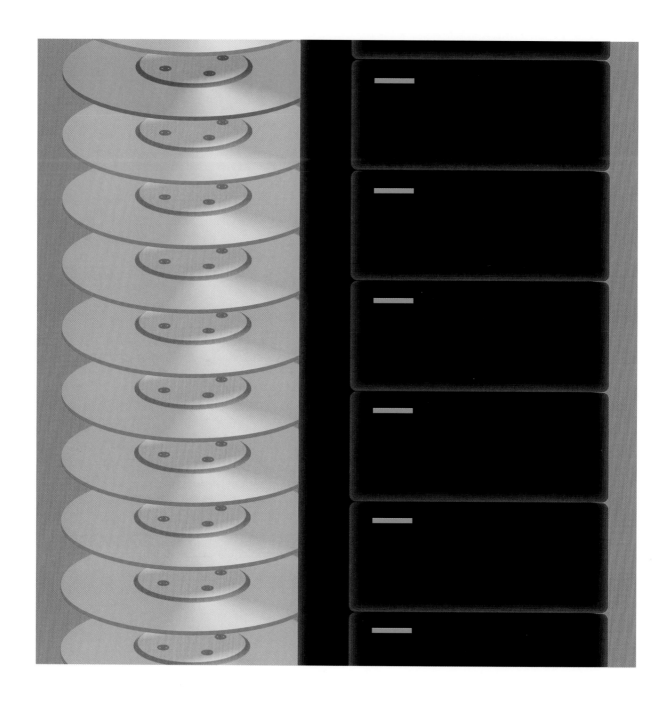

P A R T

ADVANCED INTERNET TOOLS

THE constant evolution of the Internet makes it more exciting than other communications media such as television or radio. Existing technologies are being improved and new ones are being developed every day that make the Internet a richer, more interactive, more entertaining, and more productive medium.

New technologies appear so fast on the Internet that people who work in Internet-related companies often have their own new way to measure time in "Web years" or "Internet years." Because technologies evolve so quickly on the Web, the amount of change that happens on the Internet in two months might equal the kinds of changes that happen over a year in the outside world. So a Web year might be two months in real-time.

Most of these changes occur in various advanced Internet technologies. Commonly, an idea for a new technology is hatched in a small startup company, or even by an individual. It spreads from there, usually by way of the Internet, and in a very short time what was once a mere dream becomes an Internet standard.

In this section, we'll look at some of these advanced Internet technologies. Many of them have changed the very nature of the Internet and have turned it into a truly interactive medium—one that people can navigate efficiently. The technologies also enable Web publishers and Internet developers to more effectively present information to people.

Chapter 33, "How Push Technology Works," looks at one of the newest technologies and one that may have enduring effects; it's known as *push*. In push technology, entire Web sites, customized information, and even applications can be sent straight to people's computers without them having to go out and ask for the information. In push technology, you *subscribe* to Web sites or channels of information, and they are then sent to you at intervals you specify. Subscribing doesn't mean you have to pay for information. It's the term that's used to say you've asked to receive information on a regular schedule.

No one standard for push technology exists—many companies have competing technologies and products. For example, Netscape has its own standard for push technology, called Netcasting, and Microsoft's standard is called Webcasting. Meanwhile, many other companies, notably PointCast, have their own methods of pushing information straight to people's computers. Chapter 33 looks at the most important underlying technologies that make push possible.

Chapter 34, "How Java, ActiveX, and JavaScript Work," examines three other kinds of technologies that are transforming the Internet—Java, JavaScript, and ActiveX. These three technologies may do more to transform the Internet than almost any other technologies currently available. These technologies add multimedia and interactivity, but more importantly, they begin to treat the Internet as if it were an extension of your computer. In essence, they enable your computer and the Internet to interact as if they were one large computer system. This allows for things such as news tickers, interactive games you can play with others, multimedia presentations combining animations, sounds, music, graphics, and much more.

Java, a computer language developed by Sun Microsystems, enables applications to be run from the Internet. The programs run inside your Web browser. One benefit of Java applications is that they can be run on any computer, such as a PC, a Macintosh, or a UNIX workstation.

ActiveX, a competing technology from Microsoft, can also essentially turn the Internet into an extension of your computer. Like Java applets, ActiveX controls are downloaded to your computer and run there. They can do anything that a normal application can do, and can also interact with the Web, the Internet, and other computers connected to the Internet. To run them, a browser that supports ActiveX, such as Internet Explorer, is needed.

JavaScript, which despite its name is not really related to Java, is simpler than Java and ActiveX and can be written by people who don't have substantial programming experience. JavaScript is commonly used to create interactive forms, site navigation, and similar features.

In Chapter 35, "How Agents Work," we'll look at agents on the Internet. *Agents* are programs that do your bidding across the Internet automatically, without your having to do anything. They can find the latest news and download it to your computer; they can find you the best deal on the CD you want to buy; they can perform important Web maintenance tasks; and more. They are becoming so complex that systems are being developed to allow agents to interact with one another so that they can perform jobs cooperatively.

Finally, in Chapter 36, "How CGI Scripting Works," we'll examine *CGI* (Common Gateway Interface) *scripting*. This may appear as one of the more mundane Internet technologies, but without it, very little Web interactivity would take place. CGI is a standard way in which the Web interacts with outside resources—most commonly, databases. You've probably run CGI scripts many times without knowing it. If you've filled out a form on a Web page to register to use a site and then later received an email notification with a password for you to use, you've probably run a CGI script. CGI enables programmers to write code that can access information servers (such as Web servers) on the Internet and then send the information to users.

CHAPTER

CHAPTER 33 How Push Technology Works

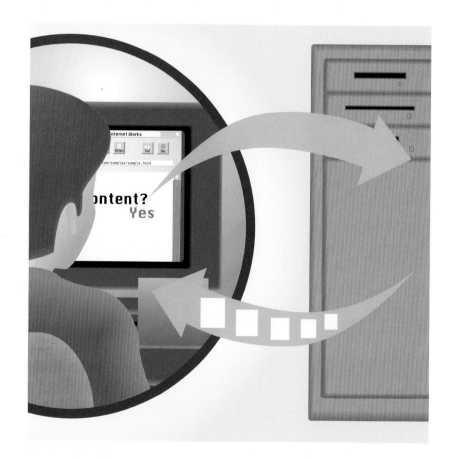

INCREASINGLY, the Internet is becoming a broadcast medium. It relies less each day on people taking it upon themselves to visit certain sites. Instead, information, entire Web sites, and applications can be sent via the Internet straight to people's computers with a variety of technologies collectively known as *push*.

In push technology, you "subscribe" to Web sites, often called channels. A *channel* generally refers to an area of interest that a publisher builds, which can include HTML pages, Java applets, ActiveX components, multimedia objects, and other information packaged together to deliver customized information to people via push technology. Those sites you subscribe to and the information they contain are sent to your computer automatically at intervals that you specify. You don't pay for these subscriptions; you merely ask to receive the desired information on a regular schedule.

Receiving these channels requires either special client software or a push-enabled browser on your desktop. This software is generally free. Push technology is built into browsers such as Netscape Communicator and Microsoft Internet Explorer. Push client software is available from companies such as PointCast and BackWeb. Most push technologies also allow you to customize the kind of information that you receive.

This kind of customization is one benefit that push technologies offer. Another benefit is the time savings—instead of you having to go out and gather the information, it's delivered right to you with no effort on your part, and it's precisely the kind of information that interests you. There's one more benefit as well: When the information is sent to you, it resides locally on your computer. So you can read it whenever you want—you don't have to be connected to the Internet. You'll also be able to view the pages and information more quickly than if they were on the Internet instead of your local computer because you're reading it at high speed from your hard disk instead of across the slow wires of the Internet.

There is no single standard for push technology. Netscape has established its own standard and software, called Netcaster, which is part of its Communicator package. Netscape refers to its version of push technology as Netcasting. Microsoft has its own version of push technology built into Internet Explorer 4.0 and above, which it refers to as Webcasting. Aside from Netscape and Microsoft there are other push technologies as well, from companies such as PointCast, Marimba, and BackWeb.

Most push technologies have a few basics in common. For example, most allow you to customize how you'll receive your information. To receive that information, you'll have to be connected to the Internet, so many push technologies will also dial into the Internet for you to get updates. They deliver the information to your computer so you can read the information locally at your leisure. Also, most use similar terminologies, such as the word, "channel."

How Internet Explorer's Webcasting Works

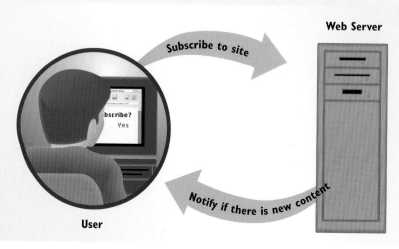

1 Internet Explorer 4.0 offers a variety of ways to use push technology and offline reading—what Microsoft calls Webcasting. In the simplest form of Webcasting, you "subscribe" to a Web site and ask to be told when the content on the site changes. Your browser will regularly visit that site and notify you if new content is available. It won't, however, automatically download any of that content.

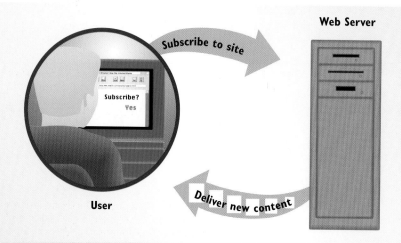

2 In a slightly more sophisticated version of Webcasting, you subscribe to a Web site and ask that whenever there is new content, it be automatically delivered to you. In this instance, your browser regularly contacts the Web site, "crawls" the pages by looking at every page, and downloads to your computer only those pages that have changed since your last visit. You'll now be able to view those pages offline, when you're not connected to the Internet.

3 A much more sophisticated form of Webcasting uses channels. A channel is designed from the ground up to be delivered via push technology, and incorporates multimedia, ActiveX, and other interactive kinds of content. To build a channel, developers create HTML files, ActiveX controls, and similar content, and post them on their Web pages. They then create a Channel Definition Format (CDF) file that describes the channel, how it functions, and where its content is on a Web server. This CDF file is linked to a button on a Web page.

```
cdf.txt - Notepad
File  Edit  Search  Help
<?XML version="1.0"?>
<!DOCTYPE Channel SYSTEM "http://www.w3c.org/Channel.dtd">

<CHANNEL HREF="http://www.hotfiles.com">
<SELF HREF="http://www.hotfiles.com/hf.cdf" />

<TITLE> ZDNet Software Library </TITLE>

<LOGOREF="http://www.hotfiles.com/hf.ico" STYLE="ICON"/>
<LOGOREF="http://www.hotfiles.com/hf.GIF" STYLE="IMAGE"/>

<SCHEDULE>
    <INTERVALTIME HOUR="2" />
    <LATESTTIME MIN'"30" />
<SCHEDULE>

<CHANNEL>
    <TITLE> Hottest New Files</TITLE>
    <ABSTRACT> Best new files.</ABSTRACT>

    <ITEM HREF="http://www.hotfiles.com/latest/new.htm">
```

Web Server

Developer/Editor

4 When someone clicks on the button, the CDF file downloads to his or her computer.

CDF File

CDF file

5 The CDF file determines how the channel functions. It contains data such as how often to schedule updates, information about the structure of the channel (such as whether it has sub-channels), and links to specific Web pages and contents, such as ActiveX controls and multimedia content.

6 The browser visits the Web site on a schedule determined in the CDF. Then it downloads the CDF file in case the file has changed, and also downloads the associated content referenced in the CDF file such as Web pages, ActiveX controls, and multimedia content.

CDF file

Get update

HTML Pages

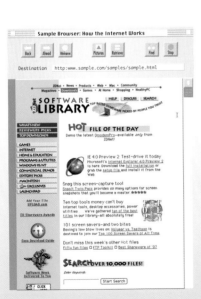

User

7 The channel pages and associated files are now on the local computer. Because the information and pages are local instead of residing on the Internet, they can be accessed while the user is not connected to the Internet. The pages and information will be accessed quickly because they are being read from a hard disk instead of across the Internet.

How Netscape's Netcasting Works

1 Netcaster is the part of Netscape Communicator that allows for information and sites to be pushed to someone's desktop, and for those sites to be browsed offline. The sites that can be pushed are called channels. Channels are built by developers using HTML and JavaScript and can also incorporate Java applets and multimedia content. Before a channel can be pushed, the developer posts all the content and channel information on a Web site, and sets default properties for that channel, such as how often Netcaster should automatically update it.

3 When the button is clicked on, an "addChannel" JavaScript call is made. A dialog box pops up, listing the properties of the channel (such as how often to update it). The user can change the properties or keep the defaults. After the user clicks on OK, the channel is added to Netcaster. The subscription to that channel is now in effect.

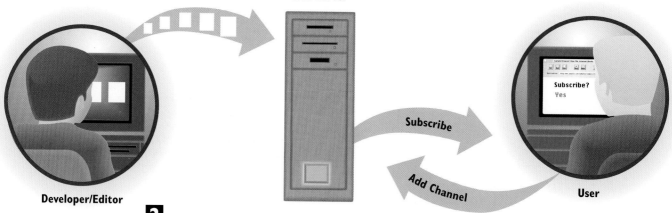

Web Server

Developer/Editor

Subscribe

Add Channel

User

2 After the channel is created, the developer creates a button on a Web site that, when clicked, will "subscribe" people to the channel.

4 Through the Channel Properties box, the user can change many aspects of how to interact with the channel, such as how often to check the channel for new content, and how many levels of Web pages should be checked.

Subscribe Button

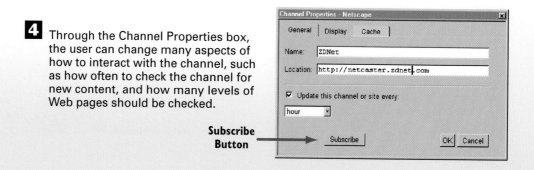

5 Netscaster connects to the channel at intervals the user specifies, or at intervals in the default information about the channel.

Web Server

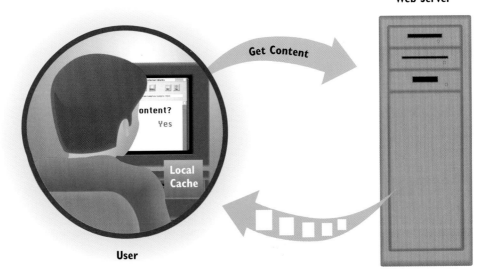

Get Content

User

6 After Netcaster connects, it "crawls" the channel—that is, it downloads the information, data, and pages in the channel. First it downloads the HTML pages, then the associated graphics, then embedded objects such as Java applets or audio and video files. The pages, graphics, and embedded objects are all put into a cache on the local machine.

7 The content of the channel can be read from the cache. Because the information and pages are local instead of on the Internet they can be accessed when the user is not connected. They can also be accessed quickly because they're being read from a hard disk instead of across the Internet.

How PointCast Works

I PointCast, the first push technology to gain widespread acceptance, delivers customized news and information to people's desktops. Publishers who want to deliver information via PointCast have to create special files and automated feeds that are placed on PointCast servers.

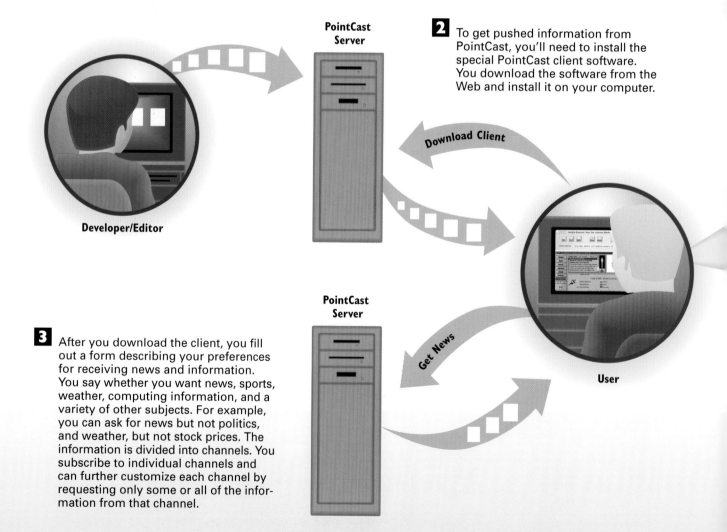

PointCast Server

Developer/Editor

2 To get pushed information from PointCast, you'll need to install the special PointCast client software. You download the software from the Web and install it on your computer.

Download Client

Get News

User

PointCast Server

3 After you download the client, you fill out a form describing your preferences for receiving news and information. You say whether you want news, sports, weather, computing information, and a variety of other subjects. For example, you can ask for news but not politics, and weather, but not stock prices. The information is divided into channels. You subscribe to individual channels and can further customize each channel by requesting only some or all of the information from that channel.

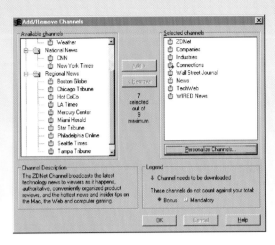

4 At set times that you determine in your preferences, the PointCast client software automatically connects to the PointCast server over the Internet. The software downloads the customized news that you've requested. You can also manually tell the client software to download the news at any time you want.

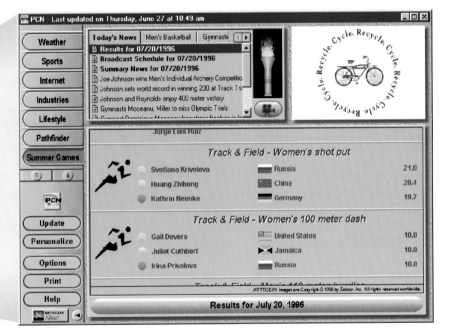

5 Using the PointCast client, you can now read the news on your own computer. The software can also be set up as a screen saver so that when the computer is idle for a certain amount of time, the news will flash across your screen.

6 Often, in news stories, there are URLs to sites that have additional information. When that link is clicked on, an Internet browser is launched, and the specified site is contacted. The person can now read more in-depth news. For example, there may be a brief news story in PointCast about a company's quarterly earnings. That story could contain links to stories on the Web with more in-depth financial information, as well as other articles about that company.

34 How Java, ActiveX, and JavaScript Work

THE Internet is no longer a place that you visit with your computer and merely look at documents or gather information—increasingly, it is an extension of your computer. You can now run programs that reside on the Internet rather than on your own computer, and tools have been developed that enable your computer and the Internet to interact as if they were one large computer system. This allows for all kinds of things never before possible: news tickers that flash breaking news; interactive games; multimedia presentations combining animation, sound, and music; and much more.

The three most important programming tools associated with Web technology are Java, ActiveX, and JavaScript. *Java*, a computer language developed by Sun Microsystems, enables applications to be run from the Internet, the same as word processing and spreadsheet programs are run on your computer. It is similar to the C++ computer programming language, and it is object-oriented, which means programs can be created by using many pre-existing components instead of by a programmer writing the entire program from scratch.

Java programs run inside your Web browser if you have a Java-enabled browser, such as Netscape. When Java programs are run inside a browser, they are called *applets*. You don't need to do anything to run a Java applet. When you visit a Web site that has a Java applet on it, the applet is downloaded automatically from a Web server, and then run automatically in your browser. Java applets can be run on any computer, such as a PC, a Macintosh, or a UNIX workstation.

ActiveX, a technology from Microsoft, allows Internet programmers to create programs—commonly referred to as ActiveX *controls* or *components*—that can essentially turn the Internet into an extension of your computer. Like Java applets, these controls are downloaded to your computer and run there. They can do anything that a normal application can do, in addition to interacting with the Web, the Internet, and other computers connected to the Internet. To run these controls, a browser that supports ActiveX, such as Internet Explorer, is needed.

One benefit of ActiveX controls is that they are written as components, which means they can be put together, much like building blocks, to build larger and more complex applications. Another benefit is that because you have already downloaded a component, you won't ever need to download it again. This means when you visit a page with a complex ActiveX application on it, you may need to download only a small portion of it because you may already have the other components on your computer.

JavaScript is a scripting language that is less complex and, therefore, much easier to learn than Java and ActiveX. People without substantial programming experience can write scripts with JavaScript. It's also an interpreted language, which means that its commands are executed by the browser in the order in which the browser reads them. It's commonly used for things such as creating drop-down boxes, navigational aids, and interactive forms, although it can be used for creating more complex applications, as well.

How Java Works

Java is a *compiled language*, which means that after a Java program is written, the program must be run through a compiler to turn the program into a language that a computer can read. Java differs from other compiled languages, however. In other compiled languages, computer-specific compilers create distinct executable binary code for all the different computers on which the program can run. In Java, by contrast, a single compiled version of the program—called Java *bytecode*—is created by a compiler. Interpreters on different computers, such as a PC, Macintosh, or SPARC workstation, understand the Java bytecode and run the program. In this way, a Java program can be created once and then used on many kinds of computers. Java programs designed to run inside a Web browser on the World Wide Web are called *applets*. Java-enabled browsers contain Java bytecode interpreters.

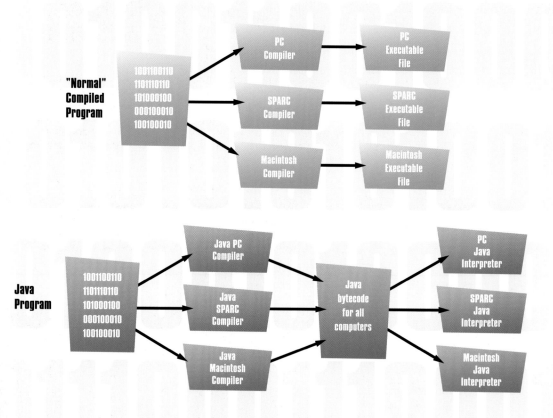

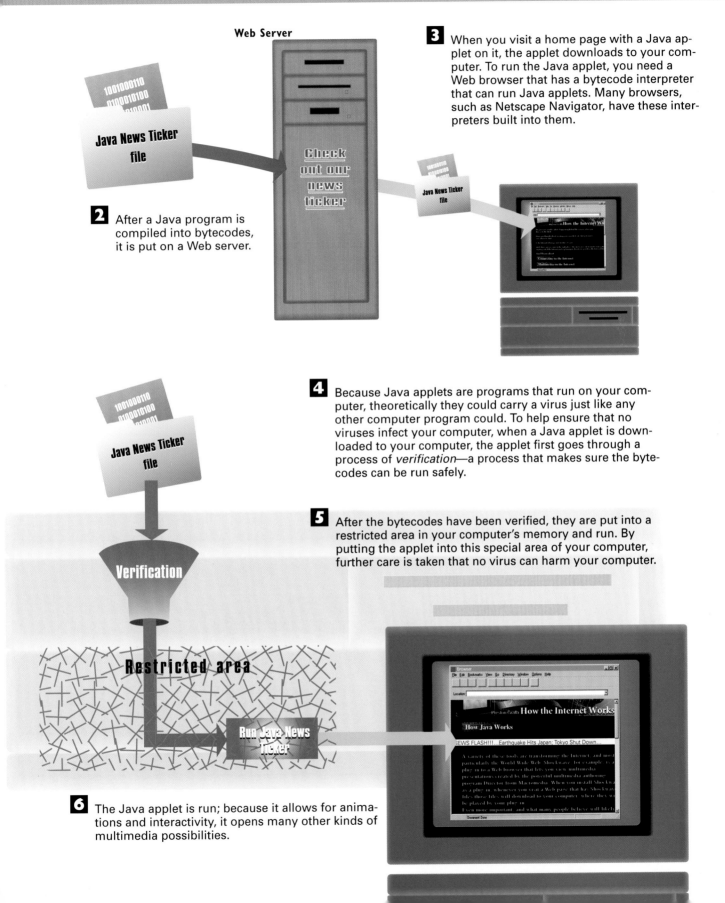

Web Server

3 When you visit a home page with a Java applet on it, the applet downloads to your computer. To run the Java applet, you need a Web browser that has a bytecode interpreter that can run Java applets. Many browsers, such as Netscape Navigator, have these interpreters built into them.

Java News Ticker file

2 After a Java program is compiled into bytecodes, it is put on a Web server.

Check out our news ticker

Java News Ticker file

4 Because Java applets are programs that run on your computer, theoretically they could carry a virus just like any other computer program could. To help ensure that no viruses infect your computer, when a Java applet is downloaded to your computer, the applet first goes through a process of *verification*—a process that makes sure the bytecodes can be run safely.

Java News Ticker file

5 After the bytecodes have been verified, they are put into a restricted area in your computer's memory and run. By putting the applet into this special area of your computer, further care is taken that no virus can harm your computer.

Verification

Restricted area

Run Java News Ticker

6 The Java applet is run; because it allows for animations and interactivity, it opens many other kinds of multimedia possibilities.

How ActiveX Works

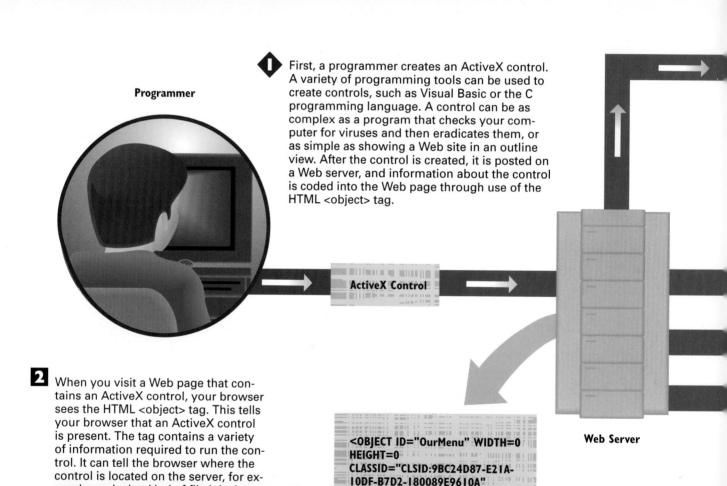

Programmer

1 First, a programmer creates an ActiveX control. A variety of programming tools can be used to create controls, such as Visual Basic or the C programming language. A control can be as complex as a program that checks your computer for viruses and then eradicates them, or as simple as showing a Web site in an outline view. After the control is created, it is posted on a Web server, and information about the control is coded into the Web page through use of the HTML <object> tag.

ActiveX Control

2 When you visit a Web page that contains an ActiveX control, your browser sees the HTML <object> tag. This tells your browser that an ActiveX control is present. The tag contains a variety of information required to run the control. It can tell the browser where the control is located on the server, for example, and what kind of file it is. It can point to the control (which has an .OCX extension); to an installation file (which has an .INF extension); to a compressed file (which has a .CAB extension); or a variety of other kinds of files.

```
<OBJECT ID="OurMenu" WIDTH=0
HEIGHT=0
CLASSID="CLSID:9BC24D87-E21A-
10DF-B7D2-180089E9610A"
CODEBASE="http://www.zdnet.co
m/ActiveX/ZDNetControls.CAB#
Version=1,0,8,0">
```

Web Server

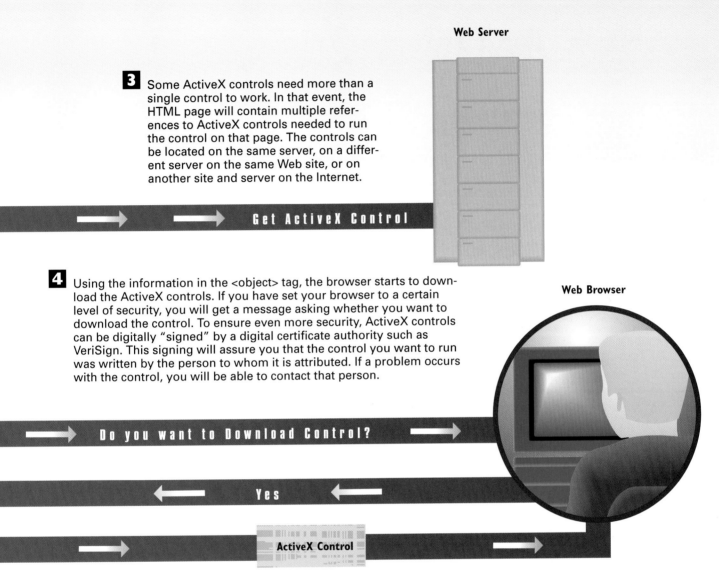

Web Server

3 Some ActiveX controls need more than a single control to work. In that event, the HTML page will contain multiple references to ActiveX controls needed to run the control on that page. The controls can be located on the same server, on a different server on the same Web site, or on another site and server on the Internet.

Get ActiveX Control

4 Using the information in the <object> tag, the browser starts to download the ActiveX controls. If you have set your browser to a certain level of security, you will get a message asking whether you want to download the control. To ensure even more security, ActiveX controls can be digitally "signed" by a digital certificate authority such as VeriSign. This signing will assure you that the control you want to run was written by the person to whom it is attributed. If a problem occurs with the control, you will be able to contact that person.

Web Browser

Do you want to Download Control?

Yes

ActiveX Control

5 If you have low security set on your browser, or if you give the okay to download the control, the control and its related ActiveX controls are downloaded to your computer. Some of the controls may already be on your system, so you won't need to download them. After the control is downloaded, the file is decompressed (if it was compressed), information about it is put into the Windows Registry, and it is installed on your computer. The control will then run. An ActiveX control can do anything that any other program can do. It can interact with your computer and with any Internet resource, such as the Web, FTP, Telnet, or virtually any other Internet resource. It can also directly use the Internet's TCP/IP protocols so that it need not ride on top of another Internet resource.

How JavaScript Works

JavaScript allows Web designers to add functionality and interactivity to Web pages that otherwise couldn't be gained with HTML, the language of the Web. It can create interactive forms, for example, or make text turn colors when a mouse moves over it, or any number of other kinds of interactivity. Despite its name, JavaScript is not a form of the Java programming language. Instead, it's a simpler scripting language. JavaScript will run only on browsers that have been explicitly designed to take advantage of it, such as Microsoft Internet Explorer and Netscape Navigator.

1 JavaScript is an object-oriented language, which means that it works by manipulating objects on a Web page, such as windows, buttons, images, and documents. It groups these objects into hierarchies, which enables programmers to manipulate them more easily.

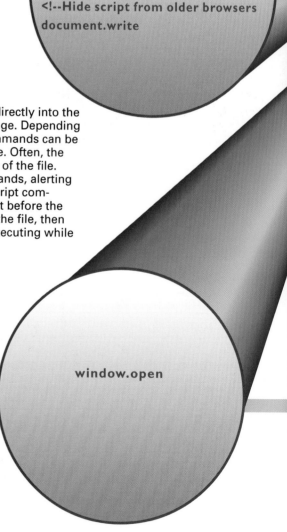

```
<HTML>
<READ>
<SCRIPT LANGUAGE="JavaScript">
<!--Hide script from older browsers
document.write
```

3 JavaScript commands are put directly into the HTML file that creates a Web page. Depending on the script being run, the commands can be put into several places in the file. Often, the commands are put near the top of the file. Special codes set off the commands, alerting the browser that they're JavaScript commands. If the commands are put before the HTML <body> tag at the top of the file, then the script will be able to start executing while the HTML page is still loading.

```
window.open
then
document.write
then
window.status=
   "These are the times that
   try men's souls"
then
```

2 JavaScript is also an interpreted language, which means that its commands are executed by the browser in the order in which the browser reads them.

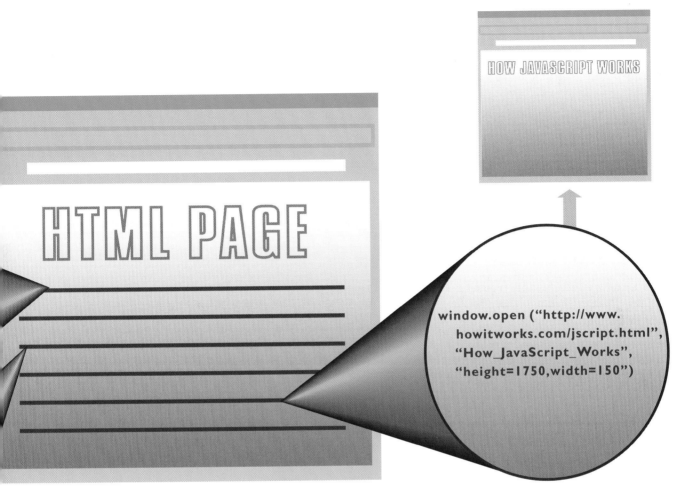

window.open ("http://www.
howitworks.com/jscript.html",
"How_JavaScript_Works",
"height=1750,width=150")

5 You can also add further instructions to the window.open command. You do this by adding parameters after the command. You put all the parameters inside one set of parentheses, put each individual parameter inside quotation marks, and then separate the parameters by commas. So, the command window.open ("http://www.howitworks.com/jscript.html","How_JavaScript_0Works","height=1750,width=150") will open a new browser window 175 pixels high and 150 pixels wide with the http://www.howitworks.com/jscript.html in it.

4 The heart of the way that JavaScript works is to take actions on objects. These actions are called methods. Using this basic concept, JavaScript can be used for a wide variety of sophisticated, interactive features, but we'll look at a simple script that opens a new browser window to a specified size, puts a specific Web page in it, and names the window. In the basic syntax of JavaScript, first the object is named, then a period appears, followed by the action taken on the object—the method. So the command to open a new window in JavaScript is window.open. In this instance, window is the object, and open is the method. This command will open a new browser window.

CHAPTER

35

How Agents Work

THE Internet has grown so quickly and its resources are so vast that we need help navigating around it. We can now use special software called *agents* to help us access the Net's resources.

While there are a lot of technical definitions for agents, put simply, agents are programs that do your bidding automatically. Many of them run over the Internet or on individual computers every day. Agents can find the latest news for you and download it to your computer; they can automatically monitor Internet traffic and report on its total usage; they can find you the best deal on the CD you want to buy; they can perform important Web maintenance tasks; and far more. They are becoming so complex that systems are being developed to allow agents to interact with one another so they can perform jobs cooperatively.

On the Internet, agents are commonly called *spiders*, *robots* (often shortened to "bots"), and *knowbots*, among other terms. Those used for searching automatically create indexes of almost every resource on the Web and then allow people to search through those indexes to find things more quickly. Common search tools such as Lycos, InfoSeek, and AltaVista use spiders in this way. We covered this specialized use of spiders in Chapter 24, "Searching the Internet."

All of these agents are software programs that are invisible to the user. You just determine the task you want done and behind the scenes the agent automatically goes off and performs that task. A variety of different languages can be used to write agent programs.

Agents may well alter the way we all use the Internet in the future. Not only will they respond to our requests, but they will also "learn" from our requests the kinds of tasks and information that interest us. They'll then go off on their own and perform those tasks and get that information, even before we make these additional requests. As we use these kinds of agents more, they'll become even smarter and more efficient.

Robots and agents can cause problems for some Web sites. For example, they can overload Web servers by swamping them with too many requests in too short a time. That means users who try to get access to those Web pages will either be denied access or access will be exceedingly slow.

Another problem has to do with the way Web sites make money. Many Web sites sell ads to support themselves and they charge advertisers based on the number of pages that have been viewed. If many of those pages "viewed" are in fact never seen by people and are instead only accessed by a computer via a robot, both advertisers and the Web site suffer.

There are several ways to solve these problems and limit robot access. One way includes creating a file called Robots.txt that describes the areas that are off limits to robots, which the robots would automatically read, adhere to, and not visit. Another is to use a technology that automatically detects whether a robot or a human has visited a page and forgo charging advertisers whenever robots visit.

Agents on the Internet

A simple Internet agent is one that gathers news from a variety of sources while you're not using your computer or while you are using your computer for another task. News agents can work in several ways. In the simplest example, you fill out a form saying what kind of news you're interested in and on what schedule you want your news delivered. Based on that information, at preset intervals, the news agent dials into news sites around the Internet and downloads news stories to your computer where you can read them as HTML pages.

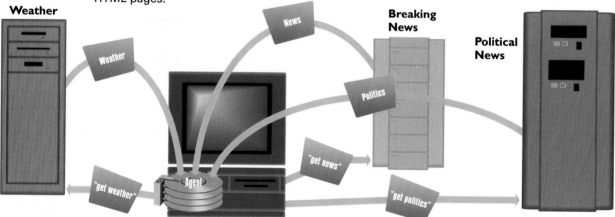

Weather

Breaking News

Political News

2 Shopping agents will let you search through all of the Internet for the best bargains. On the Web, you fill out a form detailing the product you want to buy. When you send the form, the shopping agent launches programs that search through a variety of shopping sites and databases on the Internet. The agent looks into the databases of those sites and finds the best prices. It then sends back to you the links to the sites so you can visit the sites with the best prices and order from there.

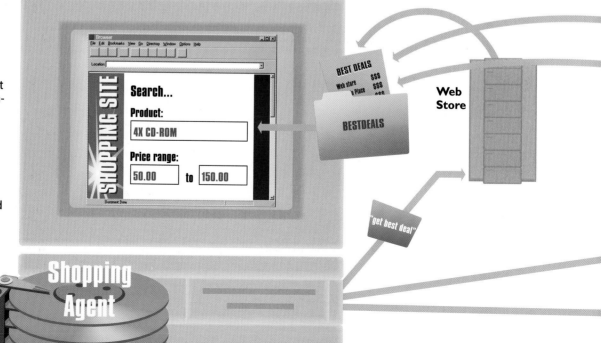

Web Store

Shopping Agent

4 When robots and spiders do their work on a remote Internet site from where they were launched, they can put an extra load on the site's system resources—for example, by swamping the server with too many requests in too short a time. Because of this, some system administrators are interested in ways of excluding robots in certain circumstances, such as not allowing robots into certain Web directories. A variety of ways have been devised to limit robot access, including creating a file called Robots.txt that describes the areas off limits to robots, which the robots would automatically read, adhere to, and not visit.

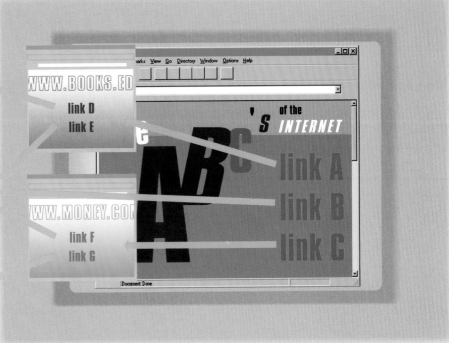

Bargain Place

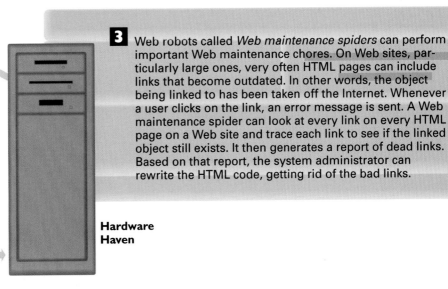

3 Web robots called *Web maintenance spiders* can perform important Web maintenance chores. On Web sites, particularly large ones, very often HTML pages can include links that become outdated. In other words, the object being linked to has been taken off the Internet. Whenever a user clicks on the link, an error message is sent. A Web maintenance spider can look at every link on every HTML page on a Web site and trace each link to see if the linked object still exists. It then generates a report of dead links. Based on that report, the system administrator can rewrite the HTML code, getting rid of the bad links.

Hardware Haven

CHAPTER

36

How CGI Scripting Works

IF you browse the Web for very long you are sure to come across the term CGI, or Common Gateway Interface. CGI refers to the communications protocol by which a Web server can communicate with other applications. For example, a CGI application, sometimes called a "script," is often used to allow Web users to access databases, or to get information from forms that people fill out. CGI can also be used to create agents that do things such as check a Web site to see whether there are any broken links on the site.

Essentially, CGI is a standard way in which the Web interacts with outside resources. Often, that outside resource is a database. You've probably run CGI scripts many times without knowing it. For example, if you've filled out a form on a Web page to register to use a site and then later received an email notification with a password for you to use, you've probably run a CGI script. In that case, the CGI script probably took the information you filled in on the form and performed several actions on it, including putting the information in a database, automatically creating a password, and then sending you mail.

CGI and CGI applications are often confused. *CGI applications* receive data from the server and return the data via the Common Gateway Interface. CGI applications are usually written in a programming language called Perl (Practical Extraction and Reporting Language), although they may be written in C, C++, Pascal, AppleScript, or others as well. CGI itself is a standardized means of communicating between a CGI application and the HTTP server. It's the "doorway" of sorts through which the Web server sends requests and the CGI application collects and returns data.

In the example of providing information on a Web page designed to accept user input, CGI performs many tasks. First, you submit unique information—like a name or email address—to the server for processing. Next, the server redirects the information to a CGI application that is called by the form "submit." CGI scripts are activated by the server in response to an HTTP request from the client. Lastly, a CGI application may send form data to another computer program, such as a database, save it to a file, or even generate a unique HTML document in response to the user's request. This is known as an *interactive form*.

In the illustration that accompanies this chapter, we'll look at a CGI program that allows someone to search a movie database for information.

How CGI Scripting Works

1 People who dial into the Web site don't need to know programming to access CGI programs. Instead, a programmer writes a CGI program. A number of different languages can be used for CGI, such as C or C++, FORTRAN, Visual Basic, and AppleScript. An application written in a programming language such as C must be passed through a program called a compiler before it can be run. The compiler turns the application into a language that CGI can understand. Other languages, called *scripting languages*, do not need to be compiled first. CGI scripts tend to be easier to debug, modify, and maintain than compiled programs so they are used more frequently. Perl is probably the most popular language used for writing CGI scripts.

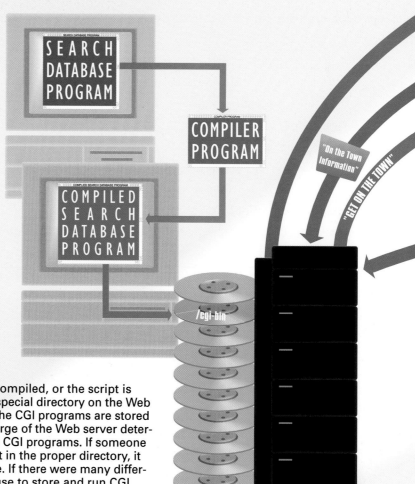

SEARCH DATABASE PROGRAM

COMPILER PROGRAM

COMPILED SEARCH DATABASE PROGRAM

/cgi-bin

"On the Town Information"

"GET ON THE TOWN"

Web Server

2 After the program is written and compiled, or the script is written, the program is put into a special directory on the Web server, such as /cgi-bin, where all the CGI programs are stored and maintained. The person in charge of the Web server determines which directory should hold CGI programs. If someone writes a program and doesn't put it in the proper directory, it won't run. This is a security feature. If there were many different directories that people could use to store and run CGI programs, it would be difficult to keep track of them all and someone from the outside could create and post a program that could be dangerous to the software that's already there.

6 The CGI program receives the data from the database and formats it in a way that will be understandable to the user. For example, the program might take the information and put it into HTML format so the user can read it using his or her Web browser. The CGI program sends the results in HTML format to the user, who displays it in a Web browser. The user can then access that HTML page. He or she can click on links to visit other pages, print pages, and view graphics and multimedia files.

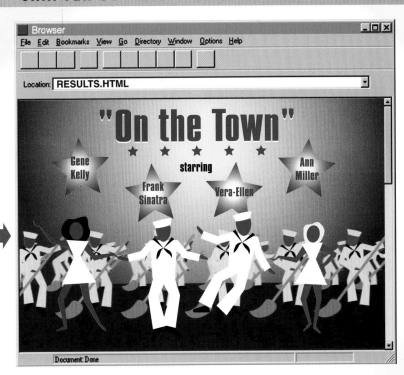

Database

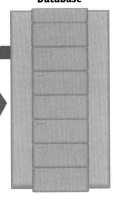

5 The CGI program contacts a database and requests the information that the user is looking for. The database sends the information to the CGI program. The information can be in a variety of formats, such as text, graphics, sound and video files, and URLs.

4 When you visit the Web site and click on the URL, the CGI program is launched. If the CGI program allows you to search a database, for example, it will send a form in HTML format. You then fill out the form detailing what you want to find. When you finish the form and click on Send, the data from the form is sent to the CGI program.

"get On the Town"

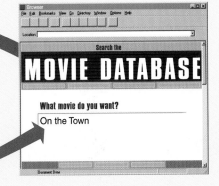

3 After the CGI program is posted to a special directory, a link to it is embedded in a URL on a Web page.

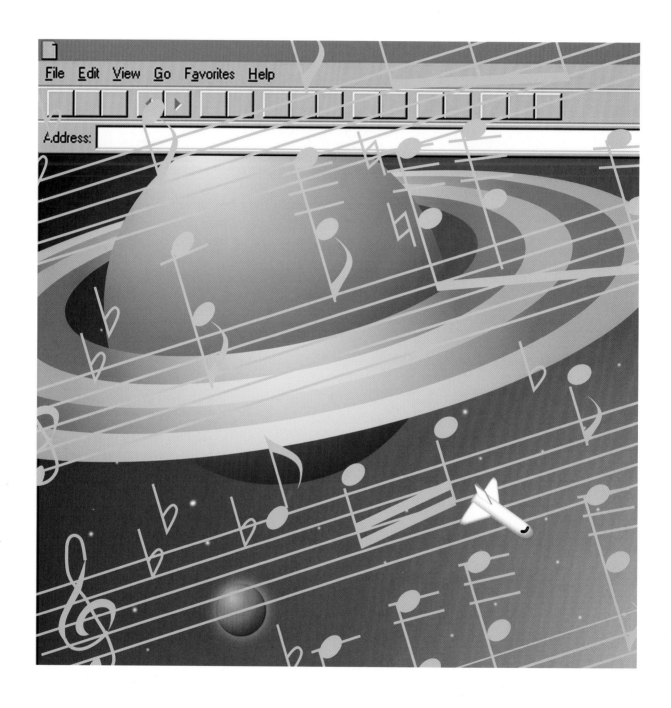

P A R T

MULTIMEDIA ON THE INTERNET

POSSIBLY the most dramatic and remarkable part of the Internet is the multimedia content. You'll be able to listen to music, sound clips, and live radio stations from your computer. You can watch astronauts live while they're on the space shuttle. You can watch video clips of the news and other events. And you can even have live videoconferencing with people from all over the world.

You can do all that with the Internet's audio and video capabilities. You won't need specialized hardware and software to do it—and in many cases, you won't even need a very high-speed Internet connection. An ordinary dial-in connection to the Internet will do, although the sound and video quality will be better at higher speeds. And you'll only need free or inexpensive software, and a sound card and speakers that ship with most computers, or that are available separately.

The Internet's multimedia capabilities go beyond mere playing of audio and video clips. You can participate in virtual worlds and join in "virtual chat" sessions in which you build your own online persona, called an *avatar*, which communicates with other avatars. The Internet allows for the creation of remarkable online multimedia content, combining animation, sound, and programming via technologies such as streaming audio and video, Shockwave, and Multicast IP.

In this section of the book, we'll look at how every aspect of multimedia on the Internet works. Chapter 37, "Audio on the Internet," covers audio. We'll see how audio files are sent to your computer and played. We'll look at how streaming audio works in detail. *Streaming audio* allows you to play sounds and music on your computer while the audio file is being transferred to your computer, so that you don't have to wait for the file to download.

Chapter 38, "Video on the Internet," details how video works. We'll look at how *streaming video* works, which (like streaming audio) lets you watch a video while it is being downloaded to your computer. Today, you're able to watch news broadcasts, music videos, and even live launches of the space shuttle through streaming video technology.

Chapter 38 also looks at videoconferencing. *Videoconferencing* enables people from different parts of the world to see each other and talk to each other—all through their computers. The voices and images are transferred over the Internet.

In addition, Chapter 38 covers a lighter topic: how NetCams work. *NetCams* are cameras on the Internet that broadcast a photograph or digital animation at regular intervals. NetCams are all over the world, from the top of Pike's Peak to the streets of Hong Kong.

Chapter 39, "How Multicast IP and the MBone Work," looks at Multicast IP and the MBone. *Multicast IP* is a technique that enables videos to be broadcast to many thousands of people simultaneously, without clogging up the Internet's backbone. And the *MBone* is a high-speed Internet backbone used for transmitting Multicast IP video across the Internet.

Chapter 40, "Virtual Reality on the Internet," examines virtual reality. *Virtual reality* allows for the creation of virtual worlds—3D creations on the Web through which you can walk or fly, interacting with your surroundings. As the bandwidth of the Internet increases, these virtual worlds may become increasingly popular.

Finally, Chapter 41, "Animation on the Web," looks at some of the most popular kinds of animation technologies, from the very simple to the very sophisticated. We'll see how *client pull* and *server push* technologies allow for the easy creation of simple animations. And we'll also look at Shockwave, an extremely sophisticated way in which animation, audio, and other kinds of interactive technologies can be used to create powerful multimedia presentations on the Web.

CHAPTER

37

Audio on the Internet

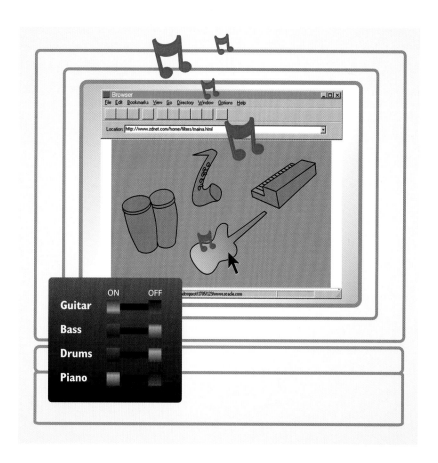

SOUNDS, voices, and music are now an everyday part of the Internet. Through the Internet, you can listen to radio stations, interviews, music, sound clips, and much more.

One of the most intriguing experimental uses of audio on the Internet was Internet Talk Radio. Modeled after National Public Radio, it featured special affairs programs, interviews, and a variety of special reports. Probably the best known show on Internet Talk Radio was "Geek of the Week," in which an Internet expert was interviewed every week. Internet Talk Radio no longer exists.

While Internet Talk Radio was popular, it was also hampered by a technology limitation. To listen to it on your computer, you had to download audio files to your system. Once they were on your computer, you could use special audio software and a sound card to listen to them. The problem was that the files were very large—often well over 10MB—so it could take hours to get them transferred to your computer before you could listen to them.

There are many other kinds of audio files you'll be able to find on the Internet. They all have one thing in common: They have been digitized so that a computer can play them. You'll find many music files and sound clips in a variety of sound formats. Each of those formats has a different extension associated with it, such as .WAV or .AU. To play those files, you'll first have to download them and then have audio player software play them on your computer. Netscape and other browsers have some of these software players built in. For additional formats, you'll have to find and download the player and then configure your browser properly to play them.

An even newer audio format, Rich Music Format (RMF) offers some intriguing possibilities. RMF allows you to interact with music in ways not possible before on the Web. For example, you can use RMF to change the music you're listening to from the Internet by eliminating some instruments or changing the music's tone and pitch.

Most sound files tend to be quite large, even after being compressed. You won't be able to listen to them until the entire file is downloaded, which can take quite awhile. It may take you 15 minutes to download a sound file that has less than a minute of sound in it.

A far better and newer use of audio on the Internet is called streaming audio. It handles audio in a much more clever way. With *streaming audio*, you don't have to wait until the entire audio file is downloaded to play it. Instead, you listen to the audio while it downloads to your computer. There are a variety of technologies that allow for streaming audio. For all of them, you'll need to have the proper audio player and you'll need a different audio player for each specific kind of streaming audio. In this chapter, we'll look at the most popular audio streaming technology, called RealAudio.

How RealAudio Streaming Audio Works

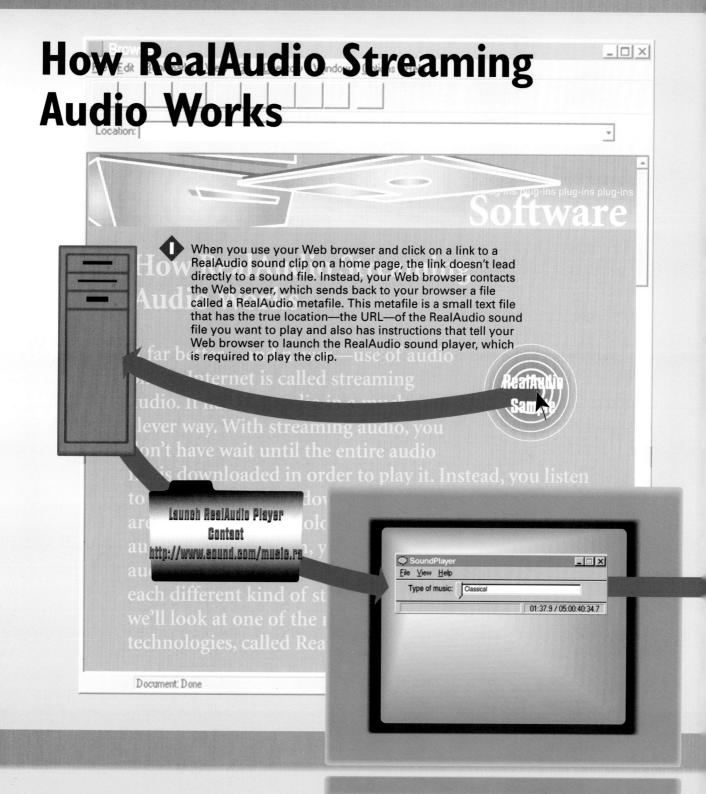

1 When you use your Web browser and click on a link to a RealAudio sound clip on a home page, the link doesn't lead directly to a sound file. Instead, your Web browser contacts the Web server, which sends back to your browser a file called a RealAudio metafile. This metafile is a small text file that has the true location—the URL—of the RealAudio sound file you want to play and also has instructions that tell your Web browser to launch the RealAudio sound player, which is required to play the clip.

Launch RealAudio Player
Contact
http://www.sound.com/music.ra

SoundPlayer
File View Help
Type of music: Classical
01:37.9 / 05:00:40:34.7

Document: Done

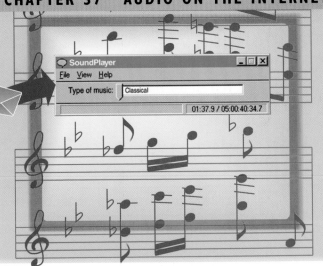

5 The packets are sent to a buffer on the receiving computer. Once the packets exceed the capacity of the buffer, they are sent to the RealAudio player, which then plays the sound file. RealAudio allows you to jump ahead or back in a sound or music clip. When you move to a different place in the clip, the RealAudio player contacts the server and tells it to start sending the file from that new place in the clip.

4 The RealAudio clip has been compressed and encoded. If the file was not compressed, the sound file would be too large and would take too long to send and be played. The clip is sent in IP packets using the UDP (User Datagram Protocol) instead of the Internet's normal TCP (Transmission Control Protocol). UDP doesn't keep resending packets if they are misplaced or other problems occur, as does TCP. If packets had to keep being re-sent, the sound player on the receiving end could be constantly interrupted with packets and could not play the clip.

3 The RealAudio server and the RealAudio sound player "talk" to one another so that the server knows at what speed the user is connected to the Internet. If the connection is a low-speed connection, a smaller RealAudio file is sent that contains less data. This will be a file of lesser quality than a file sent via a high-speed connection. If a high-speed connection is used, a larger, higher-quality sound file is sent. This will provide for better sound quality.

Get http://www.sound.com/music.ra

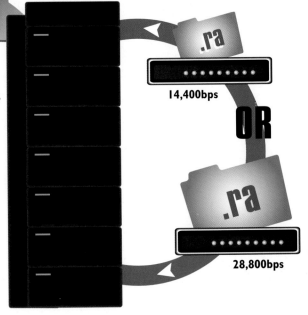

14,400bps

OR

28,800bps

2 The metafile launches the RealAudio sound player, which contacts the URL contained in the metafile. The URL it contacts is not on the Web server. Instead, it is on a different RealAudio server designed to deliver RealAudio sound clips.

RealAudio Server

CHAPTER

38

Video on the Internet

THE Internet began as a way for people to share text-based information such as email, discussion groups, and file transfers. Today, however, the technology has advanced far beyond text. Currently on the Internet, you can have video conferences in which you talk live with someone and see them live on your computer screen. You can use *whiteboard* applications that let you see and talk to other people at their computers, and you can also work on a file together live on your computer screens. You can watch live video footage of astronauts from outer space. You can also watch taped videos whenever you want—not when a national broadcaster says you must watch them.

To understand how all this works, you'll need to understand three kinds of technologies. The first is called the *MBone (Multicast Backbone)*, a special Internet high-speed backbone capable of sending vast amounts of information. Many video transmissions—especially live ones—are sent across the MBone because of its high bandwidth. Turn to Chapter 39, "How Multicast IP and the MBone Work," for more information on the MBone.

The second technology is called streaming video. *Streaming video* solves a long-standing problem of sending video signals across the Internet. Video files tend to be extremely large because they have so much information packed into them. Because of that, sending video was never very practical—it could take hours to send a single video file to someone's computer. The person on the other end would have to wait until the entire file was downloaded and then play it—and it might play for only a few minutes.

Streaming video solves the problem in two ways. First, it compresses the video file dramatically so it is much smaller as it is transmitted across the Internet. Secondly, streaming video lets the receiving computer start playing the video while the file is being transmitted. So if you receive a streaming video file, you watch the video as you receive it; no waiting for the entire file to download. Streaming video files are not usually live broadcasts. Instead, they are often files that are created ahead of time and then posted on the Internet. You can watch the video by clicking on its hypertext link. You'll need a special player to watch the video. There are a number of different ways to send streaming video across the Internet and watch it as it comes to your computer.

The third piece of technology is videoconferencing. It lets you use your computer to have live videoconferences across the Internet. Videoconferencing is done live, although the technology can also be used to broadcast taped videos as well. NASA, the National Aeronautics and Space Administration, sometimes uses the technology to broadcast live from the Space Shuttle and also to broadcast taped videos about space exploration.

NetCams, also called digital cameras, are another intriguing use of video technology. A *NetCam* is a camera attached to the Internet that automatically broadcasts photographs of moving images at certain intervals. Photos can be downloaded or browsed with your Web browser. There are hundreds of NetCams on the Internet, sending live pictures from all over the world.

How Streaming Video Works

1 Streaming video refers to video that you can play live on the Internet—you don't have to wait until the download is complete to see the video. Instead, you can play the video while it is being sent to your computer. VDOLive is an example of streaming video.

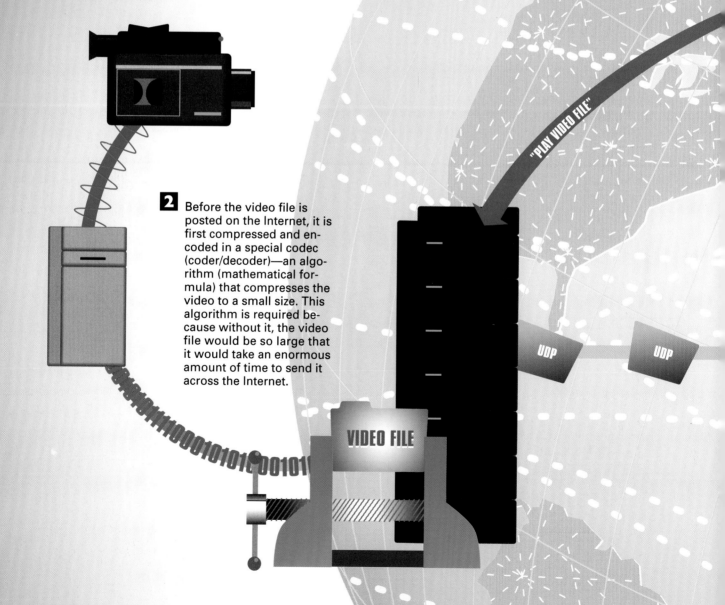

2 Before the video file is posted on the Internet, it is first compressed and encoded in a special codec (coder/decoder)—an algorithm (mathematical formula) that compresses the video to a small size. This algorithm is required because without it, the video file would be so large that it would take an enormous amount of time to send it across the Internet.

"PLAY VIDEO FILE"

UDP

UDP

VIDEO FILE

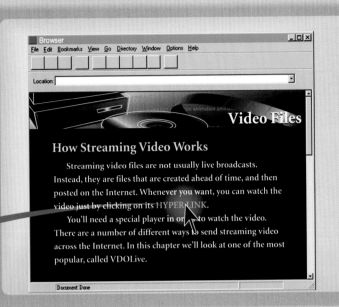

Browser

File Edit Bookmarks View Go Directory Window Options Help

Location:

Video Files

How Streaming Video Works

Streaming video files are not usually live broadcasts. Instead, they are files that are created ahead of time, and then posted on the Internet. Whenever you want, you can watch the video just by clicking on its HYPERLINK.

You'll need a special player in order to watch the video. There are a number of different ways to send streaming video across the Internet. In this chapter we'll look at one of the most popular, called VDOLive.

Document: Done

3 When you send a request to see the video by clicking on an icon or a link on a World Wide Web page, you are sending a message from your computer to a server asking for the video file. The server sends the file to you in packets across the Internet, using the IP protocol. It does not use the normal Internet TCP, though. Instead it uses the UDP (User Datagram Protocol). Unlike TCP, the UDP does not constantly check to see if data has been sent, so it results in a more uninterrupted file transfer.

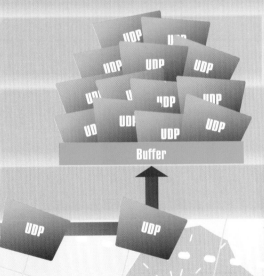

Buffer

4 The video packets are sent to a buffer in your computer—an area of memory that ranges between 5KB and 30KB. The server can tell by how fast the buffer fills up what speed connection you have to the server. At higher speeds, it will send more video data and you will get a smoother, more lifelike video. At lower speeds, it sends less data, which causes the video quality to suffer.

5 When the buffer fills up, which takes only a few seconds, a video player is launched on your computer. You can now watch the video on the player. As you watch the video, video packets are still being delivered to your buffer. Data from the buffer is continually sent to the player so that you can watch an entire video. When all the video data has been sent, the video will stop. The video file does not stay on your system; each section of the file is discarded after it is played.

How Videoconferencing Works

1 There are a variety of ways for people to videoconference across the Internet. Most require client software that allows people to send and receive video and audio signals. Also involved are special kinds of server hardware and software (sometimes called reflectors) that host the videoconference and send the signals to everyone connected to the server.

2 When one person wants to videoconference with someone else, he or she uses client software to log into a reflector. A *reflector* is an Internet computer that hosts many live video-conferences that people can join. When you log into a reflector, you can join any conference that exists. When someone is logged into a reflector, a signal goes out regularly from the person's computer to the reflector, telling everyone connected to the reflector that the person is logged in and available for a videoconference.

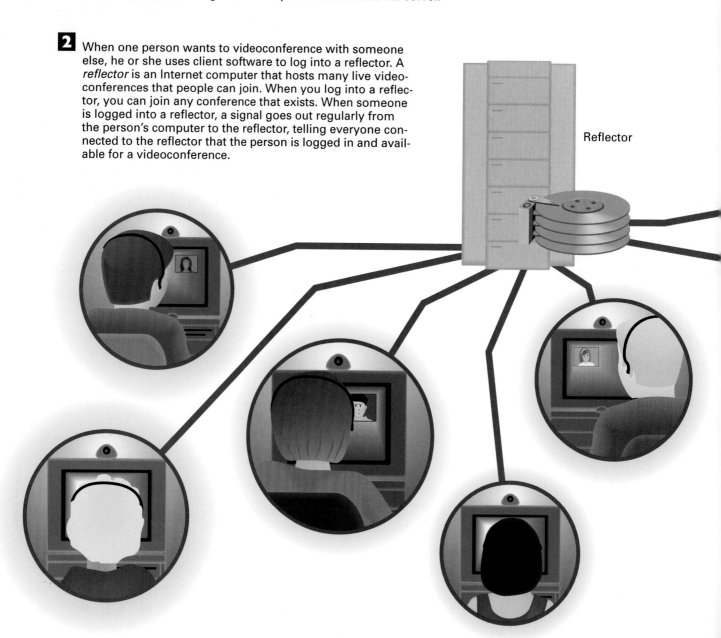

Reflector

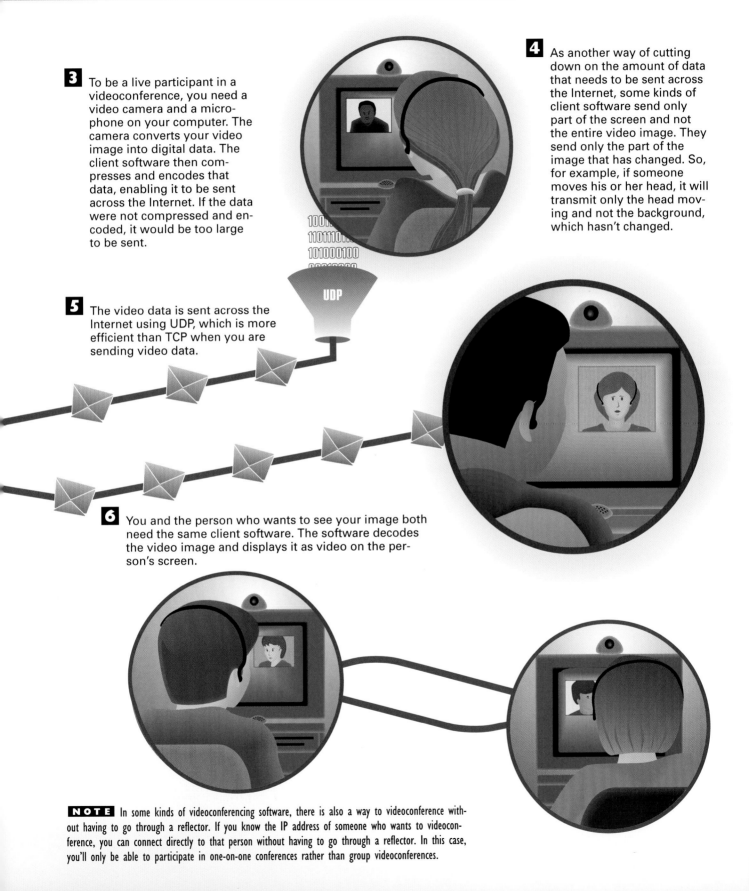

3 To be a live participant in a videoconference, you need a video camera and a microphone on your computer. The camera converts your video image into digital data. The client software then compresses and encodes that data, enabling it to be sent across the Internet. If the data were not compressed and encoded, it would be too large to be sent.

4 As another way of cutting down on the amount of data that needs to be sent across the Internet, some kinds of client software send only part of the screen and not the entire video image. They send only the part of the image that has changed. So, for example, if someone moves his or her head, it will transmit only the head moving and not the background, which hasn't changed.

5 The video data is sent across the Internet using UDP, which is more efficient than TCP when you are sending video data.

6 You and the person who wants to see your image both need the same client software. The software decodes the video image and displays it as video on the person's screen.

NOTE In some kinds of videoconferencing software, there is also a way to videoconference without having to go through a reflector. If you know the IP address of someone who wants to videoconference, you can connect directly to that person without having to go through a reflector. In this case, you'll only be able to participate in one-on-one conferences rather than group videoconferences.

How NetCams Work

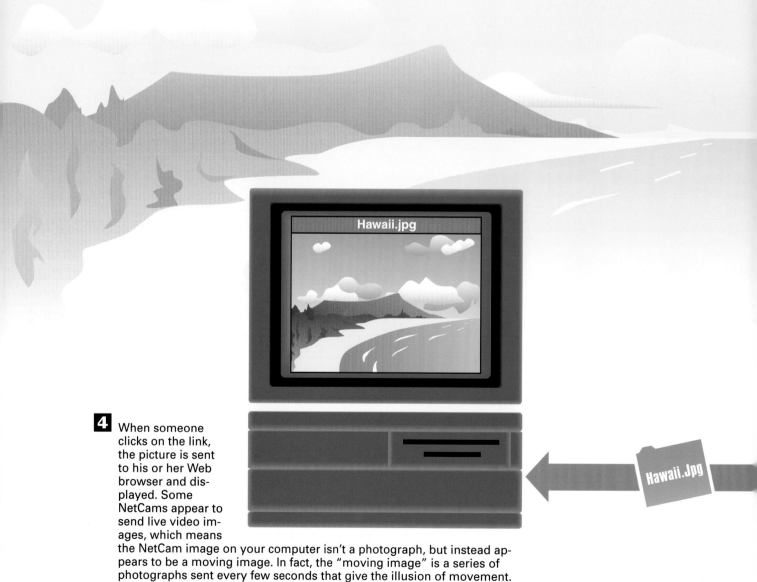

4 When someone clicks on the link, the picture is sent to his or her Web browser and displayed. Some NetCams appear to send live video images, which means the NetCam image on your computer isn't a photograph, but instead appears to be a moving image. In fact, the "moving image" is a series of photographs sent every few seconds that give the illusion of movement. When you click on the link to the image, the images will automatically be sent to your Web browser as the video camera updates them.

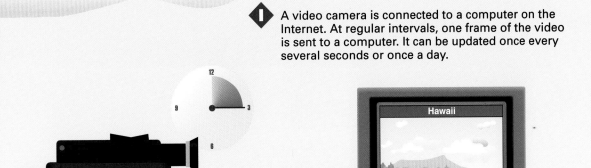

1 A video camera is connected to a computer on the Internet. At regular intervals, one frame of the video is sent to a computer. It can be updated once every several seconds or once a day.

2 The picture is sent to the computer attached to the Internet. A video capture board or other hardware captures the image by converting it into binary format that computers can read. Typically, the picture is converted into the JPEG format—a graphics format that compresses the image while still retaining a high level of detail.

Hawaii.jpg

10010110100010100101010101011010
01101000101001010101101010101011
10010111101011010010101011010
11101000101001010101110100011
10010110100010100101010101011010
01101000101001010101101010101011
10010111101011010010101011010
11101000101001010101110100011

Web Server

3 The JPEG image is linked to a specific URL on a Web home page. The link stays constant, even though the image itself changes regularly. That means whenever someone clicks on the link, that person will see the most recent picture that was taken by the NetCam.

CHAPTER

39

How Multicast IP and the MBone Work

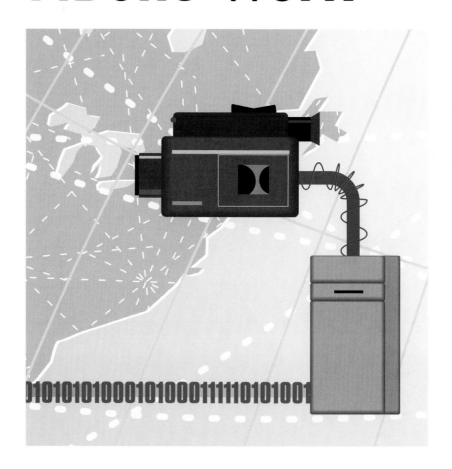

TO a great extent, the Internet of today is still in its infancy. Although multimedia elements can be found on it, it's still largely made up of text and static pictures. These text and static pictures individually take up very little space—an entire Web page made up of text and pictures, for example, is often only 50 kilobytes (KB) or less.

The Internet of tomorrow, however, will be made up of a wide variety of multimedia elements: sound, video, animation, 3D objects, and more. Web pages will become interactive, and video-based shows may be broadcast over the Internet.

All this will cause serious congestion on the wires and networks that make up the Internet. One more problem exists, as well: There's no practical way for broadcasts to be sent out over the Internet, because the files would clog up the Internet. Suppose, for example, that someone wants to broadcast a telecast of a concert. The size of the file that contains that broadcast may be 50 megabytes (MB). Now imagine that 10,000 people want to watch the concert. That 50MB file needs to be sent individually to each of those 10,000 people—and as you can imagine, that single broadcast could easily clog entire sections of the Internet, and the broadcast couldn't be delivered.

A potential answer is on the horizon, however, called the Multicast Backbone, or the MBone. The *MBone* is a high-capacity Internet backbone for transmitting broadcasts using the IP multicast protocol. It enables broadcasts to start out as a single transmission instead of, for example, 10,000 transmissions. Inside that transmission are the addresses of all the people who want to see the broadcast. As the file is sent across the Internet, it eventually makes copies of itself when necessary and delivers the broadcast to the networks and individuals who want to see it.

Suppose that 100 people want to see a broadcast of a 50MB file. Fifty people who want to see it are connected to the Internet via the WorldNet Internet Service Provider. 25 people are on a corporate network at zd.com. And another 25 use the Internet Access Company Internet Service Provider. When the broadcast goes out, it goes out as one single file, not 100 separate files. The file then splits into three parts. One part goes to WorldNet. One part goes to zd.com. One part goes to the Internet Access Company. After the file is on each of those separate networks, it is delivered to the people inside the networks who want to see it. The key here, though, is that instead of 100 files of 50MB traveling across the Internet—5 gigabytes (GB) of data—only three 50MB files travel, or 150MB of data. As you can see, the MBone can cut down tremendously the amount of traffic traveling across the Internet.

How Multicast IP Broadcasts Travel Along the MBone

1 The MBone (Multicast Backbone) is a high-speed Internet backbone capable of sending live video and audio broadcasts. It's a network of host computers that communicate with each other using a technique called IP (Internet Protocol) Multicast. An MBone multicast begins when a video signal is digitized and compressed so that it can be sent over the Internet. Without compression, the signal would be too large and take too long to deliver.

2 The compressed, digitized signal is sent in packets using the IP multicast protocol instead of the Internet's normal TCP protocol. The multicast protocol enables the signal to be sent to a number of sites on the Internet simultaneously. Normally, the Internet is unicast, which means that each signal can be sent only to a single, specific location.

3 A major advantage of the multicast protocol is that when the video packets are sent—for example, from Europe to the United States—they are sent only one time, even though they may be sent to many destinations. Normally, TCP would have to send separate video packets for each destination. The multicast protocol solves the problem by putting information about the many Internet destinations within the packet, so that later on in the transmission, the video signals will be delivered to each of the destinations.

IP

IP
Multicast
Protocol

IP
Multicast
Protocol

MBone

IP
Multicast
Protocol

IP
Multicast
Protocol

IP
Multicast
Protocol

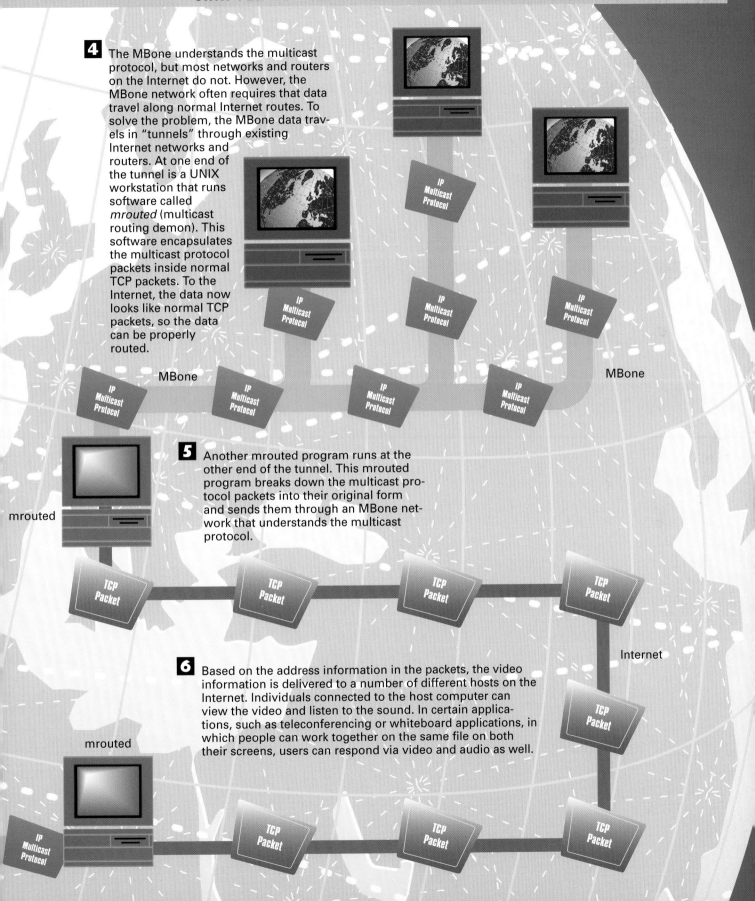

4 The MBone understands the multicast protocol, but most networks and routers on the Internet do not. However, the MBone network often requires that data travel along normal Internet routes. To solve the problem, the MBone data travels in "tunnels" through existing Internet networks and routers. At one end of the tunnel is a UNIX workstation that runs software called *mrouted* (multicast routing demon). This software encapsulates the multicast protocol packets inside normal TCP packets. To the Internet, the data now looks like normal TCP packets, so the data can be properly routed.

5 Another mrouted program runs at the other end of the tunnel. This mrouted program breaks down the multicast protocol packets into their original form and sends them through an MBone network that understands the multicast protocol.

6 Based on the address information in the packets, the video information is delivered to a number of different hosts on the Internet. Individuals connected to the host computer can view the video and listen to the sound. In certain applications, such as teleconferencing or whiteboard applications, in which people can work together on the same file on both their screens, users can respond via video and audio as well.

CHAPTER
40

Virtual Reality on the Internet

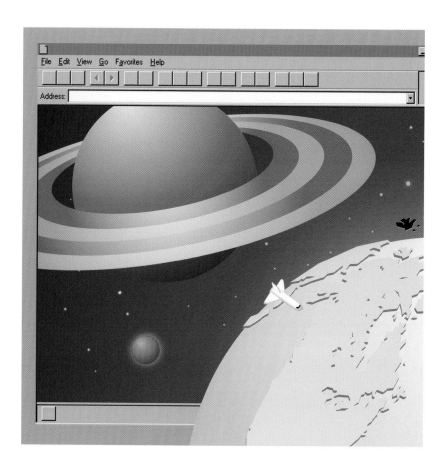

IMAGINE the Internet as a place where you could walk through three-dimensional worlds, pick up objects, examine them, and go to other Internet locations by flying or walking through doors. Picture home pages that were more than flat, two-dimensional surfaces that you could only read. What if you could be inside them, just like you can walk through a city or a building?

That's the promise of virtual reality (VR) on the Internet. In fact, it's more than just a promise—VR is already here. You'll find many virtual worlds you can explore on the Internet. You'll be able to walk through a giant computer, explore bizarre art galleries, visit outer space, go to the sites of what seem like ancient ruins, explore inside the human brain, and much more.

Virtual worlds are created using a computer language called Virtual Reality Modeling Language (VRML). This language instructs computers on how to build 3D geometric objects. Programmers and artists use the language to build complex worlds from these geometric objects. A VRML world is created by an ASCII text file containing VRML language commands—and for greater realism, graphics files can be added to this world as well. Because the virtual world is only an ASCII file, with perhaps a few graphics files, it can be downloaded quickly to your computer from the Internet, although some worlds with many graphics in them can be large.

When a virtual world is created, it is posted on an Internet server. When you want to visit that world, you either type in its URL or click on a link to it, just as you do to visit any other location on the World Wide Web. To display the virtual world, you'll need a program that is able to display the world—either a separate virtual reality browser, or more likely, a plug-in player that configures itself to your normal Web browser.

The VRML file describing the virtual world downloads to your computer. This can take a few minutes, or well over half an hour, depending on the size of the world and your connection speed. Once the file is on your computer, your CPU computes the geometry of the world, based on the VRML commands in the file. Again, depending on the size of the world and the speed of your CPU, this can take only a minute or two, or up to ten minutes or more. Once the world is computed, you can walk through it, fly through it, examine objects, and spin them. You can also visit other virtual worlds or places on the Internet by interacting with the world.

VR on the Internet is being used for far more than just creating virtual worlds that people can walk through. For example, it has been used to create views of the brain and of molecules. It has been used by astronomers to show the rotation of molecular gas in a galaxy undergoing active star formation. Finally, as with everything else related to the Internet, VR will be eventually used for things that today none of us can imagine.

Despite all its appeal, one major problem with VR worlds is that they can be very large. Because of that, they can be very slow to load and interact with due to the current limited bandwidth of the Internet. As bandwidth increases, those problems may eventually go away.

How Virtual Reality Works

1 When someone wants to create a virtual world, he or she uses the Virtual Reality Modeling Language (VRML). VRML lets people create 3D worlds not by drawing them, but instead by using the VRML computer language to describe the geometry of a scene. VRML files are much smaller than graphics files. VRML files are simply text files that contain instructions for drawing the VRML world. VRML files end in a .WRL extension. After the world is created, it is posted on a Web server.

```
==================== SPACE.WRL ====================
#VRML V1.0 ascii
Separator {
    DirectionalLight {
        direction 0 0 -1  # Light
shining from viewer into scene
    }
    PerspectiveCamera {
        position    -8.6 2.1 5.6
        orientation -0.1352 -0.9831 -
0.1233  1.1417
        focalDistance       10.84
    }
```

2 Here is an example of a VRML file describing a scene that has a red sphere and a blue cube in it, lit by a directional light.

```
==================== OBJECTS.WRL ====================
#VRML V1.0 ascii
Separator {
    DirectionalLight {
        direction 0 0 -1  # Light shining from viewer into scene
    }
    PerspectiveCamera {
        position    -8.6 2.1 5.6
        orientation -0.1352 -0.9831 -0.1233  1.1417
        focalDistance       10.84
    }
    Separator {   # The red sphere
        Material {
            diffuseColor 1 0 0   # Red
        }
        Translation { translation 3 0 1 }
        Sphere { radius 2.3 }
    }
    Separator {   # The blue cube
        Material {
            diffuseColor 0 0 1  # Blue
        }
        Transform {
            translation -2.4 .2 1
            rotation 0 1 1   .9
        }
        Cube {}
    }
}
```

1001000110
0100010100
010001

SPACE.WRL

File Edit View Go Favorites Help

Address:

6 For greater realism and detail, graphics files can be "painted" on virtual reality objects, for example, to show paintings in an art gallery. When these graphics files are painted on objects, they must be downloaded along with the .WRL file as .GIF or .JPEG files. When the browser displays the virtual world, it shows those graphics files on top of VR objects so that they look like part of the scene.

5 Objects in the virtual world can be links to sites on the Web, to other virtual worlds, and to animations. So, for example, if you walk through a door, you might be sent to a home page on the Internet, or to another virtual world. If you're sent to another virtual world, that virtual world will have to be downloaded from a Web server to your computer so your browser can compute the new world and you can interact with it.

4 As the file downloads, the VR plug-in is launched. It doesn't run separately from your Web browser. Instead, it takes over your Web browser while you're in the virtual world. After the file is downloaded, your VR plug-in creates the virtual world by taking the VRML commands in the file and having your computer compute the geometry of the scene. Once the computation is done, the scene will appear on your screen. The VRML file contains three-dimensional information that allows you to "walk" or "fly" through the scene using your browser. Depending upon the complexity of the scene, your computer may have to do computations as you move through the scene.

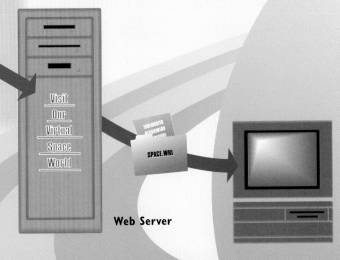

Web Server

3 When you have a VR plug-in installed on your Web browser, you can visit a virtual world by clicking on its URL. First, the VRML file is sent from the Web server to your computer. Depending on the size of the virtual world and your connection speed, the file can take from a few minutes to a half-hour or more to download to your computer.

CHAPTER
41

Animation on the Web

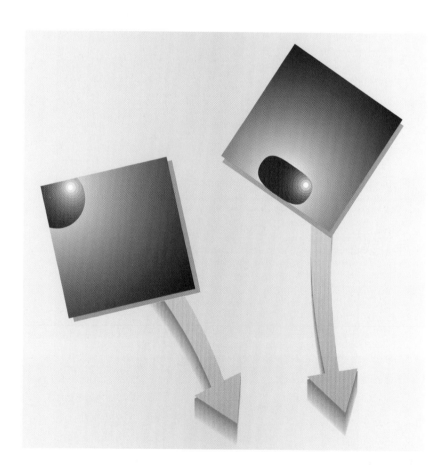

ANIMATION on the Web works no differently than animation anywhere else. Just like in a flip-book, animation is a series of still images displayed in succession to create an illusion of fluid motion. The faster the frames advance, the more fluid the animation becomes. Unfortunately, the Web can be a very slow place, and an animation that should run quickly often crawls across the screen unless special technology is used.

There are a number of different ways to create Web animations, including client pull, server push, animated GIFs, and the Shockwave multimedia plug-in. In *client pull*, an HTML page gives the browser instructions to request and load another document automatically. This feature is like a slideshow. Web pages are displayed one after the other with a specified time delay in between. This is useful for step-by-step instructions. But client pull is slowed by the need to load a whole page rather than a single cell of animation, which prevents the illusion of fluid animation.

Client pull requests are embedded within the HTTP response header of a Web page that is sent back from the server to the client. The <META> tag inserts meta-information into a response header. *Meta-information* is used to help parse a Web page, but it is not displayed by the browser. A *response header* is the beginning of each HTTP response that a server sends back to a client with the requested Web page.

Server push is a complement to client pull, though server push is the more complex of the two. Server push requires a CGI (Common Gateway Interface) script that tells the server when to automatically serve a new document or image. It requires the client browser to be able to recognize the MIME-type called multipart/x-mixed-replace. This MIME-type allows for multiple documents to be sent within one message. To understand how server push works, imagine an email message with text, hypertext, a digital movie and sound, and you can see how multiple "documents" (media types) can be sent within a single message. The multipart message is simply a series of images that displays one right after the other, each being sent or "pushed" by the server. In this way, a small animation can be embedded among the text and images of an otherwise static Web page.

Animated GIFs are a series of graphical GIF images that "roll up" into a single image—much like the flip book "animates" a series of drawings as you thumb through the pages. They load into a browser just like any GIF file, but in a series to give the illusion of motion. Animated GIFs have the benefit of speed because images are cached on the client PC and loaded from memory rather than from the Internet. They represent an easy solution to adding motion to Web pages.

More complex multimedia animation has become possible using Macromedia's Shockwave plug-in. Shockwave plays multimedia files that are created with Macromedia's popular Director and Authorware programs. You must first download and install the Shockwave plug-in before you can view any Web pages that have Shockwave animations.

How Animation Works on the Web

Client Pull

Client pull is executed by the Refresh command. A refresh command is written into an HTML document using the <META> tag. The contents of the <META> tag are added to the header's meta-information sent from the server along with the HTTP response. During a client pull sequence, the browser reads this header information, which instructs it to keep track of the time elapsed between pages retrieved with the help of your PC's internal clock. When the time has elapsed, the browser requests and displays the next page.

Refresh: 5
/page B.html

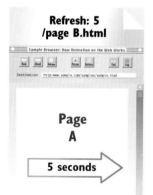

Page A

→ **5 seconds**

Refresh: 10
/page C.html

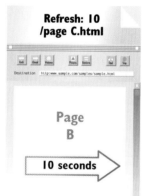

Page B

→ **10 seconds**

Refresh: 2
/page D.html

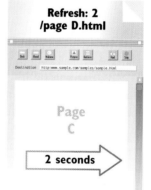

Page C

→ **2 seconds**

Refresh: 5
http://www.server.
com/folder/page E.html

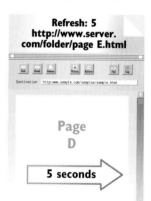

Page D

→ **5 seconds**

Refresh:
/page F.ht

Page F

 1 The Refresh command does two things. First, it indicates the time before the next page request is sent or the same page reloads. For example, page A in the illustration will refresh after five seconds. Secondly, if the URL follows the number of seconds, a request for that page will be sent automatically after five seconds. After the browser parses a document's meta-information and recognizes the Refresh command in the header, it knows to send a request for the page indicated by the URL following the command.

2 If the next document to load also has a Refresh command in the header, the browser will simply repeat the process. In this case, it will retrieve and display page C after 10 seconds.

3 Whoever writes the HTML source code can specify how long it will be until the request for the next page is made. Page C will refresh after only two seconds, followed by page D.

NOTE A client pull sequence may continue for as many or as few pages as the site designer wants. The last page will simply not have a Refresh command in the header. A user may stop the process manually by clicking the browser's Stop button.

4 Each page in a client pull sequence can be located anywhere on the Web. The URL following the Refresh command may lead the browser to any active server. Page E is located on a different server than pages A to D but will still be requested automatically after five seconds.

Server Push

Server push is more complicated than client pull, but it allows for inline animation that does not require an entire Web page to load each animation frame.

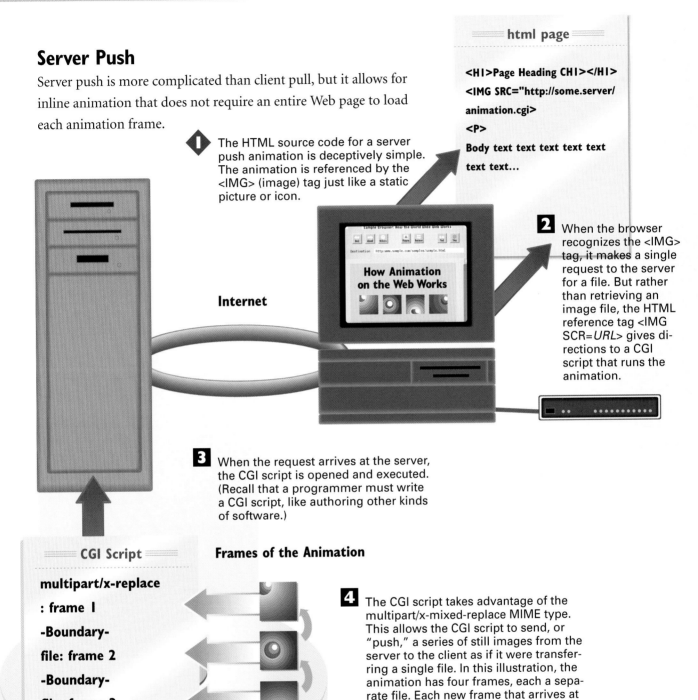

html page

```
<HI>Page Heading CHI></HI>
<IMG SRC="http://some.server/
animation.cgi>
<P>
Body text text text text text
text text...
```

1 The HTML source code for a server push animation is deceptively simple. The animation is referenced by the <IMG> (image) tag just like a static picture or icon.

2 When the browser recognizes the <IMG> tag, it makes a single request to the server for a file. But rather than retrieving an image file, the HTML reference tag <IMG SCR=*URL*> gives directions to a CGI script that runs the animation.

Internet

How Animation on the Web Works

3 When the request arrives at the server, the CGI script is opened and executed. (Recall that a programmer must write a CGI script, like authoring other kinds of software.)

CGI Script

Frames of the Animation

```
multipart/x-replace
: frame I
-Boundary-
file: frame 2
-Boundary-
file: frame 3
-Boundary-
file: frame 4 etc.
```

4 The CGI script takes advantage of the multipart/x-mixed-replace MIME type. This allows the CGI script to send, or "push," a series of still images from the server to the client as if it were transferring a single file. In this illustration, the animation has four frames, each a separate file. Each new frame that arrives at the client replaces the old one, thereby giving the illusion of fluid movement.

NOTE The server and client make one connection that is open for as long as the CGI script runs. You can manually end a server push animation by clicking the browser's Stop button.

How Shockwave Works

1 The first step in a Shockwave animation happens in a multimedia authoring program such as Director or Authorware. An animation designer must gather the raw materials necessary for a short and compelling animation, such as still images, music, and sound effects.

4 Next, the movie file must be converted and compressed into a small file that can be quickly downloaded to a user's PC. This conversion process is done with Afterburner, another Macromedia product.

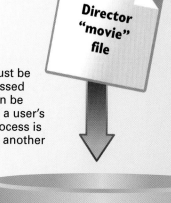

Director "movie" file

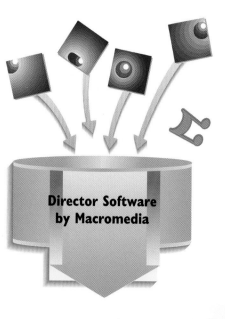

Director Software by Macromedia

Converts Director file to Shockwave file

Compress file

Timeline

frame 1   frame 2   frame 3

sound effect   sound effect

music

clickable button
stop

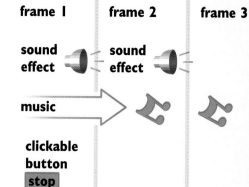

2 The authoring program then helps arrange the elements frame by frame along a time line. It also allows the designer to match a sound effect with a particular action in the animation.

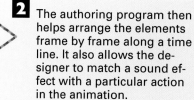

Director "movie" file

3 When this step is done, the complete animation is saved as a Director or Authorware movie file.

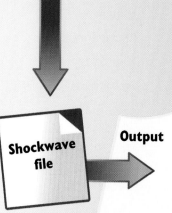

Shockwave file

Output

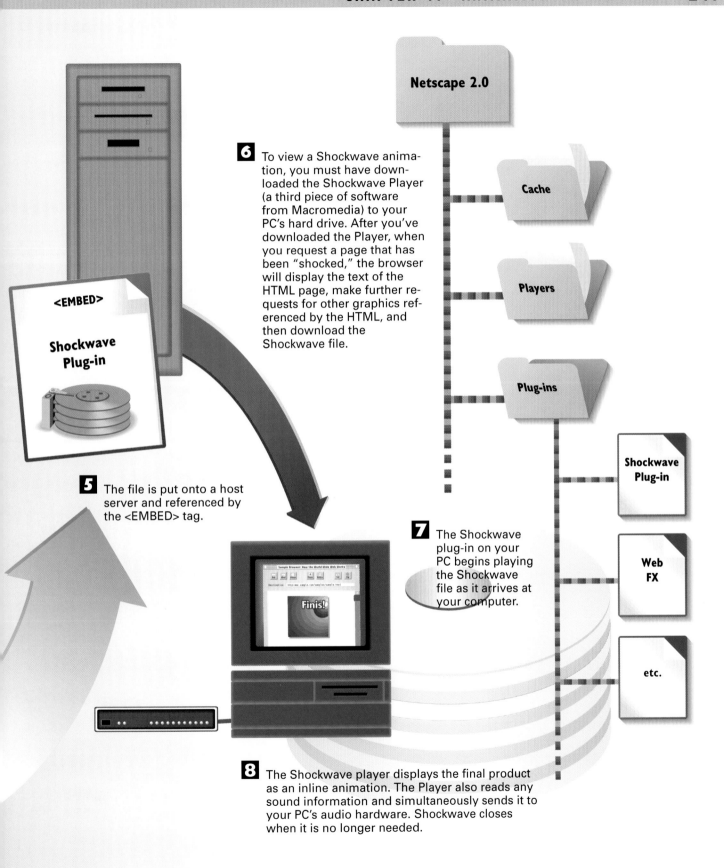

Netscape 2.0

Cache

Players

Plug-ins

6 To view a Shockwave animation, you must have downloaded the Shockwave Player (a third piece of software from Macromedia) to your PC's hard drive. After you've downloaded the Player, when you request a page that has been "shocked," the browser will display the text of the HTML page, make further requests for other graphics referenced by the HTML, and then download the Shockwave file.

<EMBED>

Shockwave Plug-in

5 The file is put onto a host server and referenced by the <EMBED> tag.

Shockwave Plug-in

Web FX

etc.

7 The Shockwave plug-in on your PC begins playing the Shockwave file as it arrives at your computer.

Finis!

8 The Shockwave player displays the final product as an inline animation. The Player also reads any sound information and simultaneously sends it to your PC's audio hardware. Shockwave closes when it is no longer needed.

P A R T

9

THE INTERNET, INTRANETS, AND THE OUTSIDE WORLD

THE Internet is no longer a self-enclosed club with no connection to the outside world. It has become intimately tied to the way we live and work, and it will become more so with each passing year. At work, for entertainment, to get information, to shop—the Internet is increasingly becoming a part of our daily lives.

The Internet may have its roots in the military and in academia, but its dramatic growth has been fueled in large part by business and consumers. The Internet may become one of the primary places in which businesses operate, and where hundreds of billions of dollars in goods and services will be bought and sold every year.

Thousands of businesses use the Internet to market and sell their products, and so many people buy things from home and from their places of business through the Internet instead of at retail stores. You can use the Internet to browse through catalogs and make purchases online; to buy and sell stock, mortgages and insurance; and even to participate in online auctions. Companies are figuring out ways not only to sell online, but also to hook those online transactions into their internal computer and billing systems.

This part of the book looks at the various ways that the Internet interacts with the outside world. It covers how the Internet is being used by businesses as their primary corporate network, and how business and commerce is being conducted on the Internet.

Chapter 42, "How Intranets Work," covers intranets. *Intranets* are private networks set up by companies for their employees, using Internet technology. Intranets are used for many purposes, including email, group brainstorming, group scheduling, and access to corporate databases and documents, among others.

Although intranets use TCP/IP networks and technologies, the network and its resources are used only by the businesses and are not available to people outside the company. Intranets are separated from the Internet by firewalls that don't allow unauthorized access to the intranet. People who work in the company can access the intranet and use its resources, but intruders are kept out by the firewalls.

Chapter 43, "How Workgroup Software Works," looks at one of the most important parts of an intranet—*workgroup software.* This kind of software ties together everyone in a corporation and enables them to work together better. Among other things, it enables people to share files and information; to cooperate more easily on projects; and in general, to work together in ways never before possible. It allows people to go beyond simply communicating, and enables them to work together on shared documents.

Chapter 43 looks at a variety of workgroup software. It covers messaging software that enables people to publicly participate in group discussions. It also looks at *whiteboard software*, which allows people to see what is on other people's computers and work together on documents. Several people could look at a spreadsheet together, for example, and one person could mark up the spreadsheet while everyone else sees what is being done.

Chapter 44, "Shopping on the Internet," covers shopping. Shopping on the Internet already accounts for billions of dollars a year in revenue, and every year many more billions are spent. One problem remains, however; by its very nature, the Internet is an insecure network, and so ways must be found to safeguard information, such as credit card numbers. Chapter 44 looks at how credit card transactions can be done securely across the Internet, and it looks at technologies such as electronic cash, also called Ecash, and anonymous payments.

CHAPTER

42

How Intranets Work

BUSINESSES will increasingly use Internet technology to create private corporate networks called *intranets* that will replace current local area networks and will be the prime computing resources of corporations.

Corporations can set up intranets for a wide variety of purposes, including email, group brainstorming, group scheduling, access to corporate databases and documents, video conferencing, as well as buying and selling goods and services.

Intranets use TCP/IP networks and technologies as well as Internet resources such as the World Wide Web, email, Telnet, and FTP. However, the network and its resources are used privately by businesses and are not available to people outside the company. An intranet is separated from the rest of the Internet by a *firewall*—a hardware and software combination that prohibits unauthorized access to the intranet. People who work in the company can access the Internet and use its resources, but intruders are kept out by the firewalls. Turn to Chapter 45, "How Firewalls Work," to learn more about firewalls.

Intranets use a combination of off-the-shelf software such as Web browsers, and customized software such as database querying tools. Because intranets are based on Internet standard protocols, it will always be possible to quickly update them with the latest in network technologies.

In the long term, companies will make the most use of intranets in *workgroup applications*— software that allows people to work cooperatively with their computers. There are many different kinds of workgroup software. These programs allow people to participate in discussions and videoconferencing across the country and across the world, share databases, track documents, and much more. For details on workgroup software, turn to Chapter 43, "How Workgroup Software Works."

Using an Intranet Within a Company

1 An intranet is separated from the rest of the Internet by a *firewall*—a hardware/software combination that protects the corporate intranet from snooping eyes and malicious attacks. The firewall allows corporate employees to use the Internet and also allows certain parts of the intranet—such as areas designed for electronic commerce—to be accessed by outsiders.

2 A key component of an intranet is an internal email system. The email system works just like Internet email. It can use normal Internet email clients, except that it is designed to route traffic within an organization so the email need not travel outside the intranet. Internal routers and mail servers send the mail to other corporate employees via the intranet. Email that travels to and from the Internet from the intranet must go through the firewall.

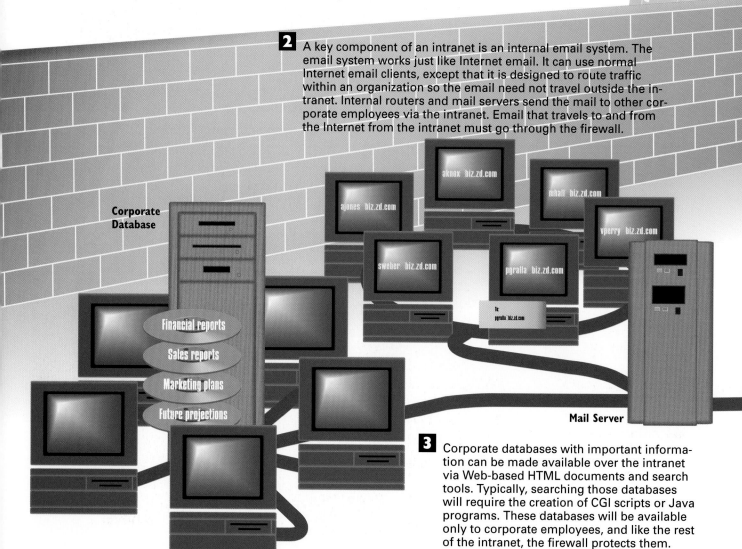

Corporate Database

Financial reports

Sales reports

Marketing plans

Future projections

aknox biz.zd.com

ajones biz.zd.com

mhall biz.zd.com

vperry biz.zd.com

sweber biz.zd.com

pgralla biz.zd.com

To:
pgralla biz.zd.com

Mail Server

3 Corporate databases with important information can be made available over the intranet via Web-based HTML documents and search tools. Typically, searching those databases will require the creation of CGI scripts or Java programs. These databases will be available only to corporate employees, and like the rest of the intranet, the firewall protects them.

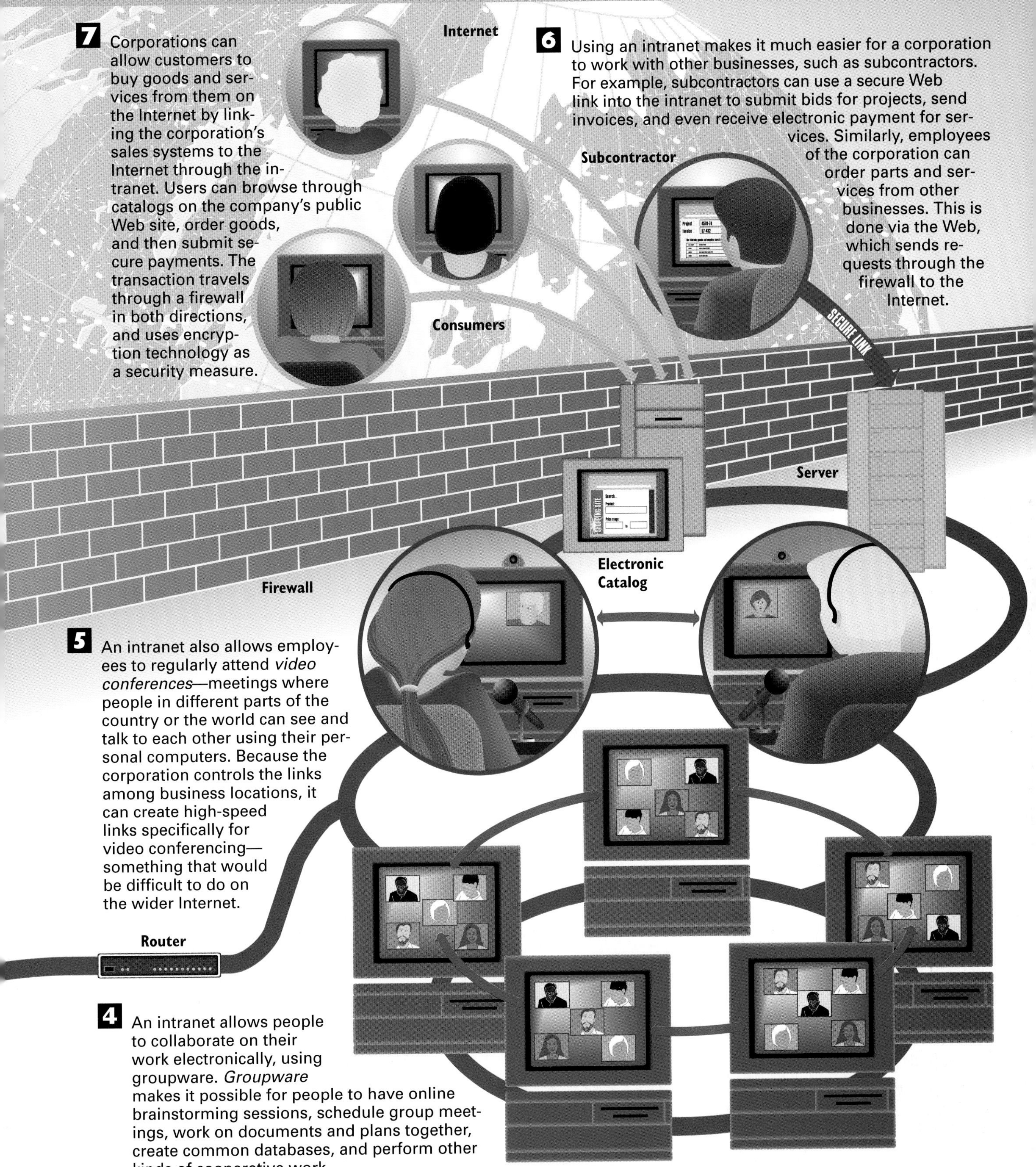

7 Corporations can allow customers to buy goods and services from them on the Internet by linking the corporation's sales systems to the Internet through the intranet. Users can browse through catalogs on the company's public Web site, order goods, and then submit secure payments. The transaction travels through a firewall in both directions, and uses encryption technology as a security measure.

Internet

Consumers

6 Using an intranet makes it much easier for a corporation to work with other businesses, such as subcontractors. For example, subcontractors can use a secure Web link into the intranet to submit bids for projects, send invoices, and even receive electronic payment for services. Similarly, employees of the corporation can order parts and services from other businesses. This is done via the Web, which sends requests through the firewall to the Internet.

Subcontractor

SECURE LINK

Server

Electronic Catalog

Firewall

5 An intranet also allows employees to regularly attend *video conferences*—meetings where people in different parts of the country or the world can see and talk to each other using their personal computers. Because the corporation controls the links among business locations, it can create high-speed links specifically for video conferencing— something that would be difficult to do on the wider Internet.

Router

4 An intranet allows people to collaborate on their work electronically, using groupware. *Groupware* makes it possible for people to have online brainstorming sessions, schedule group meetings, work on documents and plans together, create common databases, and perform other kinds of cooperative work.

C H A P T E R

43

How Workgroup Software Works

WORKGROUP software, also called groupware, is at the heart of intranets. It lets people share files and information; cooperate more easily on projects; and in general, work together in ways never before possible. The key is that it allows people to go beyond simply communicating and lets them work together on shared documents.

One of the most basic pieces of workgroup software is *messaging software*—programs that allow people to publicly participate in group discussions. These group discussions are threaded, which means that people can read and respond to individual subject areas of a discussion. For example, in a message area devoted to corporate finances, there may be one thread concerning research and development finances and another concerning engineering finances.

What makes intranet messaging software especially useful is the way it integrates with other Internet and intranet technologies. For example, some discussion software will allow the use of Hypertext Markup Language (HTML) embedded inside messages. This means that from within a discussion, someone could embed a link to a Web page or other intranet resource.

A more sophisticated workgroup application is desktop videoconferencing. It requires that everyone involved have computer-linked video cameras (which have become quite inexpensive) as well as hardware and software that allows computers to send and receive voice and sound. While sitting at computers, people can see each other and speak to each other.

A related technology is called whiteboard software. *Whiteboard software* lets people see what is on someone else's computer on an intranet while sitting at their own computer. More importantly, whiteboard software allows people to use a mouse to highlight parts of the screen, write on the screen, and otherwise mark it up. This means people on the same intranet—even if they're on opposite sides of the country from each other—can comment on each other's work easily.

Document management software and work flow groupware are useful for intranets in companies that have complicated work procedures, or where many people must cooperatively put together a single document. In intranet document management software, a document can be "locked" so that only one person at a time can use it, and so people can't overwrite each other's work. It can also give different people different kinds of rights to a particular document, so that some people may only be able to read documents, while others are able to actually work on them, edit them, and otherwise change them. The most powerful document management software allows many different people to work on different parts of the same document simultaneously.

Work flow groupware is similar to document management software. This kind of groupware manages the entire work flow of an organization in addition to handling individual documents. For example, intranet work flow groupware allows procedures for filing expense reports to be easily computerized.

How Workgroup Software Works

1 Discussion software allows people from within a corporation to exchange work and ideas. Included in the software are links to other intranet resources. From within a discussion, people can link out to a Web page on the Internet or intranet, or even link into intranet databases, servers, or shared applications. Additionally, software can replicate intranet discussions onto Internet newsgroups. From one discussion area, people on an intranet can hold discussions with people from within their company or people out on the Internet.

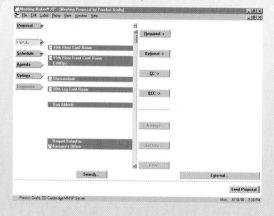

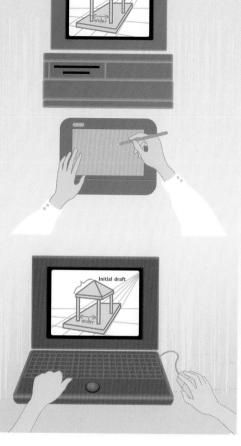

5 Whiteboard applications will be a popular workgroup use of intranets. In a whiteboard application, two or more people can see what is on each other's computer screens across the intranet and they can talk about what they see. Additionally, they can mark up what is displayed on each other's screens.

4 With intranet groupware, videoconferencing can finally be a corporate reality. Desktop conferencing software allows two or more people to see each other and talk to each other on their computer screens, as long as they have cameras connected to their computers and sound-equipped computers. Because intranets can be built using very high bandwidth connections, it's possible to have a videoconference across an intranet, while it can be much more difficult to do it across the Internet because of the lower bandwidth of the Internet.

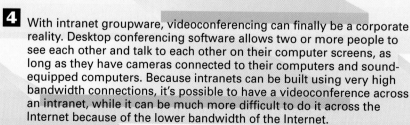

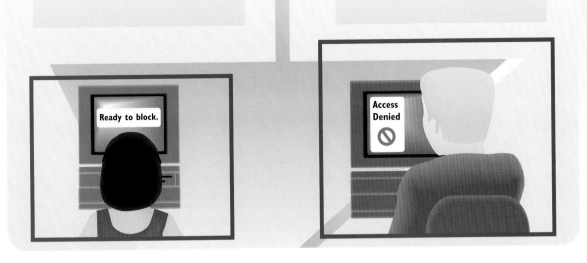

2 Document management software and work flow groupware allows intranet administrators to create systems that track and control access to documents through every aspect of their creation—for example, allowing only one person at a time to check a document out of a library. They can provide a "version history" of every document so anyone can see who has worked on it along with the changes that person made. The administrators can also give certain people the right to "lock" the document so no further changes are allowed.

3 Groupware can allow for desk-to-desk chats. People can sit at their computers and directly communicate with others sitting at their computers by typing on their keyboards. What one person types at the keyboard shows up on another person's computer screen and vice versa.

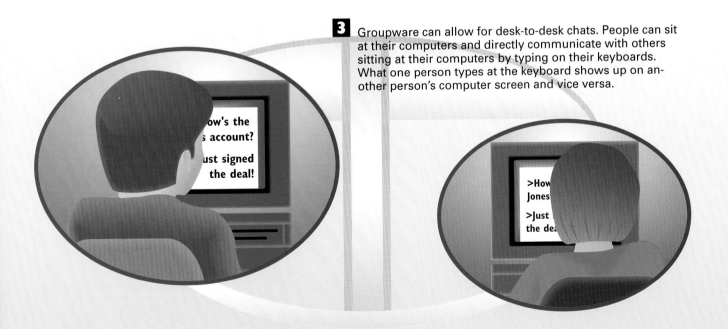

CHAPTER 44

Shopping on the Internet

BILLIONS of dollars are expected to be spent every year shopping on the Internet. You can already buy almost anything on the Internet—whether it be a book or a new car. Some day, buying over the Internet may become as common as shopping by mail or even in retail stores.

There's one problem with online shopping: The Internet is an insecure network. As packets travel across it, anyone along the way could conceivably examine those packets. Because of that, there are potential dangers to doing business online—if you pay over the Internet with a credit card, someone could snoop at it and steal your credit card number.

A number of ways to make payments across the Internet have sprung up to solve this problem. Most use procedures and protocols designed to make financial transactions on the Internet as confidential as possible, using encryption technology to make sure that no one can steal your credit card number. Dozens of organizations, including Microsoft, Netscape, the major credit card companies, automated finance services, and Internet and Web standards-setting bodies, are developing schemes to provide secure, encrypted financial transactions over the Internet.

Schemes for secure transactions take two approaches. One approach encrypts personal financial information, such as a credit card number, so that it can be transferred across the Internet in a manner that would not let prying eyes read the data. The second method creates a system of *cyber-dollars*, electronic credits that only authorized merchants can redeem for real money.

The Secure Electronic Transaction protocol (SET) has been endorsed by VISA, MasterCard, American Express, Microsoft, and Netscape, among other companies. It describes a way that people can shop online and have the purchases charged to their credit cards. Because this method of payment has gotten backing from so many major software and financial companies, there is a good chance it will become a standard for buying online in the future.

In addition to secured credit card transactions, a number of companies are working on electronic, or "cyber-dollar," scenarios that will enable consumers to purchase goods and services anonymously. That is, the consumer uses the digital equivalent of paper currency to make purchases and need not provide personal information (such as credit card or bank information) to do so. Using this method of electronic payment, consumers buy electronic "coins" or "tokens" and use these specially marked and encrypted coins to make purchases.

Both credit card systems and electronic cash systems have their advantages and disadvantages. Credit card encryption schemes are convenient and don't ask customers to change their usual purchasing methods. Transactions are charged to the credit card and appear on the customer's credit card statement as does any other purchase. Electronic cash is a little less convenient because customers have to buy electronic currency before they can use it. However, electronic currency also brings a certain amount of privacy to electronic purchases.

How Financial Transactions Work on the Internet

1 Gabriel browses through an electronic catalog on a Web site and he decides to buy a camcorder. To use the Secure Electronic Transaction protocol (SET) to pay for it, he will need a credit card from a participating bank and a unique "electronic signature" for his computer; this will verify that he is making the purchase, not an impostor. (In SET, everyone involved in the transaction needs electronic signatures identifying them.) SET also uses public-key encryption technology to encrypt all the information sent between everyone involved in the transaction.

 ORDER FORM

2 Gabriel fills out an order form detailing what he wants to buy, its price, any shipping and handling fees, and taxes. He then selects the method he wants to use to pay. In this case, he decides to pay electronically over the Internet. At this point, he doesn't send his precise credit card number, but instead indicates which credit card he wants to use. The information he sends includes his electronic signature so the merchant can verify it is really Gabriel who wants to do the ordering.

  101010 101100

3 The merchant receives the order form from Gabriel. The merchant's software creates a unique transaction identifier so the transaction can be identified and tracked. The merchant sends this identifier back to Gabriel along with two "electronic certificates," which are required to complete the transaction for his specific bank card. One certificate identifies the merchant and the other certificate identifies a specific *payment gateway*—an electronic gateway to the banking system that processes online payments.

4 Gabriel's software receives the electronic certificates and uses them to create Order Information (OI) and Payment Instructions (PI). It encrypts these messages and includes Gabriel's electronic signature in them. The OI and the PI are then sent back to the merchant.

"VERIFICATION"

5 The merchant's software decrypts Gabriel's OI and uses the electronic signature that Gabriel sent to verify that the order is from him. The merchant sends verification to Gabriel that the order has been made.

6 The merchant's software creates an authorization request for payment and includes with the merchant's digital signature the transaction identifier and the PI received from Gabriel. He encrypts all of it and sends the encrypted request to the payment gateway.

7 The payment gateway decrypts the messages and uses the merchant's digital signature to verify that the message is from the merchant. By examining the PI, it verifies that they have come from Gabriel. The payment gateway then uses a bank card payment system to send an authorization request to the bank that issued Gabriel his bank card, asking if the purchase can be made.

8 When the bank responds that the payment can be made, the payment gateway creates, digitally signs, and encrypts an authorization message, which is sent to the merchant. The merchant's software decrypts the message and uses the digital signature to verify that it came from the payment gateway. Assured of payment, the merchant now ships the camcorder to Gabriel.

9 Some time after the transaction has been completed, the merchant requests payment from the bank. The merchant's software creates a *capture request*, which includes the amount of the transaction, the transaction identifier, a digital signature, and other information about the transaction. The information is encrypted and sent to the payment gateway.

"REQUEST FOR PAYMENT"

10 The payment gateway decrypts the capture request and uses the digital signature to verify it is from the merchant. It sends a request for payment to the bank, using the bank card payment system. It receives a message authorizing payment, encrypts the message, and then sends the authorization to the merchant.

"PAYMENT AUTHORIZATION"

"PAYMENT AUTHORIZATION"

11 The merchant software decrypts the authorization and verifies that it is from the payment gateway. The software then stores the authorization that will be used to reconcile the credit card payment routinely when it is received from the bank.

LEGEND

Internet

Order form

Gabriel's digital signature

Merchant digital signature

Payment gateway electronic signature

Unique transaction identifier

101100

Merchant electronic certificate

101010

Payment gateway electronic certificate

Encryption key

Order information

Payment/instructions

Authorization request

Authorization message

Capture request

How Electronic Cash and Credit Card Encryption Work

Download Helper App
(Not necessary if browser has built-in encryption)

1 First, the customer must download an electronic payment helper application to use when shopping on the Web with "electronic cash." Some browser software already includes this application. The helper application includes an encryption key that encodes personal financial information so that it can only be decoded by the electronic payment service using a special second key.

Internet

Send Set-up Information

Sample Browser: How the Internet Works

Destination http:www.sample.com/samples/sample.html

HOW
Credit Card Encryption Works

Electronic Pay Helper Application

123456789

Insert Encryption Key

3 When a customer makes a purchase, the encrypted payment information is sent along with the purchase order to the merchant. Information is encrypted by applying a unique key to scramble the information. This scrambled information can only be unscrambled by using a special second key.

6 The merchant receives verification in a matter of seconds and then can fulfill the order and send the goods to the customer.

To:

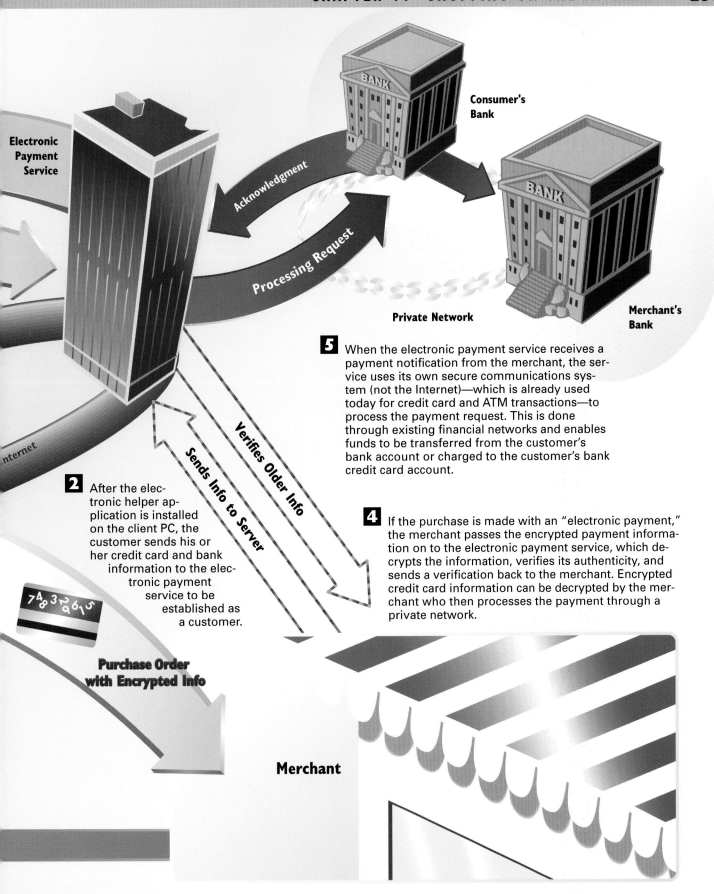

Electronic Payment Service

Consumer's Bank

BANK

BANK

Acknowledgment

Processing Request

Private Network

Merchant's Bank

Internet

5 When the electronic payment service receives a payment notification from the merchant, the service uses its own secure communications system (not the Internet)—which is already used today for credit card and ATM transactions—to process the payment request. This is done through existing financial networks and enables funds to be transferred from the customer's bank account or charged to the customer's bank credit card account.

Verifies Older Info

Sends Info to Server

2 After the electronic helper application is installed on the client PC, the customer sends his or her credit card and bank information to the electronic payment service to be established as a customer.

4 If the purchase is made with an "electronic payment," the merchant passes the encrypted payment information on to the electronic payment service, which decrypts the information, verifies its authenticity, and sends a verification back to the merchant. Encrypted credit card information can be decrypted by the merchant who then processes the payment through a private network.

74832615

Purchase Order with Encrypted Info

Merchant

How Anonymous Payment Works

1 An electronic "wallet" helper application is used to purchase electronic currency from a "bank," then pay for items using this electronic money. The bank may be an actual banking institution or a payment processing center. In either case, the customer makes a withdrawal from the bank using the wallet software.

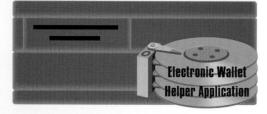

2 The software issues electronic currency, generating for each digital "coin" a unique, random serial number. The serial numbers are masked by multiplying the coins by a random number.

3 The coins are packaged into a message, digitally signed by the user's private identification key, encrypted with the bank's key, and sent to the bank. Only the bank can decrypt the message.

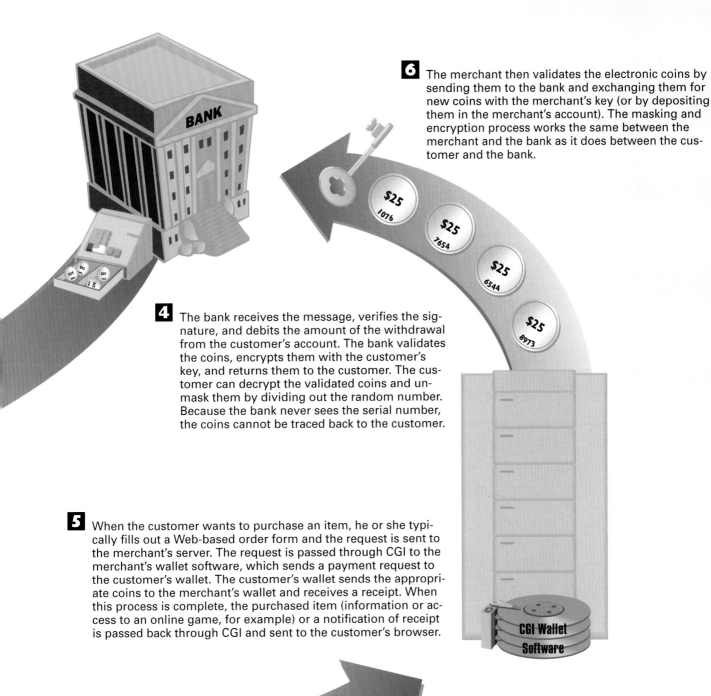

6 The merchant then validates the electronic coins by sending them to the bank and exchanging them for new coins with the merchant's key (or by depositing them in the merchant's account). The masking and encryption process works the same between the merchant and the bank as it does between the customer and the bank.

4 The bank receives the message, verifies the signature, and debits the amount of the withdrawal from the customer's account. The bank validates the coins, encrypts them with the customer's key, and returns them to the customer. The customer can decrypt the validated coins and unmask them by dividing out the random number. Because the bank never sees the serial number, the coins cannot be traced back to the customer.

5 When the customer wants to purchase an item, he or she typically fills out a Web-based order form and the request is sent to the merchant's server. The request is passed through CGI to the merchant's wallet software, which sends a payment request to the customer's wallet. The customer's wallet sends the appropriate coins to the merchant's wallet and receives a receipt. When this process is complete, the purchased item (information or access to an online game, for example) or a notification of receipt is passed back through CGI and sent to the customer's browser.

CGI Wallet Software

P A R T

SAFEGUARDING THE INTERNET

THE very nature of the Internet makes it vulnerable to attack. It was designed to allow for the freest possible exchange of information, data, and files—and it has succeeded admirably, far beyond its designers' wildest expectations. However, that freedom carries a price: Hackers and virus-writers try to attack the Internet and computers connected to the Internet; those who want to invade others' privacy attempt to crack databases of sensitive information or snoop on information as it travels across Internet routes; and distasteful and pornographic sites have sprung up on the Web and on Usenet newsgroups.

In this section of the book, we'll look at a variety of security-related issues. We'll see how various tools have been developed for making transactions on the Net more secure and helping companies protect their sensitive data. We'll examine the thorny issue of pornography versus free speech, and we'll see how software can block children from visiting obscene sites or getting obscene materials. We'll also look at some of the more controversial technologies on the Internet, such as cookies, which allow Web servers to track you as you move through their sites. And we'll look at how viruses work and how hackers attack Internet service providers (ISPs).

Chapter 45, "How Firewalls Work," looks at firewalls. Many companies whose networks are connected to the Internet have a great deal of sensitive information on their networks and want to make sure that their data and computers are safe from attack. The answer is to use *firewalls*—systems that allow people from inside a company to use the Internet, but also stop people on the Internet from getting at the company's computers.

Chapter 46, "How 'Smurf Attacks' Can Cripple ISPs," looks at attacks launched by hackers that can cripple Internet service providers. In a *Smurf attack*, also called *Smurfing*, a hacker targets an ISP and floods it with so much "garbage" traffic that none of the ISP's customers are able to use the service. Smurfing can become one of the most common kinds of hacking attacks on the Internet.

Chapter 47, "How Viruses Work," looks at viruses and how they are detected. Any program you download from the Internet has the potential for being infected with a virus, and it could, in turn, infect your computer. We'll see just how these nasty data-killers work, and we'll look at antivirus tools that can detect and kill them.

Chapter 48, "How Cookies, Passports, and Web Tracking Work," explores two controversial technologies—cookies and Web tracking—as well as a technology that may help preserve people's privacy—Internet "passports." Some people worry that cookies and Web tracking may invade people's privacy. Others say they don't and instead can help customize the Web to people's interests. *Cookies* are bits of data put on a hard disk when someone visits certain Web sites. That data can be used for many purposes. One common use is to make it easier for people to use Web sites that require a username and password by storing that information and then automatically sending the information whenever it's requested. *Passports* enable people to decide what kind of information about them may be tracked by Web sites. *Web tracking* enables those who run Web sites to see how people use their site.

In Chapter 49, "Cryptography and Privacy," we'll examine *cryptosystems*. An enormous amount of information is sent across the Internet every day—everything from personal email to corporate data to credit card information and other highly sensitive material. All that information is vulnerable to hackers and snoopers. Because the information is sent in packets along public routers, the possibility exists that someone could intercept and decipher it. As a way to ensure that the sensitive material can't be looked at, sophisticated cryptosystems have been developed so that only the sender and receiver know what's in the packets.

Chapter 50, "How Digital Certificates Work," describes digital certificates. On the Internet, no face-to-face communication takes place, so it can be difficult to know whether people really are who they say they are. *Digital certificates* are used to absolutely identify someone. If someone sends you an email, for example, a digital certificate will let you know that the person is who he says he is.

Finally, Chapter 51, "Parental Controls on the Internet," takes a detailed look at the issues of pornography and free speech on the Internet. Explicit sexual material is posted on the Internet, and some people would like to fine and jail people and organizations that allow such material to be posted. Passing those kinds of laws raises a whole host of constitutional issues about free speech. As a way to solve the problem, companies create and sell software for parents that enables them to block their children from seeing obscene and violent material on the Internet. In this chapter, we'll see how one of the most popular pieces of parental control software works.

45

How Firewalls Work

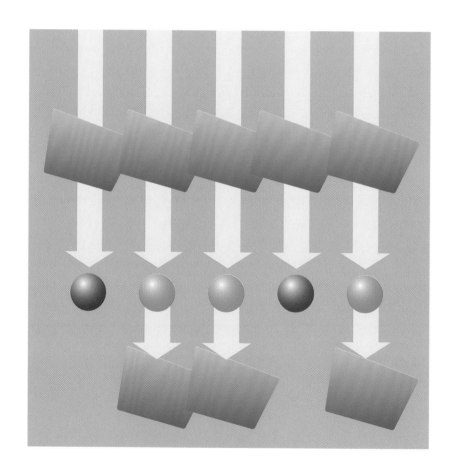

EVERY time a corporation connects its internal computer network or LAN (local area network) to the Internet it faces potential danger. Due to the Internet's openness, every corporate network connected to it is vulnerable to attack. Crackers on the Internet could theoretically break into the corporate network and do harm in a number of ways: They could steal or damage important data; damage individual computers or the entire network; use the corporate computer's resources; or use the corporate network and resources as a way of posing as a corporate employee. The solution isn't to cut off the network from the Internet. Instead, the company can build firewalls to protect its network. These firewalls allow anyone on the corporate network to access the Internet, but they stop crackers, hackers, or others on the Internet from gaining access to the corporate network and causing damage.

Firewalls are hardware and software combinations that are built using routers, servers, and a variety of software. They sit at the most vulnerable point between a corporate network and the Internet, and they can be as simple or complex as system administrators want to build them. There are many types of firewalls, but most of them have a few common elements.

One of the simplest kinds of firewalls utilizes packet filtering. In packet filtering, a screening router examines the header of every packet of data traveling between the Internet and the corporate network. Packet headers have information in them, including the IP address of the sender and receiver, the protocol being used to send the packet, and other similar information. Based on that information, the router knows what kind of Internet service—such as FTP or rlogin—is being used to send the data, as well as the identity of the sender and receiver of the data. (The command, rlogin, is similar to Telnet, allowing someone to log into a computer. It can be dangerous because it allows users to bypass having to type in a password.) After this information is determined, the router can bar certain packets from being sent between the Internet and the corporate network. For example, the router could block any traffic except for e-mail. Additionally, it could block traffic to and from suspicious destinations or from certain users.

Proxy servers are also commonly used in firewalls. A *proxy server* is server software that runs on a host in a firewall, such as a bastion host. Because only the single proxy server (instead of the many individual computers on the network) interacts with the Internet, security can be maintained. That single server can be kept more secure than can hundreds of individual computers on a network.

When someone inside the corporate network wants to access a server on the Internet, a request from the computer is sent to the proxy server, the proxy server contacts the server on the Internet, and then the proxy server sends the information from the Internet server to the computer inside the corporate network. By acting as a go-between, proxy servers can maintain security as well as log all traffic between the Internet and the network.

A *bastion host* (explained in the illustration) is another common component of firewalls.

How Firewalls Work

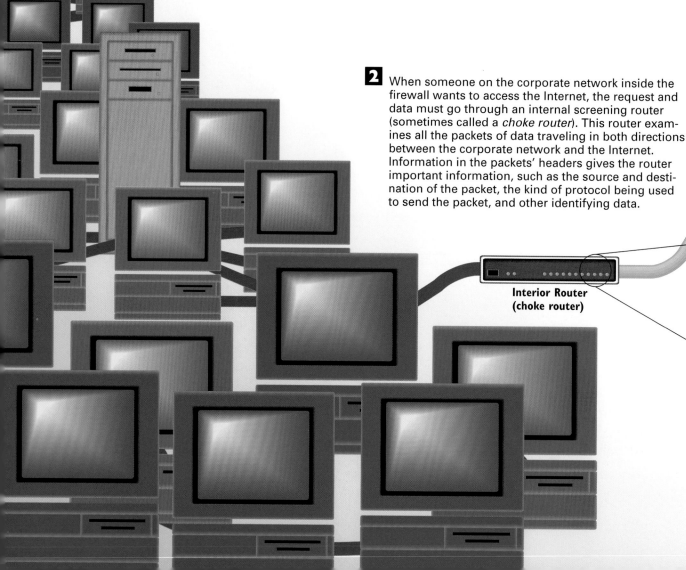

1 The firewall shields the internal corporate network from the Internet. The internal network works as networks normally do, with servers providing internal services such as email, access to corporate databases, and the capability to run programs from servers.

2 When someone on the corporate network inside the firewall wants to access the Internet, the request and data must go through an internal screening router (sometimes called a *choke router*). This router examines all the packets of data traveling in both directions between the corporate network and the Internet. Information in the packets' headers gives the router important information, such as the source and destination of the packet, the kind of protocol being used to send the packet, and other identifying data.

Interior Router (choke router)

Internet

Firewall

6 An *exterior screening router* (also called *an access router*) screens packets between the Internet and the perimeter network. It adds an extra level of protection by screening packets based on the same rules as the internal screening router. This protect the network even if the internal router fails. However, it may also add more rules for screening packets specifically designed to protect the bastion host.

5 The bastion host is placed in a perimeter network in the firewall, so it is not on the corporate network itself. This further shields the corporate network from the Internet. If the bastion host were on the normal corporate network, an intruder could conceivably gain access to every computer on the network and to all network services. Isolating the bastion server from the corporate network by putting it in a perimeter network prevents an intruder from gaining access to the internal corporate network, even if there is a server break-in.

Exterior Router (access router)

Bastion Host

4 A *bastion host* in the firewall is the primary point of contact for connections coming in from the Internet for services such as receiving email and allowing access to the corporation's FTP site. The bastion host is a heavily protected server with many security provisions built in and it is the only contact point for incoming Internet requests. In this way, none of the computers or hosts on the corporate network can be contacted directly for requests from the Internet, providing a level of security. Bastion hosts can also be set up as *proxy servers*—servers that process any requests from the internal corporate network to the Internet, such as browsing the Web or downloading files via FTP. See the next illustration for an explanation of how proxy servers work.

Screened Subnet Firewall

Internal Network

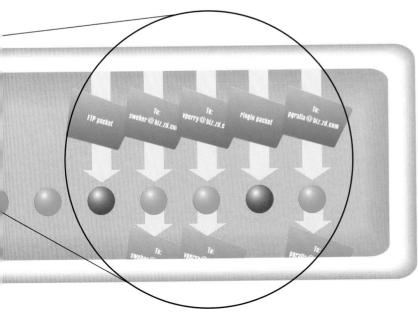

3 Based on the information in the headers, the screening router will allow certain packets to be sent or received, but will block other packets. For example, it might not allow some services such as rlogin to be run. The router also might not allow packets to be sent to and from specific Internet locations because those locations have been found to be suspicious. Conceivably, a router could be set up to block every packet traveling between the Internet and the internal network except for email. System administrators set the rules for determining which packets to allow in and which ones to block.

How Proxy Servers Work

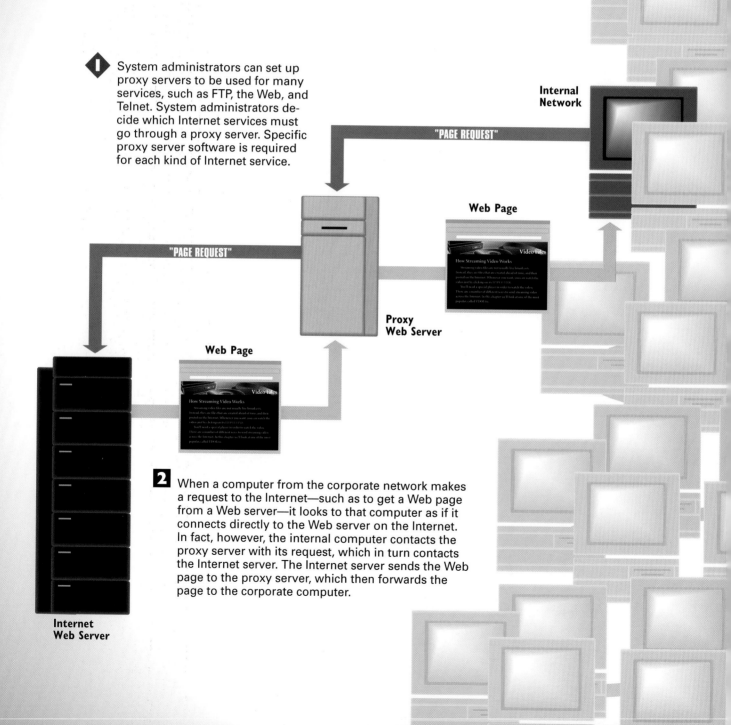

1 System administrators can set up proxy servers to be used for many services, such as FTP, the Web, and Telnet. System administrators decide which Internet services must go through a proxy server. Specific proxy server software is required for each kind of Internet service.

Internal Network

"PAGE REQUEST"

"PAGE REQUEST"

Web Page

Proxy Web Server

Web Page

2 When a computer from the corporate network makes a request to the Internet—such as to get a Web page from a Web server—it looks to that computer as if it connects directly to the Web server on the Internet. In fact, however, the internal computer contacts the proxy server with its request, which in turn contacts the Internet server. The Internet server sends the Web page to the proxy server, which then forwards the page to the corporate computer.

Internet Web Server

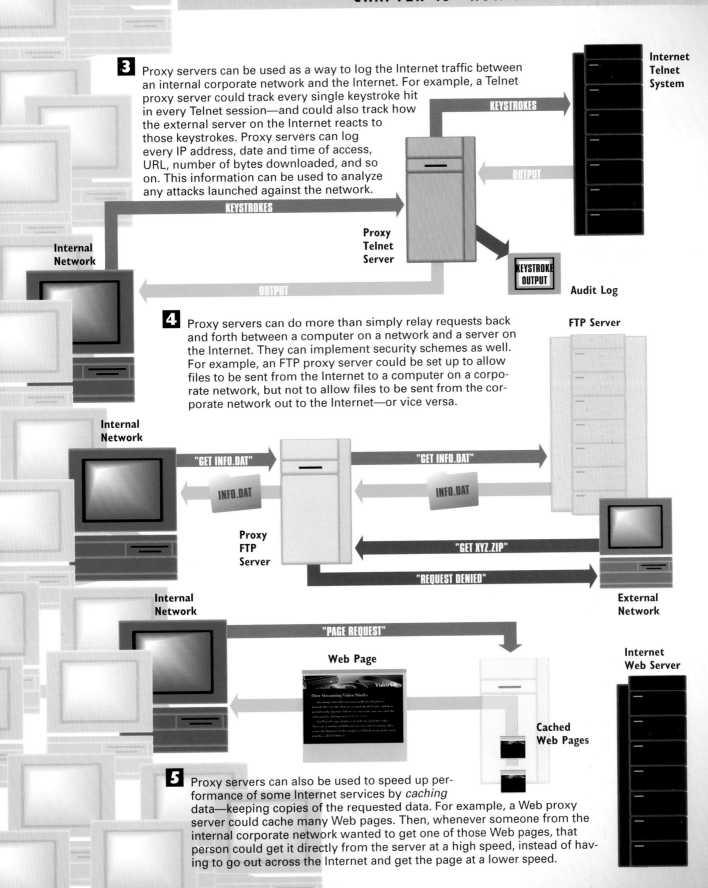

3 Proxy servers can be used as a way to log the Internet traffic between an internal corporate network and the Internet. For example, a Telnet proxy server could track every single keystroke hit in every Telnet session—and could also track how the external server on the Internet reacts to those keystrokes. Proxy servers can log every IP address, date and time of access, URL, number of bytes downloaded, and so on. This information can be used to analyze any attacks launched against the network.

Internet Telnet System

KEYSTROKES

OUTPUT

Internal Network

KEYSTROKES

Proxy Telnet Server

OUTPUT

KEYSTROKE OUTPUT

Audit Log

4 Proxy servers can do more than simply relay requests back and forth between a computer on a network and a server on the Internet. They can implement security schemes as well. For example, an FTP proxy server could be set up to allow files to be sent from the Internet to a computer on a corporate network, but not to allow files to be sent from the corporate network out to the Internet—or vice versa.

FTP Server

Internal Network

"GET INFO.DAT"

"GET INFO.DAT"

INFO.DAT

INFO.DAT

Proxy FTP Server

"GET XYZ.ZIP"

"REQUEST DENIED"

External Network

Internal Network

"PAGE REQUEST"

Web Page

Internet Web Server

Cached Web Pages

5 Proxy servers can also be used to speed up performance of some Internet services by *caching* data—keeping copies of the requested data. For example, a Web proxy server could cache many Web pages. Then, whenever someone from the internal corporate network wanted to get one of those Web pages, that person could get it directly from the server at a high speed, instead of having to go out across the Internet and get the page at a lower speed.

How "Smurf Attacks" Can Cripple ISPs

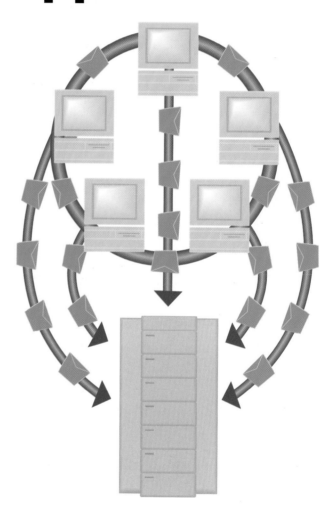

AMONG hackers' many targets are Internet Service Providers (ISPs)—companies that make a living by selling people access to the Internet. A hacker might target an ISP for several reasons: he may be angry at the ISP or at someone using the ISP, or he may attack the ISP for the mere thrill of it.

One of the most common attacks against an ISP is called a *smurf attack*, or *smurfing*. In a smurf attack, a hacker is able to flood the ISP with so many "garbage" packets that all the ISP's available bandwidth is used up, and its customers can't send or receive data by using email, browsing the Web, or any other Internet service.

In a smurf attack, hackers exploit a commonly used Internet service—ping (Internet Control Message Protocol). *Ping* is normally used by people to see whether a particular computer or server is currently attached to the Internet and working. When a computer or server is sent a ping packet, it sends a return packet to the person who sent the ping, in essence saying, "Yes, I'm alive and attached to the Internet." In a smurf attack, hackers forge the return addresses on ping requests so that those return packets go back not to them, but instead, to their target ISP. The hackers are able to use networks attached to the Internet as a way of relaying their ping requests and also to magnify each single ping request many times. In this way, a hacker can use networks attached to the Internet to flood the ISP with so many return ping packets that the ISP's customers can't use the ISP's services. Hackers can use multiple networks attached to the Internet in a single smurf attack.

It's difficult for ISPs to fight smurf attacks because the ping answering packets come from legitimate networks, not from the hacker. The ISP has to track down where the ping answering packets are coming from and then contact each of those networks, asking them to turn off the ping answering packets. Making this more difficult is that when an ISP goes down, often its customers will send ping requests to it, to see if it is alive and connected to the Internet—and so the ISP has a difficult time separating the legitimate ping packets from the smurf attack packets.

Smurf protection features and software have become available for ISPs and to put on Internet routers. But few companies are using those features and software because they have yet to gain widespread acceptance and because not everyone recognizes how big a problem smurf attacks have become. A problem is that the companies who would use this software are often backbone companies who are not the targets of smurf attacks; therefore, they have no economic reason for using the software. Until they do, smurf attacks will remain a fact of life on the Internet.

How Hackers Attack Internet Service Providers with "Smurf Attacks"

In a "smurf attack," also called "smurfing," a hacker targets an Internet Service Provider (ISP) and floods it with so much "garbage" traffic that none of the ISP's customers are able to use the service. It has become one of the most popular kinds of hacker attacks on the Internet.

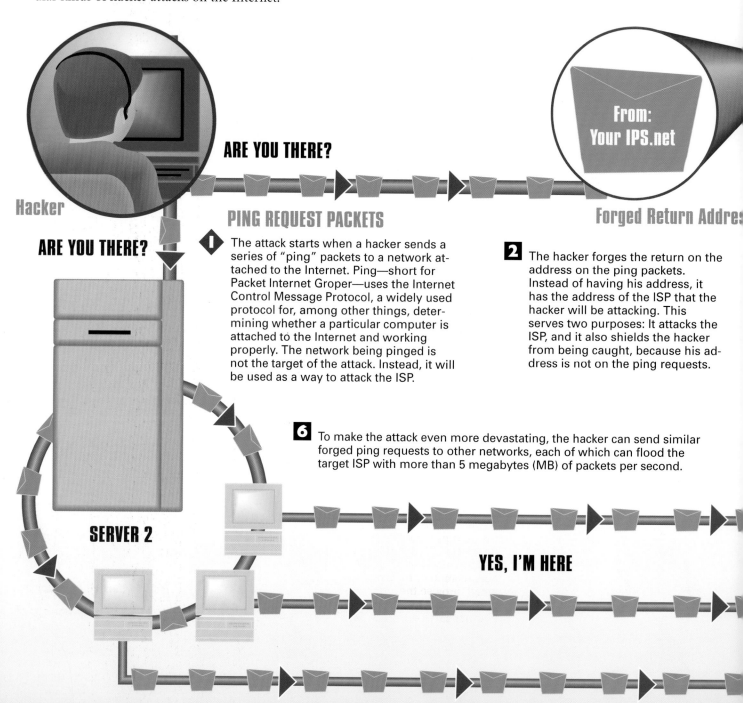

Hacker

ARE YOU THERE?

ARE YOU THERE?

PING REQUEST PACKETS

Forged Return Addres

From: Your IPS.net

SERVER 2

YES, I'M HERE

1 The attack starts when a hacker sends a series of "ping" packets to a network attached to the Internet. Ping—short for Packet Internet Groper—uses the Internet Control Message Protocol, a widely used protocol for, among other things, determining whether a particular computer is attached to the Internet and working properly. The network being pinged is not the target of the attack. Instead, it will be used as a way to attack the ISP.

2 The hacker forges the return on the address on the ping packets. Instead of having his address, it has the address of the ISP that the hacker will be attacking. This serves two purposes: It attacks the ISP, and it also shields the hacker from being caught, because his address is not on the ping requests.

6 To make the attack even more devastating, the hacker can send similar forged ping requests to other networks, each of which can flood the target ISP with more than 5 megabytes (MB) of packets per second.

DIRECTED BROADCAST ADDRESS

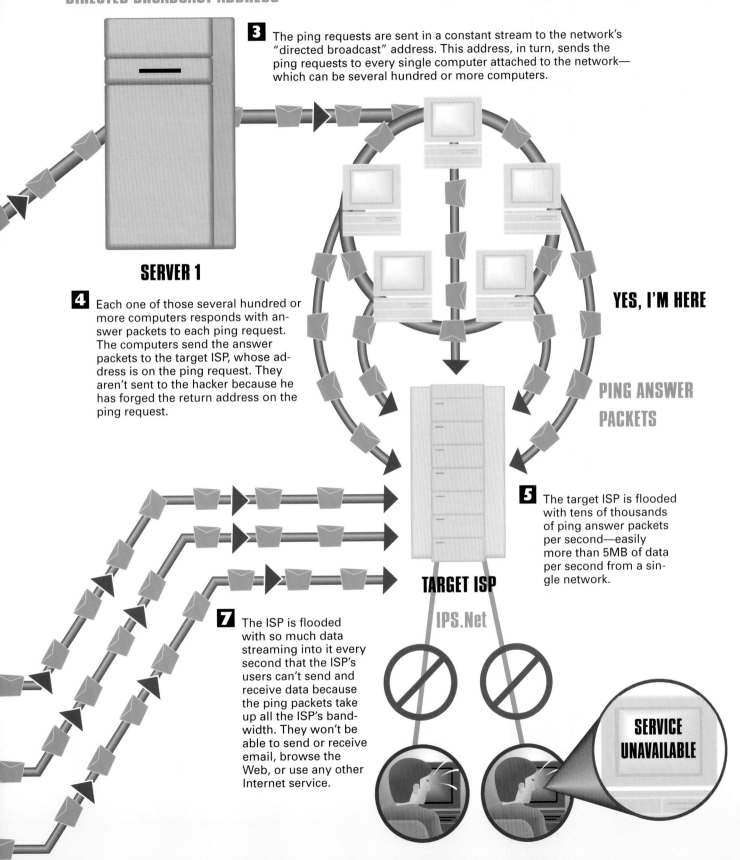

3 The ping requests are sent in a constant stream to the network's "directed broadcast" address. This address, in turn, sends the ping requests to every single computer attached to the network—which can be several hundred or more computers.

SERVER 1

4 Each one of those several hundred or more computers responds with answer packets to each ping request. The computers send the answer packets to the target ISP, whose address is on the ping request. They aren't sent to the hacker because he has forged the return address on the ping request.

YES, I'M HERE

PING ANSWER PACKETS

5 The target ISP is flooded with tens of thousands of ping answer packets per second—easily more than 5MB of data per second from a single network.

TARGET ISP

IPS.Net

7 The ISP is flooded with so much data streaming into it every second that the ISP's users can't send and receive data because the ping packets take up all the ISP's bandwidth. They won't be able to send or receive email, browse the Web, or use any other Internet service.

SERVICE UNAVAILABLE

CHAPTER

47

How Viruses Work

THE Internet, just like the rest of the world, is not a perfectly safe place to visit. If you download files from the Internet, there is a chance—a very small chance, but nonetheless a chance—that your computer could become infected with a virus.

Viruses are malicious programs that invade your computer. They can cause many different kinds of damage, such as deleting data files, erasing programs, or destroying everything they find on your hard disk. Not every virus causes damage; some simply flash annoying messages.

Although you can get a virus from the Internet by downloading files to your computer, the Internet is not the only place that viruses can be picked up. If you've sent files via email or on your company's internal network, you can get them that way as well. There have even been instances when commercially bought, shrink-wrapped software has contained viruses.

The term "virus" is a somewhat generic term applied to a wide variety of programs. Viruses are written for specific kinds of computers, such as PCs or Macintoshes, because the files they infect run only on one kind of computer.

Traditional viruses attach themselves to programs or data files, infect your computer, replicate themselves on your hard disk, and then damage your data, hard disk, or files. Viruses usually attack four parts of your computer: its executable program files; its file-directory system that tracks the location of all your computer's files (and without which, your computer won't work); its boot and system areas that are needed to start your computer; and its data files. There was a time when it was believed that data files could not be infected by viruses, but recently, viruses have been written that infect data files, too. For example, some viruses attach themselves to Word for Windows macros inside a Word for Windows data file and are launched whenever a particular macro is run.

Trojan horses are programs that disguise themselves as normal, helpful programs, but in fact are viruses. For example, if a program purported to be a financial calculator, but really deleted every file on your hard disk ending, that program would be called a Trojan horse.

Worms are programs designed to infect networks such as the Internet. They travel from networked computer to networked computer, replicating themselves along the way. The most infamous worm of all was released on November 2, 1988, and copied itself to many Internet host computers, eventually bringing the Internet to its knees.

The best way to protect your computer against viruses is to use antiviral software. There are several kinds. A *scanner* checks to see if your computer has any files that have been infected, whereas an *eradication program* will wipe the virus from your hard disk. Sometimes eradication programs can kill the virus without having to delete the infected program or data file, whereas other times those infected files must be deleted. Still other programs, sometimes called *inoculators*, do not allow a program to be run if it contains a virus, and stop your computer from being infected.

How Viruses Infect Computers

3 Viruses can corrupt program or data files so that they work oddly, not at all, or cause damage when they do run. They can destroy all the files on your computer, change the system files that your computer needs when it is turned on, and cause other types of damage.

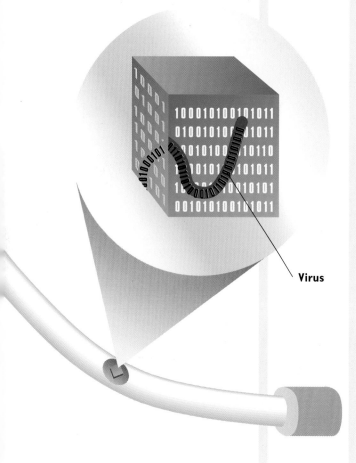

Virus

1 A virus hides inside a legitimate program where it remains dormant until you run the infected program. The virus springs into action when you actually run the infected program. Sometimes the first thing the virus will do is infect other programs on your hard disk by copying itself into them.

5 *Eradication programs* disinfect, or remove, viruses from software. Sometimes they can eradicate the virus without damaging the program that the virus has infected. In other instances, they have to destroy the program as well as the virus.

4 Software programs called *scanners* check for viruses and alert you to the viruses' presence. They work in many different ways. One method of detection is to check your program files for tell-tale virus markers that indicate the presence of a virus. Other methods include checking to see whether a program's file size has changed. Some types of antiviral programs run continuously on your computer and check any program for the presence of a virus before the program is run.

2 Some viruses place messages called *v-markers* or *virus markers* inside programs that they infect, and these help manage the viruses' activities. Each virus has a specific v-marker associated with it. If a virus encounters one of these markers in another program, it knows that the program is already infected so it doesn't replicate itself there. When a virus cannot find more unmarked files on a computer, that can signal to the virus that there are no more files to be infected. At this point, the virus may begin to damage the computer and its data.

Virus Marker

CHAPTER

48

How Cookies, Passports, and Web Tracking Work

PRIVACY issues are a big concern on the Net. Much information can be gathered about people when they use the Net, and it's not always clear who will use that information or how it will be used. In particular, two technologies that concern people are cookies and Web tracking. Both serve useful purposes, but many people worry that there is a "Big Brother" aspect to them. One technology, Internet "passports," may enable people to ensure that their privacy isn't invaded while still enabling Web sites to gather information that can be used to deliver specialized services to Web surfers.

Cookies are bits of data put on a hard disk when someone visits certain Web sites. The most common use of this data is to make it easier for people to use Web sites that require a username and password. The cookie on the hard disk has the username and password in it, so people don't have to log in to every page that requires that information. Instead, the cookie sends the information to the server and the person can visit the page freely.

Cookies can contain virtually any kind of information, such as the last time a person visited the site, the person's favorite sites, and similar, customizable information. They can be used to track people as they go through a Web site and to help gain statistics about what kinds of pages people like to visit. Although some people view them as invaders of privacy, they can also make the Web a much better place to visit by doing things such as making it easier to conduct electronic commerce.

Web sites can't read cookies that other sites have placed on a hard disk, so if you visit a certain news site, for example, no other site can get the information out of the cookie. Users always have the option of not allowing cookies to be placed on their hard disks—browsers give people this option.

Although cookies can be used to track how people use a Web site, many other methods can be used, as well. In one method, Web server logs are examined in detail. This would make it possible, for example, to identify the most popular pages on the site, the sites people have just visited, how many pages people read in a typical visit, and similar information. Other methods include using software "sniffers" that examine every packet coming into or going out of a Web site. Webmasters can use this tracking information to help create better sites—but they can also use it to assemble demographic information to sell to advertisers.

In fact, Webmasters need to know a good deal of information about how their site is being used, such as the total number of visitors per day, the total number of pages viewed, how people travel through the site, where people come to the site from, and where they go when they leave. The third illustration in this chapter shows the functionality of Web tracking software from a company called Accrue.

To allay people's privacy concerns, a variety of technologies and standards are being developed. They include the Platform for Privacy Preferences (P3P), the Internet Content and Exchange standard (ICE), and the Open Profiling Standard (OPS). Generically, we'll call them Internet passports. These Internet passports let people control which information about themselves they'll allow to be released to Web sites—and how that information can be used. And they let people control what kind of information can be gathered about their surfing and how that information can be used, as well. In general, the more information that people allow to be gathered about them, the more specialized services they'll gain on the Web, such as customized news feeds. We'll look at Internet passports in the second illustration in this chapter.

How Cookies Work

1 Cookies are pieces of data placed on a computer's hard drive by a Web server; they can be used for a variety of purposes. They can store usernames and passwords, for example, so that people don't have to continually log on to a site that requires registration; or they enable people to fill electronic "shopping carts" with goods they want to buy. Cookies also store the name of the site that placed the cookie. Only that site will be able to read the cookie information, so information from one site cannot be shared with information from another site. Cookie information is put into a special file on a hard disk. The location and files vary according to the kind of computer and the browser. On PCs using Netscape, for example, the information is put into a file called COOKIES.TXT. That single text file holds all the cookies. Each cookie is one line of data in the file.

CGI Script

www.Buyshop.com

Password:pg
Username:who

Buyshop.com cookie

2 When you visit a site, your browser examines the URL you're visiting and looks into your cookie file. If it finds a cookie associated with that URL, it sends that cookie information to the server. The server can now use that cookie information.

Buyshop.com cookie?

```
# Netscape HTTP Cookie File
# http://www.netscape.com/newsref/std/cookie_spec.html
# This is a generated file! Do not edit.
.ad-up.com          TRUE   /~barryl/public_html  FALSE  946079999    Ad-OpUser        125101
www.lego.com        TRUE   /cgi-bin/pirat  FALSE  883699199   &r       &n=unknown&pf=&b=2&t=1&f=1
.gowest.com         TRUE   /       FALSE  946684799   INTERSE  155.40.99.17113860049804657
.hotbot.com         TRUE   /       FALSE  937396800   ink      IUBOH12pEA8O36A0H5O4A8OO5395901503
.focalink.com       TRUE   /       FALSE  946641600   SB_ID    ads81.21677049801891040315
.boston.com         TRUE   /       FALSE  946684799   INTERSE  mia.tiac.net277385805621237B
.netscape.com       TRUE   /       FALSE  1609372800  HOZILLA  HOZ_ID=OFGNKGI1RJSPT5[-]HOZ_VERS=
.netscape.com       TRUE   /       FALSE  1609372800  NS_IBD   IBD_SUBSCRIPTIONS=INCOO6[INCO10]1]
.realaudio.com      TRUE   /       FALSE  946684740   uid      19927924850346722065
.nytimes.com        TRUE   /       FALSE  946684799   PW       27.7276
.nytimes.com        TRUE   /       FALSE  946684799   ID       .7,=22=0
.nytimes.com        TRUE   /       FALSE  942109160   iibuser  .7,=22=0
.nytimes.com        TRUE   /       FALSE  942109160   iibq     +6=,9'=,9cU,=22=c0ZP9=c6/=8529+6
.netscape.com       TRUE   /       FALSE  946684799   METSCAPE_ID    1000e010,13b#8f76
.doubleclick.net    FALSE  /       FALSE  942191940   IAF      1cecb58
.infoseek.com       TRUE   /       FALSE  882131378   InfoseekUserId  8A08FC0465009557036E044057
.software.net       TRUE   /       FALSE  946684799   ADURL    http://www.software.net/PKSH028051
.yahoo.com          TRUE   /       FALSE  946809208   IDAHO    domain=y&path=39312F31372F78677261
.wsj.com            TRUE   /       FALSE  946635010   user_type      subscribed
www.maricle.com     FALSE  /       FALSE  1293756608  EGSOFT_ID      155.40.99.171-1175746720.1
www.download.com    FALSE  /       FALSE  946599440   csr      /=/PG/frontDoor/8"1"0=0"01
.family.com         TRUE   /       FALSE  946601200   ck_stateID     49143.30564416.780
Buyshop.com                 TRUE   123702 132
```

Buyshop.com   True   123702   132

3 If no cookie is associated with the URL, the server will place a cookie inside the cookie file. Some sites may first ask a series of questions, such as name and password, and will then place a cookie on the hard disk with that information in it. This is typical of sites that require registration. Commonly, a CGI script on the server takes the information that the user has entered and then writes the cookie onto the hard disk.

4 As you travel through a Web site, more information may need to be put into your cookie. On a site where you can purchase goods online, for example, you might put goods into an electronic shopping cart. Every time you did this, new cookie information would be added, detailing the goods you wanted to buy. When new cookie information is put in, a CGI script deletes the old cookie information and puts in a new cookie. When you leave a site, your cookie information remains on your hard disk so that the site can recognize you the next time you decide to visit—unless the cookie has specifically been written to expire when you leave the site.

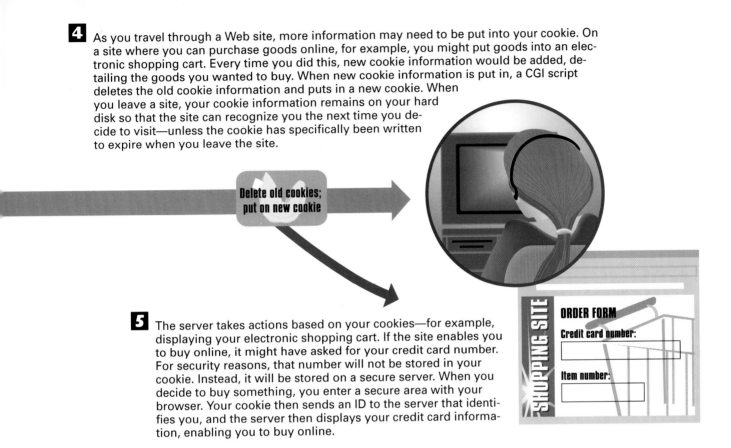

Delete old cookies; put on new cookie

ORDER FORM

SHOPPING SITE

Credit card number:

Item number:

5 The server takes actions based on your cookies—for example, displaying your electronic shopping cart. If the site enables you to buy online, it might have asked for your credit card number. For security reasons, that number will not be stored in your cookie. Instead, it will be stored on a secure server. When you decide to buy something, you enter a secure area with your browser. Your cookie then sends an ID to the server that identifies you, and the server then displays your credit card information, enabling you to buy online.

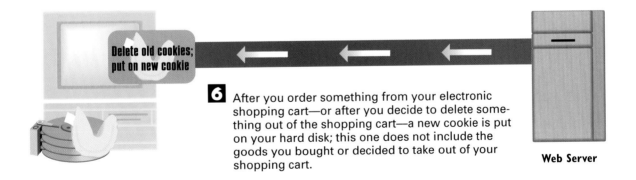

Delete old cookies; put on new cookie

6 After you order something from your electronic shopping cart—or after you decide to delete something out of the shopping cart—a new cookie is put on your hard disk; this one does not include the goods you bought or decided to take out of your shopping cart.

Web Server

The server www.amazon.com wishes to set a cookie that will be sent to any server in the domain .amazon.com The name and value of the cookie are: session-id-time=867052800

This cookie will persist until Mon Jun 23 03:55:00 1997

Do you wish to allow the cookie to be set?

[OK]   [Cancel]

7 Because some people don't like cookies to be placed on their hard disk, browsers give people control over whether to accept cookies, to not accept cookies, or to ask each time a cookie is being placed on the hard disk. Pictured is the message you get if you've asked to be told each time a cookie is placed on your hard disk.

How Internet "Passports" Work

Internet "passports" are designed to let people decide what personal information they will allow to be released to Web sites. The more information that people will allow to be released, the more sophisticated the services that can be delivered to them. The user also determines what information about their surfing habits can be gathered by Web sites and what information that's been gathered can be shared among Web sites. A variety of technologies are involved with Internet passports, including the Platform for Privacy Preferences (P3P), the Internet Content and Exchange standard (ICE), and the Open Profiling Standard (OPS).

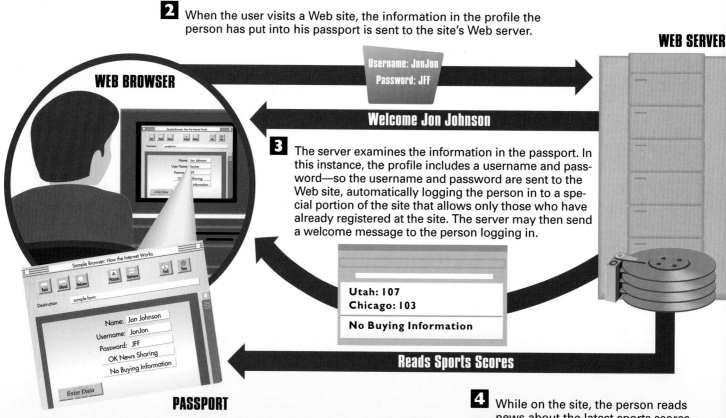

2 When the user visits a Web site, the information in the profile the person has put into his passport is sent to the site's Web server.

WEB SERVER

Username: JonJon
Password: JFF

Welcome Jon Johnson

WEB BROWSER

3 The server examines the information in the passport. In this instance, the profile includes a username and password—so the username and password are sent to the Web site, automatically logging the person in to a special portion of the site that allows only those who have already registered at the site. The server may then send a welcome message to the person logging in.

Utah: 107
Chicago: 103

No Buying Information

Reads Sports Scores

PASSPORT

Name: Jon Johnson
Username: JonJon
Password: JFF
OK News Sharing
No Buying Information

Enter Data

1 The passport lives inside a Web browser. A user fills out a profile in the browser, determining what information can be made available to Web sites, such as name, address, occupation, username and password, and age. The user also decides which kind of information about his surfing habits can be shared among Web sites—and which can't. In this instance, the person has decided that information about what news stories he reads can be shared, but not information about what products he buys.

4 While on the site, the person reads news about the latest sports scores, then buys an electric razor and a book about sailing. The Web site puts into the person's profile that he's read sports scores, but not that he's bought a razor and a book—because the person's profile said it would allow information about what news stories he reads to be shared, but not information about what he buys.

5 The person visits another Web site. The information in the profile the person has put into his passport is sent to the site's Web server. The server sees that the person has recently read a story about sports scores, and so it sends to him a daily digest of the latest sports news. Because the profile doesn't have any information about what the person has bought, it doesn't send any information about special sales on the site.

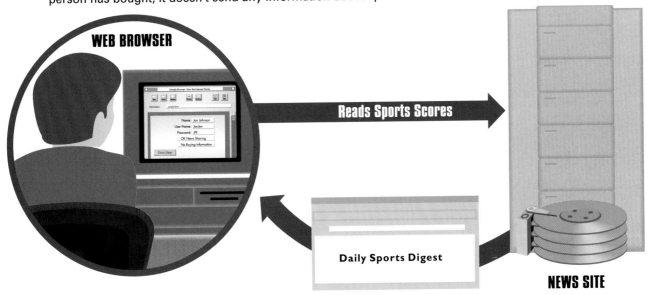

6 The person now surfs to a different Web site. This site only allows people in who have agreed, in their profile, to allow their online buying habits to be shared among sites. Because the person has said he doesn't want that information to be shared, the person is not allowed onto the site.

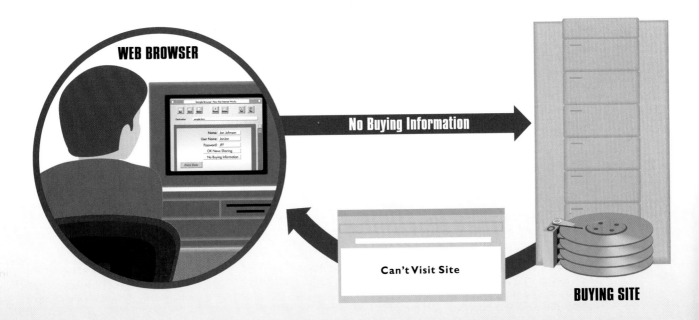

How Web Tracking Works

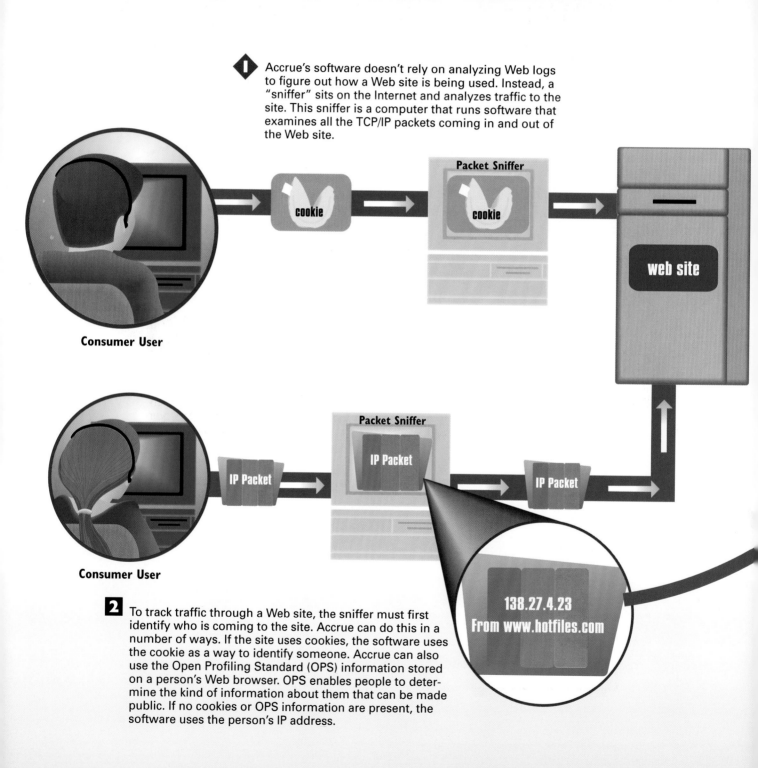

1 Accrue's software doesn't rely on analyzing Web logs to figure out how a Web site is being used. Instead, a "sniffer" sits on the Internet and analyzes traffic to the site. This sniffer is a computer that runs software that examines all the TCP/IP packets coming in and out of the Web site.

Packet Sniffer

cookie

cookie

web site

Consumer User

Packet Sniffer

IP Packet

IP Packet

IP Packet

Consumer User

138.27.4.23
From www.hotfiles.com

2 To track traffic through a Web site, the sniffer must first identify who is coming to the site. Accrue can do this in a number of ways. If the site uses cookies, the software uses the cookie as a way to identify someone. Accrue can also use the Open Profiling Standard (OPS) information stored on a person's Web browser. OPS enables people to determine the kind of information about them that can be made public. If no cookies or OPS information are present, the software uses the person's IP address.

3 The sniffer examines packets as they come into and go out of the site. It notes any time an action is taken, such as when someone requests a Web page, and whenever that action is completed, such as when the final packets from the page are delivered. It tracks who is making the requests, where they are coming from, where they are going, and similar information. This information is contained in the TCP/IP packets. The sniffer discards all the intermediate packets transmitted during each action—only the beginning and ending packets are needed. It discards all the intermediate packets because they provide no useful information.

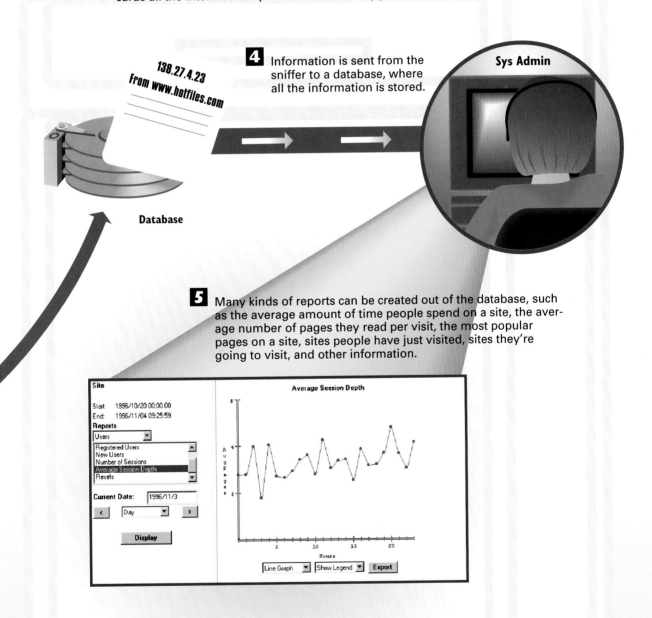

138.27.4.23
From www.hotfiles.com

4 Information is sent from the sniffer to a database, where all the information is stored.

Sys Admin

Database

5 Many kinds of reports can be created out of the database, such as the average amount of time people spend on a site, the average number of pages they read per visit, the most popular pages on a site, sites people have just visited, sites they're going to visit, and other information.

Site

Start: 1996/10/20 00:00:00
End: 1996/11/04 09:25:59

Reports
Users

Registered Users
New Users
Number of Sessions
Average Session Depth
Resets

Current Date: 1996/11/3

◄ Day ►

Display

Average Session Depth

Line Graph | Show Legend | Export

C H A P T E R
49
Cryptography and Privacy

EVERY packet of data sent over the Internet traverses many public networks, which means access to those packets is not private. This is of particular concern when highly confidential information, such as corporate data and credit card numbers, is transmitted across the Internet. Unless there is some way to protect that kind of information, the Internet will never be a secure place to do business or send private, personal correspondence.

Fortunately, software engineers have developed ways to send confidential information securely. The information needs to be *encrypted*—that is, altered so that to anyone other than the intended recipient it will look like meaningless garble. The information also needs to be *decrypted*—that is, turned back into the original message by the recipient, and only by the recipient. Many complex *cryptosystems* have been created to allow for this kind of encryption and decryption.

The heart of understanding how cryptosystems work is to understand the concept of keys. *Keys* are secret values that computers use in concert with complex mathematical formulas called *algorithms* to encrypt and decrypt messages. The idea behind keys is that if someone encrypts a message with a key, only someone else with a matching key will be able to decrypt the message.

There are two kinds of common encryption systems: *secret-key cryptography*, also called *symmetric cryptography*, and *public-key cryptography*, also called *asymmetric cryptography*. The most common secret-key cryptography system is the Data Encryption Standard (DES). The best known public-key system is known as RSA.

In secret-key cryptography, only one key is used to encrypt and decrypt messages; both the sender and the receiver need copies of the same secret key. By contrast, in public-key cryptography, two keys are involved: a public key and a private key. Every person has both a public key and a private key. The public key is made freely available, whereas the private key is kept secret on the person's computer. The public key can encrypt messages—but only the private key can decrypt messages that the public key has encrypted. If someone wanted to send a message to you, for example, he would encrypt it with your public key. But only you, with your private key, would be able to decrypt the message and read it. Your public key could not decrypt it.

It's not feasible to use private-key cryptosystems widely on the Internet for things such as electronic commerce. For a company to conduct business over the Internet with a private-key system, it would mean creating millions of different private keys—one for each person who wanted to do business—and then figuring out some way to send those private keys securely over the Internet. With a public-key system, the business only needs to create a single public/private key combination. The business would post the public key for anyone to use for encrypting information—but only the business, with the private key, would be able to decrypt the data.

How Cryptosystems Work

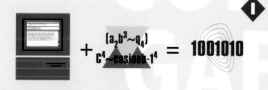

1 Gabriel wants to send a confidential message over the Internet to Mia. Mia will need some way to decrypt the message as well as a way to guarantee that Gabriel, and not an imposter, has actually sent the message. First, Gabriel runs his message through an algorithm called a *hash function*. This produces a number known as the *message digest*. The message digest acts as a sort of "digital fingerprint" that Mia will use to ensure that no one has altered the message.

2 Gabriel now uses his private key to encrypt the message digest. This produces a unique digital signature that only he, with his private key, could have created.

3 Gabriel generates a new random key. He uses this key to encrypt his original message and his digital signature. Mia will need a copy of this random key to decrypt Gabriel's message. This random key is the only key in the world that can decrypt the message—and at this point only Gabriel has the key.

4 Gabriel encrypts this new random key with Mia's public key. This encrypted random key is referred to as the *digital envelope*. Only Mia will be able to decrypt the random key because it was encrypted with her public key, so only her private key can decrypt it.

5 Gabriel sends a message over the Internet to Mia that is composed of several parts: the encrypted confidential message, the encrypted digital signature, and the encrypted digital envelope.

6 Mia gets the message. She decrypts the digital envelope with her private key and out of it gets the random key that Gabriel used to encrypt the message.

Original message

Hash function

7 Mia uses the random key to decrypt Gabriel's message. She can now read the confidential message that he sent to her. However, she can't yet be sure that the message hasn't been altered en route to her or that Gabriel was definitely the sender.

Message digest

Gabriel's public key

Gabriel's private key

8 Mia now uses the random key and Gabriel's public key to decrypt his encrypted digital signature. When she does this, she gets his message digest, the message's "digital fingerprint."

Mia's public key

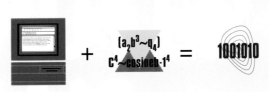

Mia's private key

Digital signature

9 Mia will use this message digest to see whether Gabriel indeed sent the message and that it was not altered in any way. She takes the message that she decrypted and runs it through the same algorithm—the hash function—that Gabriel ran the message through. This will produce a new message digest.

Random key

Encrypted message

10 Mia compares the message digest that she calculated to the one that she got out of Gabriel's digital signature. If the two match precisely, she can be sure that Gabriel signed the message and that it was not altered after he composed it. If they don't match, then she knows that either he didn't compose the message, or that someone altered the message after he wrote it.

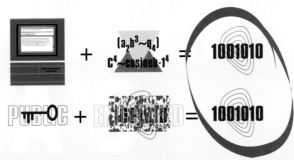

Encrypted digital signature

Encrypted random key (digital envelope)

CHAPTER

50

How Digital Certificates Work

Name: Gale Gralla
Authority: Veri Pure
Serial Number: 000516
Version Number: 3
Expires: 9/29/99
Key:

Digital Signature:

TO a great extent, the Internet is built on trust. It's a virtual world online; you don't actually see the people or institutions with whom you're communicating and getting and sending information. You don't actually see the person who's sending you email, for example, but you trust that they are who they say they are.

When it comes to financial transactions and other important communications, though, trust is not enough. There are hackers and crackers out there, con artists and scamsters who would be only too happy to take your credit card number, or who would like to learn your personal, financial, or business secrets. In the same way, businesses need to know that the person sending a credit card number really is who he says he is, and not an imposter who has managed to steal a credit card number from someone.

One of the major ways around the problem of trust is the use of "Digital Certificates." Digital certificates are used to verify that the person sending information, a credit card number, a message, or anything else over the Internet really is who he says he is. The certificates place information on a person's hard disk, and use encryption technology to create a unique digital certificate for each person. When someone with a digital certificate goes to a site, or sends email, that certificate is presented to the site or attached to the email, and it verifies that the user is who he claims to be.

Because they use powerful encryption technology, digital certificates are quite secure. In fact, they are more secure than real-life signatures. In real life, a signature can be forged. On the Internet, a digital certificate can't be.

Digital certificates are issued by Certificate Authorities. These Certificate Authorities are private companies who charge either users or companies for the issuance of the certificates. You may be familiar with one such Certificate Authority, called VeriSign. Digital certificates contain information such as your name, the name of the Certificate Authority, the certificate's serial number, and similar information. The information has been encrypted in a way that makes it unique to you. As with many other things on the Internet, there is a standard that governs digital certificates—in this case, known as X.509.

How Digital Certificates Ensure Internet Security

A digital certificate is used to guarantee that the person who sends information or email over the Internet or who makes a financial transaction really is who he says he is. This illustration shows how a digital certificate would be used to guarantee that the person sending an email is being truthful about his identity.

1 Digital certificates are issued by Certificate Authorities (CAs). To get a digital certificate, you typically visit a CA site and request a certificate. You'll provide information about yourself, such as your name and other identifying information.

Gabe Gralla requests certificate

101010

2 You'll be issued a digital certificate, which has been digitally signed to guarantee its authenticity. The certificate is data unique to you, and is put on your hard disk, along with a private key (see Chapter 49 for information about keys).

Name:	**Gale Gralla**
Authority:	**Veri Pure**
Serial Number:	**000516**
Version Number:	**3**
Expires:	**9/29/99**
Key:	
Digital Signature:	

3 The digital certificate is composed of information such as your name, the name of the CA, the unique serial number of the certificate, the version number of the certificate, the expiration date of the certificate, your public key, and the digital signature of the CA. The exact format of the certificate is defined by a standard known as X.509.

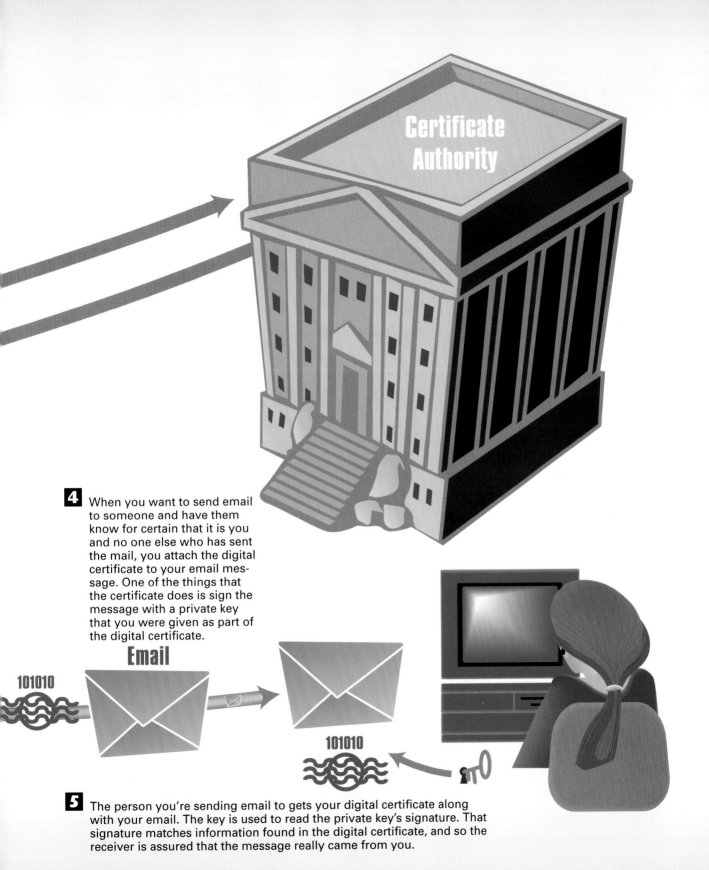

4 When you want to send email to someone and have them know for certain that it is you and no one else who has sent the mail, you attach the digital certificate to your email message. One of the things that the certificate does is sign the message with a private key that you were given as part of the digital certificate.

Email

5 The person you're sending email to gets your digital certificate along with your email. The key is used to read the private key's signature. That signature matches information found in the digital certificate, and so the receiver is assured that the message really came from you.

51

Parental Controls on the Internet

THE very nature of the Internet—the way it allows the free, unfettered flow of information among people—has gotten it a lot of bad publicity. Much has been made of the fact that erotic and pornographic information are available on the Internet, everything from pictures to discussions about subjects that many people find objectionable. The truth is, that kind of content makes up a very small part of what's available on the Internet. Furthermore, the objectionable content is not exactly in public view—you have to do a bit of digging to find it.

However, just the fact that this type of information is available to anyone who wants to see it, including children, has made people uncomfortable. In fact, Congress and other legislative bodies have tried to take steps to ban certain kinds of content from being available on the Internet. As a result of these efforts, a controversial law was passed against online pornography. The law is called the Communications Decency Act, which the Supreme Court ruled unconstitutional.

The real answer to the problem, though, doesn't lie with legislation. The answer lies with technology—software that will allow parents to make sure that their children are not seeing objectionable material. A number of companies make and sell software that will do this, such as SurfWatch, CyberNanny, and CyberPatrol. They each check sites for content and then bar children from getting to those sites that contain content that is unsuitable for them.

Online services such as CompuServe, America Online, and Prodigy have a variety of ways to block access to objectionable material on the Internet. Some allow parents to block children from using services such as the World Wide Web, chat, or newsgroups completely. Others, such as America Online, license technology from software makers like those that manufacture SurfWatch to allow anyone on their service to block Internet sites they don't want their children to visit.

One group working on the issue is PICS (Platform for Internet Content Selection), which is trying to give parents control over the kind of material that their children have access to. The group is trying to develop industry standards for technology that would allow the content of all sites and documents on the Internet to be rated according to its suitability for children. Additionally, the group would create standards to allow software to be developed for blocking sites based on those suitability ratings.

Businesses are also concerned with the type of Internet material their workers are accessing over corporate networks. There is a feeling that getting at and displaying sexual material could be interpreted as sexual harassment. Furthermore, some companies simply don't want their workers accessing that material on company time. Some companies now lease the same software that parents are buying. Instead of installing the software on individual computers, though, the software is installed on a server, and it checks all incoming Internet traffic to every computer in the company.

How Parental Controls Work

1 SurfWatch software is installed on a computer that a parent wants to monitor to make sure that children can't get to objectionable material on the Internet. When a child launches software to get onto the Internet, SurfWatch latches onto Winsock or MacTCP, depending on whether a PC or a Macintosh is being used. A SurfWatch software module sits "in front" of Winsock or MacTCP (which we'll generically call a TCP/IP stack) and monitors the TCP/IP data stream coming to the TCP/IP stack from the Internet.

2 The SurfWatch module examines the URL of every address coming toward the TCP/IP stack. It looks specifically for five kinds of URLs: https, nntps, ftps, gophers, and IRCs. It takes each of those five types of URLs and puts them in its own separate "box." It allows the rest of the Internet information coming in to go through. SurfWatch checks for these types of URLs because they are the ones that are the most likely to contain objectionable material.

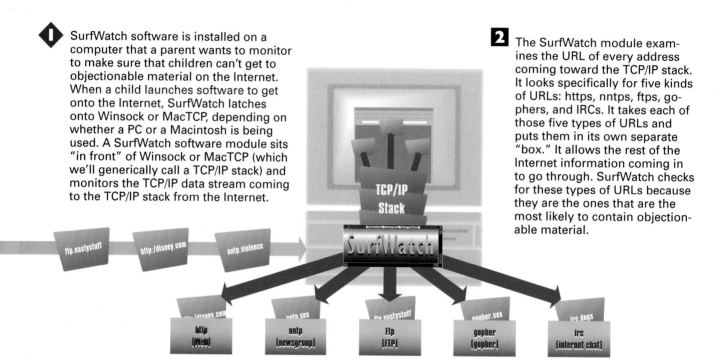

3 Every URL in each of the boxes is checked against a database of the URLs of objectionable sites. If SurfWatch finds that any of the URLs are from objectionable sites, it won't allow that information to be passed on to the TCP/IP stack, blocking the site and preventing information from being viewed. It alerts the child that the site has been blocked. SurfWatch checks thousands of sites and lists in its database the ones that are found objectionable.

4 If the URL is not in the database, SurfWatch does another check of the URL. This is called *pattern matching*. It looks at the words in the URL and checks them against a database of words to see if any of them indicates a request for objectionable material. Often, people creating objectionable material put representative words in the URL to draw attention to the site. If SurfWatch finds a matching pattern, it won't allow that information to be passed on to the TCP/IP stack, blocking the site and preventing information from being viewed. It alerts the child that the site has been blocked.

5 There is another way that SurfWatch may eventually check for objectionable sites. A rating system called PICS (Platform for Internet Content Selection) is being developed that will embed information about the content in its documents—saying, for example, whether objectionable material can be found there. If SurfWatch uses this system and finds that the URL is of a site that contains objectionable material, it won't allow that information to be passed on to the TCP/IP stack, blocking the site and information from being viewed. It alerts the child that the site has been blocked.

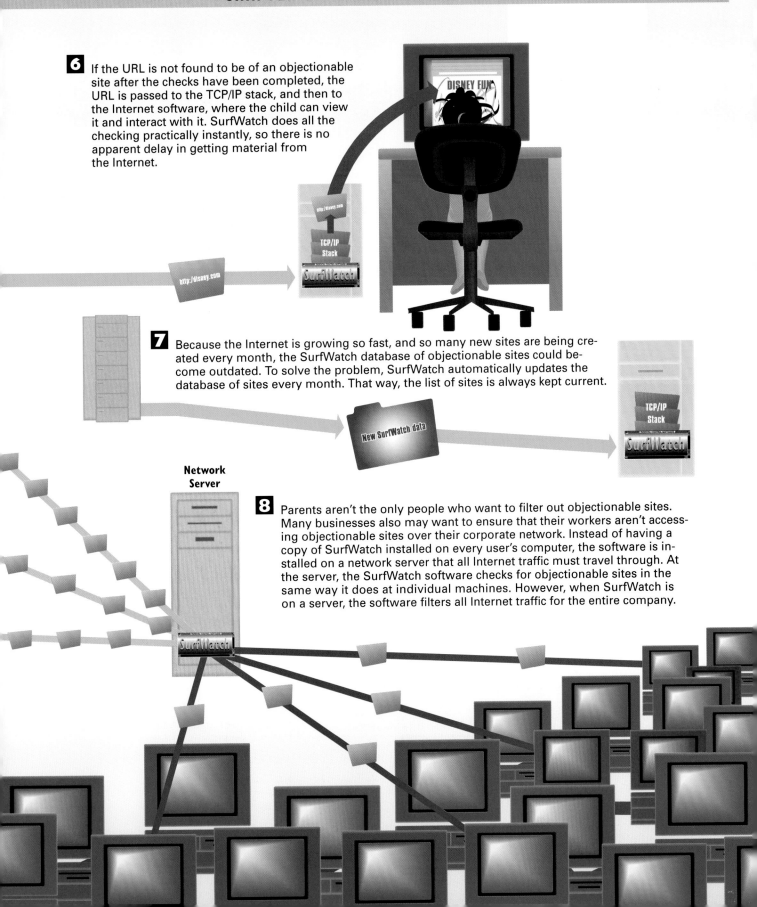

6 If the URL is not found to be of an objectionable site after the checks have been completed, the URL is passed to the TCP/IP stack, and then to the Internet software, where the child can view it and interact with it. SurfWatch does all the checking practically instantly, so there is no apparent delay in getting material from the Internet.

7 Because the Internet is growing so fast, and so many new sites are being created every month, the SurfWatch database of objectionable sites could become outdated. To solve the problem, SurfWatch automatically updates the database of sites every month. That way, the list of sites is always kept current.

8 Parents aren't the only people who want to filter out objectionable sites. Many businesses also may want to ensure that their workers aren't accessing objectionable sites over their corporate network. Instead of having a copy of SurfWatch installed on every user's computer, the software is installed on a network server that all Internet traffic must travel through. At the server, the SurfWatch software checks for objectionable sites in the same way it does at individual machines. However, when SurfWatch is on a server, the software filters all Internet traffic for the entire company.

Network Server

Q-R

X-Z